Leadership as Masterpiece Creation

Leadership as Masterpiece Creation

What Business Leaders Can Learn from the Humanities about
Moral Risk-Taking

Charles Spinosa, Matthew Hancocks, and Haridimos Tsoukas

The MIT Press
Cambridge, Massachusetts
London, England

The MIT Press would like to thank the anonymous peer reviewers who provided comments on drafts of this book. The generous work of academic experts is essential for establishing the authority and quality of our publications. We acknowledge with gratitude the contributions of these otherwise uncredited readers.

This book was set in ITC Stone Serif Std and ITC Stone Sans Std by New Best-set Typesetters Ltd. Printed and bound in the United States of America.

Library of Congress Cataloging-in-Publication Data

Names: Spinosa, Charles, author. | Hancocks, Matthew, author. | Tsoukas, Haridimos, author.
Title: Leadership as masterpiece creation : what business leaders can learn from the humanities about moral risk-taking / Charles Spinosa, Matthew Hancocks, and Haridimos Tsoukas.
Description: Cambridge, Massachusetts : The MIT Press, [2024] | Includes bibliographical references and index.
Identifiers: LCCN 2023019245 (print) | LCCN 2023019246 (ebook) | ISBN 9780262048965 (hardcover) | ISBN 9780262378406 (epub) | ISBN 9780262378413 (pdf)
Subjects: LCSH: Leadership. | Executive ability. | Creative ability in business.
Classification: LCC HD57.7 .S69485 2024 (print) | LCC HD57.7 (ebook) | DDC 658.4/092—dc23/eng/20230421
LC record available at https://lccn.loc.gov/2023019245
LC ebook record available at https://lccn.loc.gov/2023019246

10 9 8 7 6 5 4 3 2 1

In memory of Hubert (Bert) Dreyfus

Contents

Preface: Why Should We See Leadership as Masterpiece Creation?

"The best lack all conviction, while the worst
Are full of passionate intensity."
—W. B. Yeats, "The Second Coming"

The world is not in a good state. We have a climate crisis, a threat of nuclear war, pandemics, high inflation, disrupted global supply chains, fentanyl use, political polarization, displacement by artificial intelligence, and the decay of truth seeking. We face unsettling uncertainty. Many want resolution of these difficulties and those that will follow. But something holds us back. We do not have sufficient collective will. We value the social goods of convenience, efficiency, flexibility, and safety more than we like to admit. Although they are genuine goods, they stand in the way of the resolutions many want. Can business leaders contribute to the collective effort by improving our moral fiber? We believe they can, and not just by making us all become more entrepreneurial.

How? Here is our core thesis. Business leaders can change our moral fiber so far as they create masterpiece organizations: businesses worthy of admiration by diverse communities. Masterpieces resonate with our heritage, produce wonder, and are technically superb. A few words of clarification before we proceed. We acknowledge that some might hear strongly masculine overtones in "masterpiece." Still, etymology apart, mastery need not be a strictly masculine trait. We can just as easily speak of Anita Roddick's or Oprah Winfrey's masterpieces as of Jeff Bezos's or Steve Jobs's or of Marie Skłodowska-Curie's as of Hendrik Lorentz's. Do we want to say that Jane Austen, George Eliot, Charlotte and Emily Brontë, and Virginia Woolf wrote no masterpieces because of the male implication of the term *master*? Since the Renaissance inspired our notion of masterpiece, we certainly want to say that Artemisia Gentileschi painted masterpieces. The same goes for businesses. We credit women in business who shaped organizations of resonance, wonder, and technical proficiency. As of 2021 in the United States, for example, women started 49 percent of the new businesses, and women own around 42 percent of small businesses. Small businesses generally display the owner's vision. For many owners, success amounts to having customers (and suppliers) admire the vision and the business enough to sustain the business. Together the vision and business produce resonance and wonder as well as technical commercial excellence. We call those businesses "masterpieces." Just because "mastery" has been associated with white masculinity does not make it conceptually bankrupt. That association points to the sociopolitical conditions that have historically given the term a particular twist. However, concepts such as "nation," "masterpiece," "justice," and so forth are inherently malleable, and we depend on them to make sense of our world.

Masterpiece organizations command our attention primarily by the gratitude we feel for them and the admiration we give. That we describe quite different admirable organizational masterpieces is important because we all do not admire the same things, and we certainly will not embrace many things we admire. Our point is that if you are a business leader, you ought to strive to create an organization that a sizable number of people will deem worthy of admiration.

However, we expect some to disagree with us. There is a widespread view that business leaders—except for mold-breaking, celebrity business leaders and small-business leaders—should strive mainly for operational excellence. Anything more ambitious might be considered self-aggrandizement or narcissism.[1] We do not agree. From our work, we know that for-profit business leaders can (and do) create masterpieces, and so we focus on them. We know, too, from our experience that some nonprofit leaders can do the same, and we advise them to do so.

Why would creating business masterpieces help us develop new moral fiber? Bear with us for a few moments while we explain. Martin Heidegger's account of our postmodern age as deeply technological strikes a chord with us. Heidegger was one of the most important philosophers of the past century. He argued that, unlike in other ages, the moral goods we seek now—the ones that we think could give us a good life—are convenience, efficiency, flexibility, and safety. "Was this not always the case?" you might ask. To some degree it was. But people at different historical times did not seek these goods as their *highest* goods.

In the modern age (from the European Renaissance of the fifteenth and sixteenth centuries to the beginning of the twentieth century), people sought *understanding* and *ordering* as the top goods in life. They wanted to know the essential categories and laws governing people and things. People wanted encyclopedic knowledge. They wanted to arrange things in periodic tables. They wanted certain knowledge, and the one thing they felt they could be certain of was their own thinking. "I think, therefore I am," Descartes famously wrote. That is why in the modern age, the greatest fear was the Cartesian anxiety—namely, that a genie (a brain disorder) could fool you even in your own thinking. In the age before modernity (the Middle Ages), people primarily sought *salvation* from their sinful lives. Going further back, the ancient world valued *heroic struggle* and the beautiful poetry and art that celebrated such struggle. In the ancient world, the struggle was mostly seen as martial, but the struggle could also be for truth. Seneca famously said life was a test.[2]

So it seems obvious that the top goods of those ages are no longer the top goods for us, although they are still around and cared for by some people. Nevertheless, why should we believe that Heidegger is right that our top goods are convenience, efficiency, flexibility, and safety? Some will say that they value work highly. Others will say that they value family. Still others will say that they value freedom or equality (or both). No doubt they do. But what happens when work becomes inflexible and dangerous? What happens when the family is no longer convenient? What happens when our business (or a business where we are customers or employees) or our home life makes us feel as though we are slogging through molasses? What happens when it becomes dangerous to exercise freedom? What happens when becoming more unequal and less free makes our lives more convenient and efficient? The point is not that we will always choose convenience, efficiency, flexibility, and safety over the other goods. But *in general* we do. That is the technological ethos.

Further, look at what today's innovations provide us with. Consider new cars, new phones, new computers, new kitchen appliances, new social media features, new homes, new experiences of nature, new vacations, and new retail experiences. In all these cases, the regular upgrade gives us more convenience, more efficiency, more flexibility, and more safety. Even our education works that way. Our educators train us to look at situations with ever more flexibility. Consider the plane on the runway: We can conceive of it as a mechanical object. We can see it as an element in a transportation system. We can see it as a means for globalized business. We can see it as part of the vacation and entertainment industries. Where generations before would want to know what a plane is really, we have learned to get in tune with the diverse ways it can be and switch among them as the situation warrants. In our estimation, we have become very good at that. The anthropologist and philosopher Ernest Gellner described this type of person as "modular man": we divide ourselves in different modules of thought and action and configure ourselves according to the circumstances.[3]

We might think that such modular lives are fairly appealing. But Heidegger and Nietzsche saw us as trapped in something deeper, which they called "the eternal return of the same." Change brings—and brings only— more of the same: more convenience, more efficiency, more flexibility, and more safety. We miss what can be called "infinite commitments": "I will be with you forever"; "I will never leave this vocation, career, or craft"; "I will love this constitution and will preserve it no matter what." Some of us say those words, but as we say them, we can contemplate situations where we will break our oaths or at least consider doing so. We tend to make our commitments, no matter how strong, contingent.

We are deeply critical of foundations and foundational commitments in our postmodern lives. Heidegger and Nietzsche call this state a form of nihilism. There is nothing worth dying for. There is nothing that we are infinitely obliged to stay true to. That is our cultural tragedy. That is what leaves us irresolute in facing our crises. In facing crises, we think we need those infinite commitments that we postmoderns cannot easily make. It is, however, just this tragedy of infinite commitment that we can look for masterpiece-creating business leaders to address. Before we go directly to the form of the solution, we need to say a little more about the typical way of thinking of our postmodern age.

We postmoderns think deconstructively. Deconstructive thinkers examine what seem like enduring, important, hierarchical distinctions—good over bad, true over false, man over woman, thinking over emotion, leader over follower, among others. These thinkers correctly see that each of the higher elements in the distinction is irremediably founded on the lower element and, indeed, conceals that it contains the lower as constitutive of itself. To see how this argument works, take, for example, good over bad. It generally takes a shockingly *bad* act to establish a way of acting that we call *good*. Few good states are founded without violence. Similarly, to establish peace, we must disable those who would fight against each other. To maintain freedom, we must give a monopoly of controlling power to the state. Likewise, *leaders* must pay attention to the cues of what matters among their *followers*. Deconstructive thinking works because there is, indeed, an intimate, co-constitutive connection between the two members of the distinction. We do not know good without knowing evil.[4] You are not a leader unless you have followers and can follow what they are up to. So far so good, but deconstructive thinking goes beyond undermining hierarchical distinctions. Deconstructive thinking leaves us in a world of fluidity, where we establish distinctions as important for only a brief time and then weaken them. Consider, for instance, the increasing fluidity of marriage, family, gender, and career and work life today. These distinctions are not part of nature but held in place, when they are held in place, by social conventions based on relationships frequently involving political or market dominance.

How could business leaders help us out of this situation? Are they not in it for the money? Are they not interested in market dominance? Look around you. In mold-breaking businesses and in small local businesses, we can see that it is not just market or political power that enables leaders to hold their positions, especially now. With remote working, employees can leave a job far more easily today than in the past. Customers can do the same. Various other stakeholders can easily point the finger at and back away from business practices they find objectionable. Thus, leaders cannot simply dictate their terms to employees, customers, or stakeholders. Leaders can no longer say, as Henry Ford did, "Any customer can have a car painted any color that he wants, so long as it is black." In liberal democracies, we expect business leaders to be legally and morally accountable. But in our postmodern times, we also expect more. Business leaders today make their leadership legitimate by making and keeping themselves and their organizations worthy of admiration. Leaders and their organizations must act and be seen to act in a way that inspires admiration and gratitude. In the global, interconnected, incessantly communicating village, organizations need to strive to stand out, to make themselves discernible in the noise. Heidegger loved quoting the poet Friedrich Hölderlin: "But where danger is, grows / The saving power also."[5] We interpret that to mean that where the danger of having lives of flexibility without real commitment is high, we see clearly etched in our circumstances that there is a saving power in the gratitude and admiration we feel for masterpieces. Heidegger also thought that in the postmodern era "creativity finally passes over into business enterprise."[6]

An economy of gratitude and admiration (as the Nietzsche scholar Bernard Williams observed) enables such distinctions as those between *leaders* and *followers* and between *truth* and *falsehood* to remain in place within communities and organizations so long as there are admired masterpieces that reinforce those distinctions. Consider what happens in today's world when a leader loses admiration and gratitude. Liz Truss had the shortest premiership in British history. As soon as her chancellor of the exchequer (minister of finance) Kwasi Kwarteng announced a mini budget consisting of extensive tax cuts on the wealthy (funded by public borrowing), the prime minister's capacity to have people follow her collapsed in days. Public-borrowing costs increased; the sterling dropped to its lowest point; the Bank of England had to step in. She had done what she had said she would do. But in seeing it happen, people lost admiration for it. What is remarkable is how quickly admiration and gratitude fell away. The end came quickly, and she resigned after only 44 days in office!

If you accept our claim that gratitude and admiration can give us some stability and hold important distinctions in place, the following question naturally arises: How do business leaders gain such gratitude and admiration? We address this question head-on in this book. Please make no mistake: This is emphatically not a book about public relations or gaining celebrity status. We are writing about moral masterpieces to renew our moral fiber. We claim that leaders strive in their companies and communities to create distinctive *moral orders*, each reflecting a conception of the *good life*, and that leaders consequently must take *moral risks* to establish those new moral orders. (Much of our book is about the preparation for and activity of taking successful moral risks.) Here are a few examples of masterpieces: Amazon is relentless in raising the bar on employee performance; a good life at Amazon requires a person to live relentlessly. In contrast, Google lavishes benefits on employees who are made to feel psychologically safe. A good life at Google means dreaming new dreams in its dreamy atmosphere.

The Body Shop exudes fun, compassion, and an emphasis on taking care of one's body. A good life there will require buoyant purity and care. Individuals can admire all three moral orders and their associated good lives, although these individuals might embrace only one or none of them.

As more business leaders begin creating distinctive moral spaces for their organizations, we will find ourselves living in a world where we can again feel drawn and committed to a way of life without disparaging other ways of life. We will no longer live in the eternal return of the same because new, distinctively moral organizations will arrive with new moral evaluations. The beauty of the market economy, constrained by the moral framework of liberal democracy and its associated institutions (rule of law, state bureaucracy, and civil society), is that it enables a plurality of morally distinctive organizations to flourish. To these organizations, people in their gratitude can give their moral commitment. And in liberal states (on which this book focuses), our capacity to admire morally distinctive organizations will also require that they be inclusive, have equal respect for individuals, and seek diversity.

So, in this book, we help business leaders figure out what moral personality they would like their organizations to have. We ask: What would you want people inside and outside the organization to admire? What do you think is the right way to treat employees, customers, suppliers, and owners? How do you want to cultivate your leadership style so that it is a masterpiece worthy of admiration? Once such questions are posed, the abiding moral goods that surface will not be convenience, efficiency, flexibility, and safety, though those goods will remain.

Leaders and followers alike will then be able to find an infinite passion (or at least an abiding one) to commit to other goods. With business leaders creating masterpieces, we can have salvation from the eternal return of the same and lead lives where we can experience infinite commitment again. With that we can better address the challenges and crises mentioned at the beginning of this preface. With that kind of infinite passion, we will not need universal agreements. Rather, our businesses will manifest their moral-aesthetic distinctiveness as do the palaces lining the streets of Genoa or Venice. The promise of this book is to help business leaders do that. This promise is bold. We believe it is necessary. We are grateful to any who will entertain it.

Authors

Charles Spinosa was a Renaissance scholar who taught Shakespeare at Miami University in Ohio and then philosophy as a visiting assistant professor at the University of California, Berkeley, where he worked and wrote with the philosopher Hubert Dreyfus. Together they taught and wrote on Heidegger, Nietzsche, Foucault, Rorty, Merleau-Ponty, Wittgenstein, and Derrida. Once *Disclosing New Worlds*, which they coauthored with Fernando Flores, came out in 1997, Charles Spinosa gave up teaching for management consulting and has been a consultant for 26 years, first with Fernando Flores's company BDA, then with VISION Consulting, and later with Stratam. He has tested the lessons of this book with diverse clients in the senior- and middle-management ranks in companies ranging from start-ups to the Global 1000 in the United States, Canada, the United Kingdom, Europe, Latin America, and China.

Matthew Hancocks is a corporate strategist, consultant, and C-suite leadership coach who since 2001 has written and consulted with Charles Spinosa. His consulting work focuses on the practices of leaders who reconfigure the moral orders in which they, their organizations, and their sectors exist. His doctoral research explores the strategic and leadership practices of companies reconfiguring the agile norms of contemporary business to cultivate infinite commitment and avoid nihilism.

Haridimos Tsoukas is a professor of strategic management and organizational behavior at the University of Cyprus and Warwick Business School. He is the scientific adviser to the Association of Chief Executive Officers in Greece. He takes a strong interest in how philosophy can illuminate our understanding of leadership and organizational behavior. His course "Leadership and the Art of Judgment," which draws on Aristotle and Heidegger, has been one of the most popular courses at Warwick Business School. He is the author of the books *Complex Knowledge* (2005) and *Philosophical Organization Theory* (2019). His book *If Aristotle Were a CEO* (2005) in Greek was reprinted several times. He was the editor in chief of the leading academic journal *Organization Studies*. As well as a scholar and educator, he is an engaged citizen regularly commenting on Greek and international politics. He once ran (unsuccessfully) for the Greek Parliament.

Christopher Davis, who joined the team in writing chapter 7, is the founder and CEO of Stratam, a consulting firm that works with clients to turn their cultures into masterpieces. He has been involved for decades with bringing philosophical ideas into business. He started by being part of the team, led by Fernando Flores, that developed the practice of commitment-based management. It was inspired by speech act theory as developed by the philosophers John Austin and John Searle. Chris and his team have participated in more than a hundred consulting engagements and have helped create or enhance masterpiece cultures in companies across multiple industries, including tech, biotech, health care, finance, manufacturing, and entertainment. He is coauthor with Charles Spinosa of a paper on organizational moods, "Transforming Crippling Company Politics" (2014), published in the journal *Organizational Dynamics*.

A Note on the Text

We intend our book for organizational leaders, team leaders, and scholars. We have written the main content of chapters with an erudite informality that would suit readers of such publications as the *Financial Times*, the *New York Times*, the *New York Review of Books*, and *The Economist*. The more contrarian the chapter, the longer. Our endnotes make distinctions and add references that scholars will find useful.

Introduction

Someday, everything is gonna be different
When I paint my masterpiece.
　—Bob Dylan, "When I Paint My Masterpiece"

This book is primarily for leaders and aspiring leaders who want to reflect on what their leadership is all about and to make it better. It seeks to help leaders turn their organizations or parts of them, whatever the size, into masterpieces.

Who are these leaders? You might think that you need to be a chief executive officer (CEO) or at least a vice president to be a leader. That is not true. If you oversee an organizational unit, you are de facto its leader: you articulate valued ends and provide direction for the people in it; you focus on the big picture and the long term; you want your unit uniquely to serve its purpose. The people we conventionally call leaders most obviously hold these responsibilities. They are typically individuals who are formally in charge of an entire organization, and that is why we draw on their experience. But the argument applies to all levels of business leadership and a wide range of activity domains. If you can effectively, either formally or informally, set standards for treating employees, customers, suppliers, *and* owners in your area, then you are a leader for the purposes of this book. You might not take actions that have the consequences of those taken by a Churchill, Bezos, Madam Walker, or Roddick, but many of your key actions are leaderly nonetheless. We will return to this important point.

Why "masterpieces"? Think of a masterpiece as a work of art. Think of your organization as *your* work of art. Doing so is not new. Consider the city-states of the Italian Renaissance. In Jacob Burckhardt's magisterial book *The Civilization of the Renaissance in Italy*, his first section is "The State as a Work of Art."[1] He describes an age when leaders—princes and condottieri (leaders of mercenaries)—boldly and imaginatively led and shaped admirable city-states in multiple styles that reflected their varied moral senses and leadership approaches, which ranged all the way from seeking to be loved to seeking to be feared.

Niccolò Machiavelli, the renowned chancery officer, diplomat, thinker, author, and promoter of Italian Renaissance rulers, saw things the way Burckhardt did. His thinking is exemplary for us. He accepted the diversity of leaderly styles. In *The Prince*, Machiavelli was not *against* a leader who ruled by love if the leader could do so. He simply thought ruling by fear safer. Successful leadership was Machiavelli's goal, at least in *The Prince*.[2] In his *Discourses*, he makes it clear that he prefers, for their stability, republics where princes, nobles, and the people join in government. Moreover, in *The Discourses*, he gives cases where princes both need to be loved and, at some moments, need to be feared.[3] He sought stable masterpieces. Often mistaken as an immoralist, Machiavelli was quite the opposite: he was a pragmatist who knew that great cities arise from the tough choices made by great leaders.[4] He saw leaders as artists.[5] Like Burckhardt, who came much later, Machiavelli saw that leaders developed city-states with distinctive personalities—Florence (run by Medici bankers), Venice, Padua, Bologna, Urbino, and so forth. They have a majesty that remains today. Unlike today's organizations that sport nice-sounding values and soothing consistency, an Italian city-state that became a masterpiece would have *discordia concors*, or inharmonious harmony, as one of its animating principles.[6] That speaks to the passions of those leaders. They are not unlike the passions and contradictions of today's leaders who create masterpiece organizations such as Amazon and Apple. Those leaders do not grow their organizations out of crowd-pleasing "aligned" platitudes but out of values such as loving customers and loving frugality. Those values jar against each other but nonetheless, at Amazon at least, deliver a distinctive, admirable, majestic energy.[7]

Do postmodern leaders *want* to turn their leadership styles and organizations into masterpieces? Our answer is yes, but we concede that it is not self-evidently the case. Let us start to make the case. Consider small businesses. Though business schools do not spend much research and teaching time on them (unless they are high-tech start-ups), small businesses constituted more than 99 percent of the 27,281,452 businesses in the United States in 2018.[8] (The percentage for the United Kingdom is approximately the same.) When we consider our local restaurants, hardware stores, grocery stores, cafés, dry cleaners, salons, and so forth, we have little intuitive trouble seeing that the owners are expressing their visions in the design of their businesses.

On the Upper East Side of Manhattan, there are, for instance, two hardware stores within walking distance of each other. In one, the minute you walk in, you hear highly curated classic jazz music; you smell soaps; and as you walk down the main aisle, at least one salesperson asks if you need help. It is a high-touch customer-service store. There are many salespeople throughout the small store. There is no question but that it is right—morally right—that in this store an employee *ought to* spend as much time with the customer as the customer wants. Prices are higher than at the other store, where there might be one service person restocking shelves and another behind the cash register. In that store, there is a faint smell of electric-motor oil. Pop music plays. There is no question but that it is right—morally right—for salespeople in this second store to treat customers efficiently.

These are two different visions of hardware stores. Each vision includes not just the décor, pricing, and display but also the moral norms that guide the treatment of customers and fellow employees, managers, and even suppliers. That is what makes each a masterpiece like an Italian Renaissance city-state. It is a careful articulation of an aesthetic, economic, and moral vision intended to draw admiration from various sets of stakeholders. No doubt some of you have worked for a small business and experienced the force of the leader's vision firsthand. You know that such leaders want to test their visions and prove their visions worthy by making a profit. Vision comes first; profit (or some other measure of success) comes second.

At the other end of the spectrum from small-business owners, we have mold-breaking leaders: Bill Gates of Microsoft, Steve Jobs of Apple, Jeff Bezos of Amazon, Ray Dalio of Bridgewater, Anita Roddick of the Body Shop, Jack Welch of GE, Larry Page and Sergey Brin of Google, Madam C. J. Walker of the Madam C. J. Walker Manufacturing Company, Reed Hastings of Netflix, and Ed Catmull and John Lasseter of Pixar. People concede that such leaders create organizations that are distinctive aesthetically, economically, and morally, especially in their norms of management. The right thing to do at

Google is quite different from the right thing to do at Amazon or the Body Shop or Pixar. In the rest of the book, we draw on such companies (because they are well known) to clarify how leaders create masterpieces. But our argument holds more generally—for the hardware stores in Manhattan as well as for Amazon or Apple.

Why Do We Focus on Moral Norms and Moral Orders?

You might have been surprised that we called the right way of doing things in a company "moral." After all, companies can have prescriptive policies about all sorts of things, including the specific colors to use in presentations and the emptying of bins at the end of the day. However, those policies are not moral norms, though it is right to follow them. Moral norms are the ones that a company holds inviolable or nearly so. Breaking with them means preventing people associated with the company from having a good life as offered by the company. A lexicon of our key terms will help here.

There are *moral* norms, *legal* norms, *conventional* norms (including aesthetic and instrumental ones), and *prudential* norms.[9] Moral norms involve good and evil or good and bad. To repeat, breaking them impairs the ability of people associated with an organization to lead the good life offered by the organization. Except for cases of mental illness, if one violates a moral norm, one demeans all who hold the moral norm; one is doing something bad or evil to oneself, others, and the community that holds the norm. We generally consider moral norms inviolable. One step down from moral norms are legal norms, very many of which are codifications of moral norms, while others are no more than arbitrary but binding agreements, such as about when one is allowed to drive or vote. Someone who violates a legal norm is a wrongdoer but not necessarily bad or evil unless the law is a codification of a moral norm. Next down are conventions that do not have the force of morality or law. When one violates these norms, one is a nuisance and might suffer ostracism but will not normally be judged a wrongdoer, bad, or evil. Last, prudential norms are the norms for making trade-offs based on moral, legal, and conventional norms and involve what to do *now*. For instance, if I have someone terribly ill in my car, I run the red light to get to the hospital, but I do not take the curve so fast that I might lose control of the car. Of course, the distinctions among these norms are not like those among natural kinds. The norms have some overlap.

In organizations, what seems like a mere prudential or conventional norm can be, and in a masterpiece becomes, a moral norm. For example, when Bezos made relentlessness a moral norm at Amazon, it started out as a prudential norm. In the trade-off between going home when your day is done or working until the task is done, working won. But Bezos saw it as a norm that defined his organization. By threatening to fire his most talented employee who had the habit of going home before finishing a task, he turned this standard into a moral norm at Amazon.[10] At Amazon, one worked at least 60 hours per week or longer until the work got done, and if one did not, one was understood as violating the whole Amazon community; such a violation was an evil that stopped people from having good lives at Amazon.

People frequently think that moral norms need to be binding for everyone in various senses: moral norms cover all deliberative, embodied, rational beings or cover all of God's creatures or cover all those who live in a national culture. This definition leads to thinking that moral norms are the minimal ones for general, peaceable welfare. However, we see this view as mistaken. Thinking this way leaves out much of what we consider the right thing for a moral person to do, which varies not only across history but also across organizations on opposite sides of the street.[11] Consider the two hardware stores. For them to have distinctive moral orders, the stores must have clusters of coherent norms that mean that people inside the organizations do morally different things to have good lives. This does not mean that everyone always follows them, but it does mean that the norms come together enough so that we can see clearly different moral orders. Consider, for instance, a psychologically safe Google with lavish benefits for all employees in contrast to a relentless and frugal Amazon, where employees feel insecure and pay (or paid) for snacks and parking.[12]

Additionally, as already suggested, moral norms are not, in our usage, simply minimal grounds for getting along peacefully; they are rules or ways for living a *good life*.[13] So, for instance, we have widespread negative moral norms, such as those interdicting murder and stealing, and positive ones, such as the responsibility to take care of one's children. These norms enable us to live peaceably, but they don't necessarily create good lives. In one kind of society, creating and preserving family dynasties might be a way of having a good life. In another, sharing neighborhood goods in common might be a requirement for a good life. We are claiming that those norms for making a good life are moral norms just as the ones for getting along peacefully are and that the good-life norms inflect the more standard, getting-along-peacefully ones. The good-life norms will determine, for instance, what counts as theft or nuisance and even the degree to which murder or theft is evil. To show how this works for businesses, we will consider Google and Amazon again.

Because creating a psychologically safe environment is morally required at Google and creating a relentless one is required at Amazon, a good life (of leisure for thought) at Google is different from a good life (of struggling to push boundaries) at Amazon. These different moral norms for creating a good life also inflect the meaning and normative power of more widely shared economic and liberal norms or conventions. Giving employees free time might well be a right at Google. Treating one's time as free would plausibly be immoral at Amazon. Thus, how one treats another and how one shapes a good life are inextricably bound together, at least in morally coherent organizations, and these moral norms are not universal in any sense beyond covering all of Google or all of Amazon. Because we can have such morally different organizations in proximity, listening for and bridging differences, as described in chapter 4, are important for avoiding continual hostility among the organizations in which we shape good lives. These norms for interpersonal obligations and shaping good lives are different from legal or conventional norms. By making a prudential, conventional, or even legal norm take on moral force (where violating it means committing a wrong against the whole organization), leaders give their organizations distinctive moral orders.

Once we accept that the moral norms for securing interpersonal peace and justice are intertwined with norms for leading a good life, there is one more important distinction to make. We take it from the philosopher Martin Heidegger, and we elaborate on it in chapter 7. We have three different kinds of moral norms that work together and produce and manage a tension in any rich moral order.

There are moral norms that are clearly articulated and that people feel they stand for. In the United States and many other parts of the world, we call these moral norms "rights." We have the right to free assembly. We have the right of free speech. We call them *clarifying norms* because court cases, trials, and legislative actions frequently try to bring more clarity to them. Even families have clarifying moral norms. Parents rightfully insist on proper hygiene and an education for their children.

These clarifying norms rest on *grounding norms*, which are more subtle and live more at the level of communal or neighborly micro-norms. They are largely unarticulated and govern the extent to which we assert clarifying norms and how we do so. Grounding norms are the moral norms of neighborly give-and-take and of reciprocity. They determine when, for instance, assertion of free speech becomes a nuisance to a community. They determine how we let each other speak when we assemble. In families, there are grounding norms of respect for parents and love of children. (Many people in the United States credit Alexis de Tocqueville and, more recently, Robert Putnam with sympathetically showing these grounding norms in the shape of American community or neighborhood organizations.[14]) Clearly, at all levels, grounding norms are frequently in tension with clarifying norms. As we write, in the United States, there is the clarifying moral norm that businesses open to the public should serve all customers and the grounding moral norm that you do not push people to violate their religious obligations.

The conflict between these norms gets tacitly or expressly adjudicated by *organizing norms*. In the United States, the organizing norms, which you find in government, business, and families, are norms for deliberation with respect to precedent.

These distinctions give us a powerful way to classify different moral orders. We look to an organization's primary clarifying, grounding, and organizing moral norms to understand that organization. When *any of these norms* is different from those of another organization, then the two organizations have different moral orders.

Do Ordinary Leaders (Not Just Mold Breakers) Take Moral Risks?

Managers tell us that between the small-business entrepreneurs and the sophisticated, large-scale, mold-breaking entrepreneurs lies rational, prosaic management, consensus building, and the use of rational influence to achieve incremental changes.[15] Managers of these businesses are not the sort who will threaten to fire a brilliant loyal employee for working fewer than 60 hours per week. That action seems nearly absurd to them. They would not take the moral risk of such a firing to turn a prudential norm into a moral one. Is this description really accurate? We think not, but let us start with what boards and senior managers do when they appoint leaders in their organizations. Do boards or senior managers appoint leaders who say that they are seeking the position merely to maintain the status quo and to make incremental changes when forced by competition? We know of none that do so. Boards typically ask what distinctive change a potential leader will bring and why it will be good for the organization. Why do they do that? They see the world changing and uncertainty increasing. They see competitors, especially the mold-breaking ones, shifting the rules of the game. They see political uncertainty, pandemics, climatic change, and disruption in supply chains. They see difficulty in acquiring and maintaining the best employees and in keeping shareholders happy with equity valuations. Perhaps they are wrong in what they see, but in our experience that is what they claim to be seeing. Boards and senior managers entrust leadership to potential leaders only when the latter explain how they will make the company thrive in a distinctive way. What difference will the new leader make? How will the new leader uniquely shape the way the company or department will respond to the challenges it faces?

It is often hard to see the moral risk-taking implicit in the answers that potential leaders give to boards and senior managers. Aspiring leaders usually explain how they will make their companies distinctive by deploying new technologies, bringing in new processes, hiring better and more diverse workforces, making new offerings to customers, entering new market segments, introducing new supply-chain-management techniques, making shifts in competitive advantage and strategy, and so on. However, as they set out their visions and make their promises, they tend to do so as servants following fashions, not as masterpiece creators following their spirits and taking moral risks. Those who promise higher market returns generally see themselves by the lights of Milton Friedman, where they serve the owners mostly by maximizing financial value for shareholders.[16] Those who promise to distinguish the organization by serving additional social purposes tend to see themselves as following the 182 CEO signers of the Business Roundtable's "Statement on the Purpose of a Corporation" by claiming they maximize value to customers, employees, suppliers, communities, shareholders, the environment, and social justice concerns. They speak of environmental, governance, and social leadership. In short, these potential leaders see themselves as *serving* financial performance, dignity-saving performance, planet-saving performance, or some other performance, but they make themselves sound as though they are acting as servants to shareholders or stakeholders.

Servants do not think of themselves as creating new moral orders. They see their tasks as far more prosaic and operational. However, it is virtually impossible to implement significant new technologies, introduce new processes, or make new offers to customers without changing at the same time an organization's moral order. These tasks cannot be done without changing the moral norms of how to treat customers, colleagues, subordinates, managers, and others. Different companies have different moral codes, and significant alterations in operations change those codes. Thus, as part of the implementation of their changes, these leaders make many small, morally laden decisions about what it is right to do in their companies. Notice that moral changes necessarily bring along with them aesthetic effects. As people feel obliged to behave in new ways, so their descriptions of good behavior and poor behavior change. People must develop glamorizing stories of good and bad behavior to imitate the good and to avoid the bad. These stories will determine the look and feel of the organization. If getting stuff done is highly valued, then there will be floor plans that show people abuzz with activity. If the organization values perfectionism, the layout will include areas for small working groups to work intensely on details. In both cases, there will be heroic stories of getting stuff done or of coming up with the perfect product.

What does this account of moral-norm creation mean in practice for middle-management leaders? Are we writing only to members of top teams or the CEOs and boards they report to in unregulated private enterprises? No, we are not. We are writing to middle managers and to managers in highly regulated public-service organizations. We have spent more than 75 years combined bringing these lessons mostly to general managers and middle managers and frequently to ones working in heavily regulated public utilities. We have tested our thinking in these milieus as well as others. Here is what we have found.

In our experience, managers in general have distinctive moral stances on the treatment of customers, employees, suppliers, more senior managers, shareholders, and members of the community. They have a sense of what is right and what is not. They have interactions with some set of those stakeholders, and they, in almost every case, have the leeway to start instituting their moral intuitions. These leaders establish them, at least at first, as new *prudential* norms and then transform them into *conventional* norms and subsequently into *moral* norms for their areas.

In commerce, most of the boundaries between prudential and conventional and between conventional and moral are gray. So, once the new prudential or conventional norm is in place, leaders persuade their team or take the moral risks necessary to give, say, the conventional norm moral force. In the three examples that follow, the middle manager started the norm change without senior-management support and gained that support once the norm became moral in the middle manager's area.

(a) At a public utility company, a middle manager transformed the moral norm of having engineers follow process meticulously (to create audit trails) into a moral norm of expert engineers reflectively and responsibly exercising their judgment. For engineers, the norm of audit-trail creation was not only seemingly legal (what the regulator and government required) but also moral, the right thing to do. This leader asked the senior members of his team to start making prudent judgments in cases where they were sure they had enough experience to know what the right thing to do was. Then he gradually asked them to increase the range covered by their judgments based on experience. Finally, he made it the case that managers in his organization hire, promote, and praise for good judgments, not for extensive audit trails. Yes, he had to persuade, cajole, and even exert some risky pressure, which might have led to a disciplinary action, but with the increased productivity he gained free rein in his area. His team members went from having the moral norms of order takers to having those of judicious decision makers, and, as frequently happens, these team members were eager to have others in their organization make the same change.

(b) In a medical company, a middle manager transformed the moral norm of laissez-faire management in a business-development team into a norm of brilliant teamwork. Such a transformation was difficult because the business developers prided themselves on bold, heroic actions that required nerve and skill. So this leader started by instituting conventions of weekly reporting and checking in. People in these meetings had to stop talking as though they were freewheeling, "anything-goes-so-long-as-I-make-my-numbers" employees and start talking as though they were collaborators who took advice from each other and the manager and then received more resources for their actions. There were clear benefits to collaborating, but these benefits only meant that the new behavior was merely prudential and conventional. To make the new convention moral, the middle manager dramatically let go of two people who irregularly attended the weekly check-in meetings but regularly hit their numbers. That move was dramatic because most cases of terminating employees in this company involved clear legal wrongs or massively missing the numbers. She took the chance of facing appeals and even legal action, but she was able to make the reasons clear enough (and the severance fair enough) to get them to walk away.

(c) Finally, in a high-tech case the manager of a small unit broke the moral norm of silence in which no functional area head would comment on the workings of another area. This middle manager told colleagues what she thought was wrong and then went on to tell senior management. Her colleagues vilified her for breaking this norm. It was not the right thing to do in that company at the time, and people wanted her terminated. But when her truth telling averted crises, senior managers started appreciating it and encouraged others to imitate her. It took months, but senior management removed people until the new moral norm was born: "If you see it, say it." People went from secretive, sullen believers in omertà to open collaborators.

These middle managers received the typical plaudits and bonuses for raising productivity, increasing deal sizes and volumes, and enabling product enhancements to go to market on time. But their true sense of accomplishment took place in the gut-wrenching moments of making the moral change to do—as they all felt—the right thing. That is why we say leaders are creating masterpieces, frequently without knowing they are doing it and without being able to say so. These middle-management leaders also became valued advisers of their senior leaders because the middle managers could speak with sensitivity to the moral-norm-changing dimension of leadership. Thus, though they did not receive admiration for transforming whole companies, industries, or nations, they took the same kinds of actions as those of the leaders we shall describe and who made larger-dimension changes.

One might think there is not much moral risk involved in insisting that people follow their best judgment, work collaboratively as a team, or tell the truth to senior management. We believe that is a misunderstanding. To drive the change that creates a distinctive organization, a masterpiece—whether the unit of a company, an entire company, a city-state, or a nation—one generally must shock people morally. Though moral change can in principle and in practice come about by rational persuasion, people generally must see the new moral norm in place and notice that it is providing a good life before they embrace it.

Creating Morally Distinctive, Admired Organizational Masterpieces: A Framework

To put it in broad strokes, we shall describe the path that masterpiece-creating leaders follow: (1) Living in their organization's or culture's moral order, they (2) encounter a moral anomaly (where there is no right thing to do), (3) conceive it in a way that allows them to act, and then (4) take increasingly risky, shocking actions to overcome the anomaly. If the shocking actions are in practice successful, (5) they become acceptable actions for maintaining the new moral norm (giving it its force) or are seen as an example of the new moral norm, which with its establishment changes the organization's entire moral order. Figure 0.1 shows the change of one moral order to another through successful moral risk-taking.

A moral anomaly occurs when one is confronted with a situation where under the current understanding of what is morally right, *no* morally right action will bring about a practically good result.[17] In chapter 1, we provide two historical examples: one from Winston's Churchill's decision-making during World War II, and a more extensive one of Madam C. J. Walker's norm-breaking beauty business in the early twentieth century.

The Skills of Masterpiece Creation and the Course of the Book

This book sets out the skills leaders need to create masterpieces. We start in chapter 1 with two historical examples—Churchill and Walker—that will help us to illustrate what leaders as masterpiece creators do. In the remaining chapters, we present the required skills. In chapter 2, we set out more completely our view of the current postmodern situation, the good lives available to us, and the wonder of business. Then we take up the major objections we expect people to raise against our thinking. In chapter 3, we move beyond today's emotional intelligence to describe practices for intervening in moods. In chapter 4, we cover trust and listening for difference.

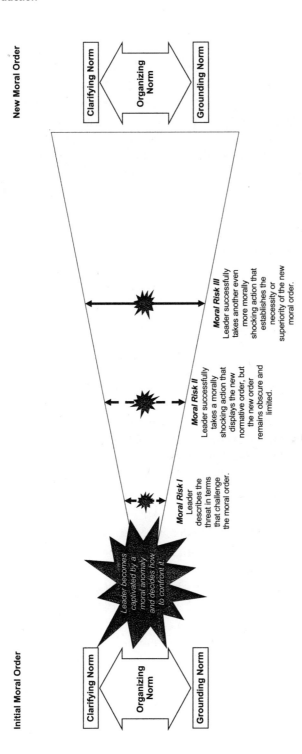

Figure 0.1

The general steps of establishing a new moral order. Vertical lines show the new moral order displacing the original one as moral risks are taken one after another.

We move beyond the trust brought about by being reliable to the trust, which can occur even at first sight, brought about by exhibiting admirable virtues. To move beyond today's empathetic listening, we explore listening for difference, which is listening with such care that we understand where others would think us terribly wrong. We then examine the practice—essential in a world of moral diversity—of building bridges across such moral differences. In chapter 5, we push ourselves beyond openness and transparency to adopt the disciplines of seeking truth and speaking truth to power. In place of the cultivation of psychological safety, chapter 6 explores a key concept of this book: moral risk-taking. Chapter 7 takes us beyond creating "happy" organizations, which provide the greatest good to the greatest number, to creating organizations where people cultivate a distinctive mood and style. Such organizations have such distinctive cultures that they feel like different worlds. Chapter 8 goes beyond the normal strategy of applying operational strength against operational weakness to show how moral-risk-taking leaders compete based on the appeal of a new, distinctive, admirable moral order. We draw on Anita Roddick and Julia Robertson as our exemplars. Then, chapter 9 goes beyond cultivating one of the typical leaderly styles such as servant or authentic leadership and shows the self-critical disciplines for cultivating a personal leadership style worthy of admiration. In such cultivation, masterpiece-creating leaders give up parts of themselves that they love. That is the character of a moral risk-taker. Last, in chapter 10 we summarize the book and then turn to the crucial issue of whether we have simply reinvented the old heroic, autocratic, patriarchal leader. We draw on Thomas Carlyle, who developed the "great man" view of leadership, and show—as Carlyle himself says—that it lives in an economy of obedience. Our leader, however, has many nonpatriarchal behaviors such as listening, attending to moods, being receptive to anomalies, and cultivating and changing personal styles, but, most importantly, our leader dwells in an economy of gratitude. People follow the leaders because they are grateful for the moral change the leader brought about. Our leader is a poet of action who creates a morally distinct and attractive organizational masterpiece.

1 Leaders as Masterpiece Creators: Churchill and Madam Walker

Tomorrow,
I'll be at the table
When company comes.
Nobody'll dare
Say to me,
"Eat in the kitchen,"
Then.

Besides,
They'll see how beautiful I am
And be ashamed—

I, too, am America.
—Langston Hughes, "I, Too"

In this chapter, we show how two quite different leaders—Winston Churchill and Madam C. J. Walker—nevertheless acted in a similar fashion, although in hugely different contexts, to take moral risks and create new moral norms and a new moral order. They exemplify our thesis that genuine organizational leaders create organizations that bring the wonder of a new moral order that resonates with our lives, and they do so with technical and practical proficiency. In short, they create masterpieces through their moral risk-taking. Establishing the connection between moral risk-taking and new moral-norms creation will enable us to discuss how business leaders today, such as Ray Dalio, Jeff Bezos, Anita Roddick, and Julia Robertson, less dramatically, also broke the then prevailing moral norms in order to create new moral orders within their organizations and wider communities. Given our central interest in *business* leadership that enables a greater plurality of moral orders, we will devote significantly more space to the case of Walker.

Churchill

Adolf Hitler in the 1930s is the simplest, clearest example of a moral anomaly. At that time, the moral order of the British elite consisted of grounding norms of buoyant bonhomie with high-minded judgment as the clarifying moral norm and affability as the organizing norm. Within that moral order, it made complete sense to think that Hitler would become a gentleman as soon as he led Germany to recover from its humiliation at Versailles.[1] Thus, virtually all elite thinking (in Britain and elsewhere) saw appeasement as the morally right thing to do. Indeed, it was a version of the elite's organizing norm of affability. Anything else, such as Churchill's call for a military buildup, looked like immoral warmongering.[2]

Indeed, the morally correct elite wanted to negotiate a settlement with Hitler even after Dunkirk in 1940. In dealing with Hitler, however, Churchill could not see under the prevailing moral norms any morally right action that could yield an end to Hitler's conquest. Churchill saw Hitler as having a brutal thirst for conquest, but the English broadly reviled Churchill for calling for a military buildup during the 1930s. People vividly remembered that Churchill's aggressive leadership had driven the disaster at Gallipoli in World War I. In 1940, though, when it became apparent that the Tories' appeasement politics was in trouble, the Tories appointed Churchill prime minister. Churchill not only had to save the British army but also had to change the way the British saw Hitler and the war.

With the largest part of the British army huddled in Dunkirk awaiting transport, the approaching German army would likely wipe out most of the British troops. Churchill took his first morally shocking action, which was much like the one he had been condemned for at Gallipoli 15 years earlier. To delay the German army, he ordered the British troops stationed in Calais to fight to the death. No calculation could show that the action was likely to work. Hence, it was shocking, but Churchill's luck held, and it worked. The gambit saved the troops at Dunkirk. Nevertheless, only those closest to Churchill saw the change he was trying to make. He knew that the only way to survive and win would be to adopt brutal realism instead of high-mindedness and ruthlessness instead of appeasement. But Churchill's own speeches clouded the issue.

When France fell, Churchill faced an even harder decision. Most of the French fleet lay in the harbor at Oran and could be seized by the Germans to build their own fleet and add a significant challenge for the British navy. Churchill had his admirals issue orders that the French had to sail to safe ports, sink their ships, or have them sunk by the British navy. The French admiral delayed, Churchill issued the order, and in 10 minutes the British navy sunk the ships and killed 1,297 French sailors who were allies. Churchill called the action a Greek tragedy. But when he grimly reported to a silent, shocked Parliament, the MPs and virtually all the English understood his decision. As Churchill said, "The elimination of the French Navy as an important factor almost at a single stroke by violent action produced a profound impression in every country. . . . It was made plain that the British War Cabinet feared nothing and would stop at nothing."[3] Buoyancy, brutal realism, and ruthlessness became key to the new moral order that lasted through World War II and so long as the strategy of mutually assured destruction remained a cornerstone of peace. Figure 1.1 draws on these three different kinds of moral norms and shows the main steps in establishing a new moral order.

Madam C. J. Walker

Churchill's heroic vigor may create the misimpression that masterpiece-creating leadership is masculine—indeed, based on a remorseless masculinity. Not at all. Walker is a good example. Before we expand on the issue of gendered masterpiece-creating leadership, we want to stress that she is important to us for another reason. Walker created a moral norm that reverberated through the 1920s: that Black women (really, women in general) should make themselves and their lives into masterpieces. In short, she had a more radical claim to make about masterpieces than we make. Ours is for leaders, not for everybody or for women generally. However, she anticipated the core of our view and provides a good example of the feminine side of masterpiece creation.

Around 1905, Walker, along with her husband and daughter, started selling her hair-growing treatment door-to-door, by mail order, and through her salon. By 1910, she established the Madam C. J. Walker Manufacturing Company. Through her entrepreneurial activity as one of the inventors of the cosmetics industry, she is one of the first Black American women to become a millionaire in the United States. Like Churchill, she faced a moral anomaly and took moral risks to overcome it. So far as we assess leaderly

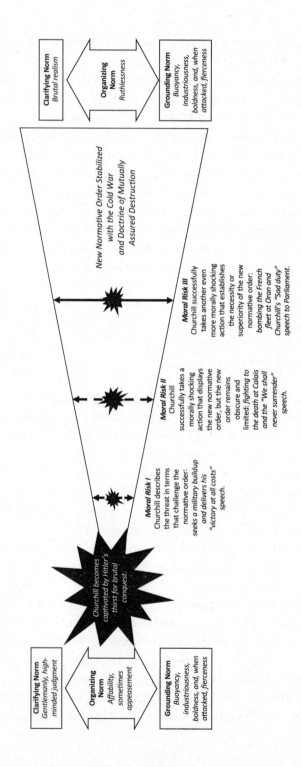

Initial British Normative Order

Clarifying Norm
Gentlemanly, high-minded judgment

Organizing Norm
Affability, sometimes appeasement

Grounding Norm
Buoyancy, industriousness, boldness, and, when attacked, fierceness

Churchill becomes captivated by Hitler's thirst for brutal conquest.

Moral Risk I
Churchill describes the threat in terms that challenge the normative order: *seeks a military buildup and delivers his "victory at all costs" speech.*

Moral Risk II
Churchill successfully takes a morally shocking action that displays the new normative order, but the new order remains obscure and limited: *fighting to the death at Calais and the "We shall never surrender" speech.*

Moral Risk III
Churchill successfully takes another even more morally shocking action that establishes the necessity or superiority of the new normative order: *bombing the French fleet at Oran and Churchill's "Sad duty" speech to Parliament.*

New Normative Order Stabilized with the Cold War and Doctrine of Mutually Assured Destruction

New British Normative Order

Clarifying Norm
Brutal realism

Organizing Norm
Ruthlessness

Grounding Norm
Buoyancy, industriousness, boldness, and, when attacked, fierceness

Figure 1.1
How Winston Churchill changed the British moral order. Vertical lines show the new normative order displacing the original one as moral risks are taken one after another.

behavior as gendered, then Churchill's opening himself up to moral anomalies and becoming captivated by one—Hitler—had the feminine capability we find in all masterpiece creators, but he did not fully express it publicly. Walker gives us a more gender-balanced leadership. To give a quick view of Walker's blended leadership, we will look at her company convention in 1917, two years before she died.

On the first day, she quelled a rebellion of her agents who were upset that she started selling her Madam Walker's Wonderful Hair Grower in drugstores instead of strictly through them: "I have conducted my business this year almost at a loss owing to the unusual cost of material, heavy taxes, etc. I have not raised prices because I did not want my agents to suffer. . . . You have been loyal to me and by the help of God, I am trying to be loyal to you." She admitted her vulnerability. However, on the second day she advised them on their business endeavors in a speech that sounds as masculine as Churchill's later famous speeches: "My advice to everyone expecting to go into business is to hit often and hit hard; in other words; strike with all your might."[4] One cannot help but hear in this speech a business version of "We shall fight on the beaches." This blending is notable throughout her facing of her moral anomaly and her moral risk-taking. It is a model that serves well for illuminating the other masterpiece-creating leaders we mention.

Like Churchill, she faced a key moral anomaly. Though lynchings, peonage, segregation, and general race-based contempt made life hellish at the turn of the twentieth century, the Black community had developed resources to survive. First, members of these communities grounded their lives in norms of mutual help, education, thrift, and charity. The institutions that drove these moral practices were the churches (the African Methodist Episcopal Church, which Walker attended, the Baptist Church, and the African Methodist Zion Church) and the fraternal organizations (the Knights of Pythias and its sister organization, the Court of Calanth, of which Walker was also an active member). The churches exemplified the grounding norms in weekly services, Bible classes, recitals, and revivals. Together with the fraternal organizations, the churches understood that they were competing against "alley crap games and all-night dives." Members of these churches and clubs upheld the moral norms of middle-class life.[5]

Walker's community also had the clearly etched aspirational, clarifying moral norms of self-reliance and industriousness. Booker T. Washington was the exemplar of such moral norms, and his Tuskegee Institute trained people to teach and to succeed at farming and other trades typical of the rural South. But this training was not simply vocational. It was also moral and aesthetic. Washington wanted the students to be beautiful and digni-fied.[6] For Walker, Washington was the most "well-known advocate of Black entrepreneurs," and in 1912, with her business established, she sought his endorsement.[7] Within the Black community, there was also the clarifying norm of political activism to achieve equal rights. W. E. B. Du Bois stood for this norm's primacy. Though Walker was politically active, this clari-fying moral norm never became primary for her: first and foremost, she ran her business. Another clarifying norm in the Black community (fitting closely with industrious self-reliance) applied especially to women. Helena Rubinstein stated it succinctly with one of her famous, powerful aphorisms: "There are no ugly women," she said, "only lazy ones."[8] Any woman with a work ethic could look good, and for women brought up on the Bible, such as those in communities Walker sold to, hair was particularly important. "Does not Nature herself teach you that while flowing locks disgrace a man, they are a woman's glory?" (1 Corinthians, 11.14–15).[9]

In the Black community, the grounding moral norm of mutual care and the clarifying norm of industrious self-reliance were bound together by an organizing norm of self-promotion. This combination and particularly the organizing norm of self-promotion came out most clearly in the speeches made in the meetings of Booker T. Washington's National Negro Business League. One Black entrepreneur after another spoke about his financial suc-cess, the size of his business, where he sold products, the number of his customers, and so forth.[10] These commercial reports seem brash and even conceited to our ears today. But marketing was much more brass-knuckled then. Such self-promoting bragging connected industrious self-reliance with the mutual-support organizations because a critical part of the brag was the size of support for those organizations and their charities. One pro-moted oneself as an industrious, successful, wealthy (with the trappings of wealth), outstanding member of the community who gave significant amounts of money to mutual-support organizations. That opened the ques-tion of what self a Black woman entrepreneur could promote.

Annie Pope-Turnbo (later Turnbo Malone) was a model for such a self. She was also Sarah Breedlove McWilliams Davis's—Walker's—mentor, model, and competitor. Though Annie Malone became a millionaire entrepreneur in the Black haircare, cosmetics industry around the same time as did Walker, Malone promoted herself as a forthright, financially successful Black woman who made her employees financially independent. By the time Walker started her business in 1906, Malone had already made good on the promise of growing hair and linking well-groomed hair with money. Better grooming did open the job market, and by training women to sell her hair growers and to work in and run her salons, she made these sales agents and salon operators financially independent through self-reliance. With Malone's and soon Walker's techniques, these hairdressers could earn between $15 and $40 per week, comparable to good factory work and far better than the 40 cents per day paid to farmworkers in the South.[11] Malone promoted her business prowess and its value to her customers and workers, but she lived modestly, later shared the ownership of her business with her husband, Aaron Malone, and made charitable contributions with less fanfare than Booker T. Washington's mostly male acolytes. In short, her self-promotion accepted feminine compliance, subordination, and, to a certain extent, meekness. Given the hard edge of the times and the coming Jazz Age, the self she promoted did not seem a distinctive masterpiece. She certainly did not, as Walker did, proclaim herself to be on a divine mission.

To see the qualitative difference between the self as a masterpiece and the self as a role model, we need to look at Walker's development, what she learned from Malone, her moral risk-taking in her betrayal of Malone, Walker's creation of the new Black American woman, and the consequent shift in the moral order. First, we need to answer one question. Could Malone and Walker really grow hair? Yes. Because hair hygiene was poor and treatment of it harsh at the time, Black women especially (including Walker) had scalp diseases—primarily seborrhea and psoriasis—that caused hair loss. Malone's Wonderful Hair Grower and later Madam C. J. Walker's Wonderful Hair Grower contained sulfur and disinfecting carbolic acid to heal scalps. Other ingredients made for a pleasing ointment and covered the smell of the sulfur. With regular shampooing and these women entrepreneurs' hair growers, hair did grow.[12] And within the prevailing moral order, taking care of one's hair was, for a woman, an aesthetic, financial, and moral good. It showed self-reliance and industriousness. It was the right thing to do.

Second, to see the difference between these two entrepreneurial women, it is critical to know that Walker had earlier in her life lost most of her hair;

Malone never did. Malone started out loving chemistry and hairdressing, which she did with her sister. In the early 1900s, she developed her own hair-growing product, which she called Wonderful Hair Grower.[13] (Note the near identity in name of Walker's product.) Then, around 1902 Walker met Malone. Walker had by that time lost most of her hair, and Malone offered her services. Walker's hair grew back.[14] Malone then trained Walker in her hair-treatment techniques and showed her how to be a sales agent. Walker thrived as Malone's sales agent and in 1905 decided to represent her boss in Denver.

Malone promised her customers that "better appearance means greater business opportunities, higher social standing, cleaner living and beautiful homes."[15] It was so. But her promise and the self she promoted seemed empty to Walker, who knew not only the despair of losing hair and having no glory as a woman but also the joy of gaining her hair and glory back. To appreciate the difference in sensibility between the chemist turned hairdresser-entrepreneur and the sensibility of a desperate, balding washerwoman who received a new outlook and life, we need only listen to Walker's story of her development of her own hair treatment, as told by her biographer and great-great-granddaughter A'Lelia Bundles:

> "I was on the verge of becoming entirely bald," Sarah often told other women. Ashamed of the "frightful" appearance of her hair and desperate for a solution, she "prayed to the Lord" for guidance. "He answered my prayer," she vouched. "For one night I had a dream, and in that dream a big black man appeared to me and told me what to mix for my hair. Some of the remedy was from Africa, but I sent for it, mixed it, put it on my scalp and in a few weeks my hair was coming in faster than it had ever fallen out. . . . When I made my discovery, I had no idea of placing it on the market for the benefit of others. . . ." [However, this] miraculous concoction, she believed, was nothing less than "an inspiration from God," a heaven-sent gift for her to "place in the reach of those who appreciate beautiful hair and healthy scalps, which is the glory of woman."[16]

Walker was not out merely to grow hair and increase a woman's status. Her aim was a religious fervor to bring a miracle to women, to raise their glory to a new level. In our interpretation, bringing out the glory of women meant making them into masterpieces. She saw her hair grower as a miracle that would be a road-to-Damascus moment of regeneration for women.

Fulfilling her mission would require that Walker take the most significant moral risk of her life in betraying Malone. Walker did not have a formula for making her hair grower. She probably learned Malone's formula through the analysis services of Edmond Scholtz of the Scholtz Drug Company in Denver. Likewise, Walker did not have her own business model: salons, a training institution, sales agents, and mail order. She adopted Malone's. Walker did not even feel up to training her own daughter, whom she sent to Malone's training program in St. Louis shortly before Walker made her break with Malone. But in mid-May 1905, Walker stopped her weekly advertising of herself as one of Malone's agents and remained silent until mid-September 1905. Then she completely broke off her relationship with Malone. She made her own version of Malone's (unpatented) formula and began to develop the same business model. Malone denounced Walker in the popular Black newspaper *The Statesman*: "The proof of the value of our work is that we are being imitated and largely by persons whose own hair we have actually grown. They have very frequently mentioned us when trying to sell their goods (saying that 'theirs is the same' or 'just as good'). . . . BEWARE OF IMITATIONS."[17]

Given the brass-knuckled marketing of the time and Malone's capacity to name other competitors and blame them for harming people, her tone in *The Statesman* was relatively mild.[18] She did not name Walker. She did not go into the details of the betrayal. Although others claimed that Walker "filched" the formula, Malone did not press that claim. She did not liken Walker to Judas or try to poison Walker's reputation within her church. Malone certainly did not follow Walker's maxim of "hit often," "hit hard," "strike with all your might." We can easily suppose that, as with Machiavelli's bold heroes, Walker's brazenness stunned Malone. Still, Walker was a genuine churchgoing, believing, traditional Christian. She had to know the wickedness of her betrayal. She had to have felt that there was no other way for her to create a business that would bring glory to women. To make her action good, she had to succeed at the mission set for her of giving women the capacity to appear as the receivers of a miracle—to appear, we shall say, as admirably distinctive masterpieces of their own self-reliant and self-promoting self-creation. Unlike Churchill, whose morally shocking actions themselves became the new norms, Walker's morally shocking betrayal and theft as well as her self-transformation into "Madam C. J. Walker" set the level of moral intensity that the good to come of the betrayal and theft would have to have. Giving women their sense of glory—enabling them to become masterpieces—had to have sufficient moral value to offset the wrongs.

Walker had to take other moral risks, which again could have back-fired. When she treated her husband, C. J. Walker, as a mere salesperson and then divorced him because he did not want so much growth as she did, she faced not only legal risks but claims that she was unwomanly and purely self-aggrandizing. Again, her brazenness won the day.[19] Everyone had to accept her uncompromising control over a growth company. She sliced through the question of whether a Black woman could become an independent, successful leader. Another moral risk came when Walker used her wealth to pressure (bully) a poor neighbor into giving up her beautiful daughter and perfect hair model for adoption by Walker's daughter, Lelia. It appeared to some critics that Walker and Lelia simply wanted a model they could control. But they were, like Roman emperors, adopting the perfect heir for the empire. Making these matters right would depend on using her hair-growing company to create a new moral order. In it, Black women (and other women generally) would include in self-promotion becoming financially, intellectually, and politically independent. They would culti-vate their own beauty and become miraculously self-confident in making their lives masterpieces.

Malone promoted herself as a financially independent Black entrepre-neur with an otherwise upright and conventional life. We might want to claim that by our current lights her life and business were masterpieces. But that was not what Malone promoted herself as. Madam C. J. Walker (con-sider the name alone) promoted every aspect of her life for admiration so that people would see it as a masterpiece.

While Malone held half her business with her husband, Walker let her husband be no more than a sales agent when she learned that he was sat-isfied with their $10 per day in earnings, and then she carefully divorced him, leaving a little settlement and a strong threat from her attorney against trying to make any legal claims.[20] When Aaron Malone divorced Annie, he sued her for half the value of the business and settled for a huge $200,000. Meanwhile, Annie led a modest life with relatively little engagement in politics. She quietly gave thousands of dollars to the YMCA, the Howard University College of Medicine, and the St. Louis Colored Orphans Home.[21] Walker stood firmly and outspokenly against lynching and for the rights of Black men returning from the war; she also carved out carefully calculated political stands to wind a course between Bookerites and followers of W. E. B. Du Bois. Further, she expected and pushed her agents to take thoughtful political stands. Walker gave generously and boisterously to charities from first to last and made sure her charitable giving enhanced her own and her business's identity. She also gave with the expectation of influencing the spending of her gift.[22] No one would accuse her of modesty.

After her divorce, Malone moved her business to Chicago, where she bought a whole block. In contrast, at the beginning of the Harlem Renaissance Walker purchased Harlem properties, and with her daughter, Lelia, who would become a famous hostess of Harlem Renaissance figures, she created a stunningly beautiful salon. "The decorators said that of all the work they had done . . . there is nothing equal to it, not even on Fifth Avenue," which included the midtown salons of Elizabeth Arden and Helena Rubinstein. Walker then built her Italianate palace, Villa Lewaro, so christened by Enrico Caruso, in Irvington-on-Hudson, the neighborhood of the Rockefellers, Goulds, Tiffanys, Astors, Vanderbilts, and Morgans. (Note the ease in comparing Walker's palace to those in Nietzsche's Genoa.) She told her longtime lawyer and general manager, Freeman B. Ransom, to tell reporters that "the Irvington home, after my death, will be left to some cause that will be beneficial to the race—a sort of monument." But though Villa Lewaro is surely monumental, it was Walker's own personal transformation that amazed most. Bundles writes: "Madam Walker herself continued to impress others with her own personal transformation. . . . *Freeman* reporter William Lewis had described her as 'splendidly poised[, wearing] her wealth and honors with ease as if she had [them] for all the years. . . . Madam Walker can hold her own in any gathering of women.' Through her new organization she meant to help other women develop the same self-acquired confidence."[23] Hers was a masterpiece of confident beauty, grace, wealth, independence, marketing brilliance, political moral thoughtfulness—an entrepreneurial rags-to-riches transformation that brought many other women along. She created a "washtub to the boardroom" masterpiece on the back of her moral risk-taking. She was at the end of her life a distinctive icon. As Erica Ball writes, "And by the time of her death in 1919, the name and image of Madam C. J. Walker conjured up a wealth of meaning—both personal and political—for black Americans." Ball claims that Walker defined what it would mean to be a "race woman," one who lifted up her race, and that Villa Lewaro showed that she also became a celebrity.[24] We believe that as a masterpiece creator Walker became a member of the American aristocracy, which seems clearly implicit in Bundles's description of her.

Did Walker change her moral order? She did, but she did not live to see it fully. She died on the eve of the Roaring Twenties and the Harlem Renaissance. She displaced the organizing norm of conventional self-promotion with making oneself a miraculous masterpiece.[25] Lelia's life shows that she understood her mother's example, that the moral norm of masterpiece making displaced that of conventional self-promotion. After living in her mother's shadow and constantly losing the tug-of-war with her mother, Lelia Walker had to transform herself. She did not have her mother's marketing acumen and abdicated her corporate responsibilities to her mother's loyal, brilliant lawyer and general manager, Freeman B. Ransom. After a trip to Europe, she returned transformed into "A'Lelia Walker" and became the leading hostess of the Harlem Renaissance who was celebrated by poet Langston Hughes as the "joy-goddess of Harlem's 1920s."[26] Ball describes her as the "type of edgy and avant garde New Negro Womanhood fit for the glory days of the Harlem Renaissance."[27]

It is commonplace to say that Virginia Woolf, Dorothy Parker, Edna St. Vincent Millay, Ernest Hemingway, and F. Scott Fitzgerald are among the main voices that chronicled and brought about the transformation of women in the Jazz Age of the 1920s. Black women in the United States transformed themselves as well; for that, we owe Walker (as well as perhaps her daughter, Zora Neale Hurston, and few others) our gratitude. Even while Malone's forthright, modest form of self-promotion remained, notable women of the age promoted themselves as masterpieces. Unlike state builders such as Churchill, whose new moral orders *replace* the old, business leaders tend to create new moral orders that *displace* the older orders, leaving them in place in some organizations. Hence, we have the moral pluralism enabled by business.

Figure 1.2 illustrates the ways Walker changed the Black American entrepreneurial moral order. But did her changes last? Did Walker's moral order last beyond the Jazz Age? The human potential movement of the 1960s owes something to the moral order left by Walker, but perhaps the most noteworthy representative of this form of masterpiece selfhood is Oprah Winfrey. Oprah Winfrey found the financially perfect medium for promoting herself as a masterpiece, the talk show, and she constantly carefully choreographed her revelations—stories supposedly from her own life—which

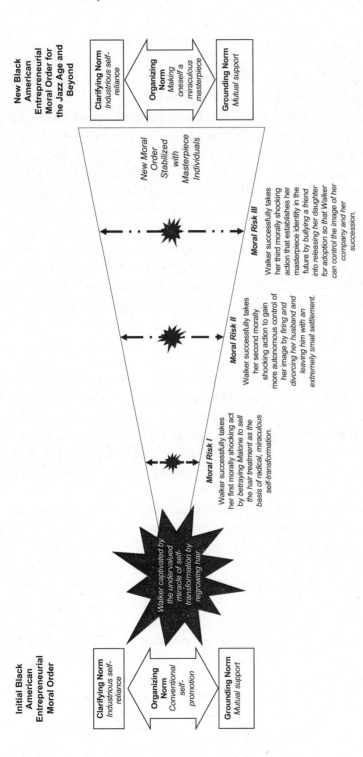

Figure 1.2

How Madam Walker changed the Black American entrepreneurial moral order. Vertical lines show the new moral order displacing the original one as moral risks are taken one after another.

rang true and brought wonder to the lives of her audience. Like Walker and the story of her invention of her hair grower, Winfrey is a walking literary masterpiece and, as such, evidence that the moral order of Madam C. J. Walker lives. Nancy F. Koehn and her coauthors write: "In the image-driven world of television, Winfrey was candid about her flaws and vulnerabilities. From early on, for example, she talked on air about her lifelong struggle to lose weight. Occasionally, Winfrey also made surprising confessions. In 1995, she startled viewers and media observers by revealing that she had used cocaine in her 20s. . . . Winfrey shared such details of her personal battles because, she said, 'I've experienced what everyone else has experienced.'"[28] Thus, Winfrey's point is that everyone should become a literary masterpiece like her. Her mission says the same: "Our intention is to create moments in which people can connect to their truest sense of themselves and build from there."[29] Winfrey's family members often feel betrayed by the fanciful elements of her stories, but they accept this cost.[30]

The Limits of Rational Persuasion and Expediency

The Churchill and Walker cases show why rational persuasion does not usually change moral norms to create new moral orders. Churchill had unsuccessfully tried to reason with the British elite for 10 years, and he could be brilliantly persuasive. Imagine Walker trying to persuade chemistry-loving Malone to leverage her hair-growing ointment into a transformative miracle. We adopt new moral norms when a morally shocking action succeeds and shows us a new, workable moral order.

The stories raise two additional questions. First, in drawing on the actions of these leaders, are we simply saying that ends justify any means? No. In this book, we examine moral risk-taking *in the face of moral anomalies*. We believe that is the proper place for such risk-taking because no other action will have a good outcome. However, in life as in literature, moral risk-taking frequently occurs for the sake of expediency. Odysseus's deceits—such as telling the Cyclops his name is "Nobody"—are expedient immoral actions not taken in the face of a *moral* anomaly, where doing any of the traditionally right things would lead to evil. Odysseus's actions, typical of *metis*, are cases of a moral risk taken for expediency's sake.[31] This expedient moral risk-taking is what desperate leaders take in liberal democracies and what authoritarian and totalitarian leaders frequently take as a matter of course.

In these cases, practical ends justify practical means. Our focus is on changing moral orders and not on expedience.

Second, by advocating for moral risk-taking in the face of moral anomalies, are we condoning businesses engaging in illegal practices? Our moral risk-taking involves a shocking immoral action that must itself be clearly visible (unlike most criminal actions), and the results must be so widely admired by various groups that they excuse or celebrate the shocking action. Additionally, we focus on cases where the action not only produces a change in moral order but also produces a morally distinctive organization. We cannot imagine every business scenario, but it seems likely that the only kind of crimes that could meet these criteria for our moral risk-taking would be acts of civil disobedience. However, neither of our answers implies that the form of moral risk-taking we advocate cannot lead to evil actions; it can. We will look at that issue in chapter 8 when we discuss Andrew Fastow, Enron's former chief financial officer.

Masterpiece-creating business leaders have to take shocking moral risks that could threaten their and others' careers and personal well-being, and they do so to change moral orders as Churchill and Walker did. They must take them because they face moral anomalies, where no attempt to resolve the anomaly with good practical consequences is morally acceptable under the prevailing moral order. Thus, rational persuasion is uncommon. Changing people's minds about what is right generally requires bringing them into another world either in imagination, as artists and even dissidents do, or in fact, as organizational leaders do. We do not justify every action in the name of masterpiece creation, but we do justify those sometimes seemingly unethical actions taken in the face of moral anomalies and resulting in the establishment of a new moral order.[32]

Consider, for example, the case of Jeff Bezos. By creating a humiliating retirement for his founding employee Shel Kaphan, who created the initial Amazon site, Bezos made raising the bar on job qualifications a moral norm at Amazon and enabled Amazon to become an everything store that brought order to online retail.[33] Ray Dalio terminated his initial thinking partner Paul Colman and later demoted his chosen successor (whom he had treated like a son) to establish the moral norm of radical transparency.[34] Anita Roddick took the moral risk of betraying her husband and business partner's trust by giving away—potentially irresponsibly squandering—half the ownership of the Body Shop in order to fund growth. Thus, she made growth a moral norm at the Body Shop, as important as compassion, love, and fun.[35] Phil Knight took the moral risk of lying to his bankers, manufacturers, and closest associates to make just-do-it athleticism into a moral norm.[36] These terminations (including the ones made by Julia Robertson, which we discuss in chapter 8) and betrayals are the milder children of Churchill's and Walker's moral risk-taking.

Jerks and Assholes and the Current View of Leadership as Influence

Even if we accept that such mold-breaking, masterpiece-creating leaders get us out of moral messes, are these leaders not still, in the end, jerks and assholes? The leaders might have done something morally good for their community, but should they be able to look at themselves in the mirror at night and feel good about themselves?

As an empirical matter, these leaders do seem able to look at themselves in the mirror at night. They seem self-admiring. These leaders act (and write about their actions) with clear awareness that they are creating organizations and leadership styles that are masterpieces. In effect, they become practical philosophers by developing distinctive comprehensive views concerning human behavior, success, and the meaning of life. Ray Dalio of Bridgewater loves his bold, frank assessment processes for creating an idea meritocracy and keeps those processes through thick and thin.[37] Throughout the working day at Bridgewater, people are constantly making blunt assessments of each other and each other's ideas. Many companies still copy Jack Welch's GE practices because managers think that efficient performance is what business is about and that managers need to remove deadwood regularly and quickly.[38] They believe that every bit as much as Anita Roddick believed that business should be fun.[39] Steve Jobs is famous for joining the humanities to technology and for setting impossible perfectionist goals to do so. Reed Hastings's commitment to his "no rules rules" culture at Netflix is well known.[40]

Nevertheless, many believe that these mold-breaking leaders are jerks and assholes and that their successes did not require their shocking moral-convention-breaking behavior.[41] Many have condemned Steve Jobs for creating a reality-distortion field around himself as he expected the impossible of his people.[42] The press and others have described Ray Dalio as a cult leader.[43] Jack Welch is "Neutron Jack." Reed Hastings is famous for saying,

"Do not tolerate brilliant jerks. The cost to teamwork is too high"—but his insistence on candor and truth telling as well as on terminating those who do not deserve pay above their current level could easily in many quarters earn him the title of brilliant jerk.

Could these leaders have achieved moral and economic successes through milder means? Our masterpiece-creating leaders put their necks on the line in taking bold risks to resolve moral anomalies. The reigning orthodoxy claims that risk-taking, even if it is sometimes required, is not the essence of leadership: leadership is essentially influence. True leaders influence others to act appropriately. Jerks and assholes push people around. One of us was recently in a conversation with the leader who transformed a small company into a company with $1 billion in revenue. He had taken tough moral risks to create a team that could drive the company to its current size. However, when asked to give a talk on leadership, he said it was a hard talk to give because he could not settle on a narrative for it. However, he recalled a course he took at Berkeley where the professor explained that in the past people thought of leaders as heroic individuals who issued directives, but in the 1970s that view changed. Leaders became understood as influencers who coached and cultivated the talents of their teams. So this leader, who had transformed the company against persistent opposition, said that he spoke about his moments where he had influenced others with persuasion and had helped members of his team succeed. The speech on leadership went over well, but it captured little of what he had done as he transformed his organization. It left out his moral risk-taking entirely. We find leaders frequently going along with the common account and ignoring what they have done. They do not want others to see them as assholes, jerks, or tyrants.

Can influence be the essence of leadership? Who has not influenced another person? If influence is the essence of leadership, there is nothing particularly special about leaders. Salespeople influence every day. To influence another, a person builds trust by carefully cultivating normal personal or professional virtues. So, unsurprisingly, today's leadership literature emphasizes such virtues: Ronald Heifetz sees leaders as good doctors who know how much truth to tell a patient and when; Robert K. Greenleaf and James Burns see leaders as coaches; Herminia Ibarra as daring self-experimenters; Bill George as authentic (he really means dutiful) individuals; Robert Kegan and Lisa Laskow Lahey as self-transforming

actualizers; Jim Collins as humble team builders.[44] Although these virtues
are good virtues, there is nothing especially leaderly about them. People
with such virtues do influence us, but there is nothing about these virtues
that would enable one to take on a moral anomaly. Are these the virtues
that could face down Hitler? Are they the virtues that could face down the
beauty business in Anita Roddick's day?

Many academic theorists follow the insight that leadership is essentially
influence to its natural and problematic conclusion: because leadership is
merely influence, leadership is distributed among many people in an organization so that anyone can be a leader.[45] This form of thinking has other
insidious consequences. Because leadership is influence, the mark of a great
leader turns out to be that the leader can achieve consensus and influence
everyone.[46] That argument presumes influence by rational persuasion.
Rational influence sometimes works, but when it does, it is not necessarily a manifestation of leadership. What such thinking forgets are the hard
choices that organizational leaders must make. Such thinking forgets the
captain of a naval vessel who sends one band of sailors to repair a breach
and then, to save the ship, must send another band to close the hole farther
in and thereby drown the first team. If the ship is saved, the captain will
be a hero; if not, the captain will be considered to have acted callously and
likely immorally. Such leaderly actions do not come down to influence.

Somehow the way artists and dissidents work to change our moral orders
has migrated over to organizational leaders. Artists, particularly literary
ones, create worlds where we imaginatively see ourselves behaving and
thinking differently. Seeing is still believing, but we see imaginatively. Dissidents are much the same. They have a life story that is quite different from
our own but compellingly connects in such a way that we feel the necessity
for new moral evaluations. Martin Luther King Jr. did that brilliantly with
his capacity to mix the violence of racism against him with a Christian forgiveness. Most organizational leaders, in particular business leaders, do not
have that imaginative, poetic capacity. They are action takers. Thus, without the poet's abilities or the dissident's special life circumstances or burning sense of a wrong, organizational leaders will find building consensus
arduous work and likely will end up achieving consensus by hewing close
to the current moral order. So, we end up where deconstructive thinkers
said we would: to lead is to follow.

Accordingly, most who write about business do not see it as a place for moral invention but rather as a place for prudent sense making. Under these writers' influence, business leaders look at those parts of work where prudence is most at home: operational processes, organization of work and roles, strategies that simply pit technical strengths against technical weaknesses, and positive team and individual building. These business leaders supplement their prudence with emotional intelligence, empathetic listening, trust as reliability, openness, transparency (without hard truth seeking), safety, and authenticity or servant (caring) leadership. They search for the greatest happiness for the greatest number. All those attributes are good to have, and if used well, they will produce an operationally and financially successful organization where people get along. But they will not give a leader an organization that is admirable for and competes on its *moral* difference. The building of moral difference requires different or more sophisticated skills, which we set out in the rest of this book. Leaders cannot build moral masterpieces without morally shocking actions.

2 Philosophy, Literature, History, and a Leader's Good Life

I want to learn more and more to see as beautiful what is necessary in things; then I shall be one of those who make things beautiful.

—Friedrich Nietzsche, *The Gay Science*

Most philosophers and literary writers have had a dim view of business. Plato and his successors saw people in business as living in a world of necessity and providing only what people needed. People in business did not have spirits that soared to see pure ideas. It was up to creative people, thinkers, and political leaders to think freely about the world and design the ways in which to live. The good thing about this philosophical (civic humanist) mistake in judging business is that it shows us what we should look for in our business leaders. We should look for them, as the Victorian philosopher John Ruskin did, to design new ways to live, just as thinkers and state builders were supposed to do in the ancient world. This lofty view of business started arising in the Renaissance. William Shakespeare was the first artist to support himself through his business, the Globe Theatre. As he designed ways for theater owners and players to live, his tragedies taught people to live for their personal narratives, the stories that made them who they were. He made us the kind of people we were in modernity—lead characters in our own lives. Such are "modern" people: self-conscious, autonomous, free subjects. By creating this new kind of good life, Shakespeare made himself and his actors extremely successful in commerce; there are more records of how Shakespeare conducted his theater business than of how he composed his poetry and plays.

For this chapter, from the Renaissance, we draw on Shakespeare, Niccolò Machiavelli, and John Milton. From philosophy, we draw mostly from the twentieth-century Continental tradition with Friedrich Nietzsche, Martin Heidegger, and Michel Foucault as our main inspirations.[1] We also pay attention to Anglo-American philosophers such as Martha Nussbaum, Bernard Williams, Charles Taylor, William James, Hilary Putnam, Richard Rorty, John McDowell, and especially Hubert Dreyfus. Other writers from the humanities will appear along the way.[2] Some of these writers and scholars may be from the distant past, but their works have a surprising resonance for us today if we are to become masterpiece creators. If you have not engaged with their writings before, do not worry: we will explain them and show why they matter for business leadership.

You may justifiably ask: What does such attention to philosophers and literary lions get us? We answer: It enables us to see businesses as masterpieces and leaders as masterpiece creators who take moral risks. It enables us to see conceptual frameworks and practices that can be used in helping leaders create their masterpieces. It enables us to open an alternative, morally creative view of business, which we do in this chapter.

First, drawing on the humanities, as we do, leaves us among a small band of contrarian scholars who not only use traditions of thinking from the humanities to understand leadership, especially business leadership, but also, critically, do so to make sense of moral risk-taking—a version of Machiavelli's *virtù* (aggressive effectiveness) as a critical part of leadership. Absent this knowledge from the humanities, the reality of moral risk-taking remains a mystery or even a moral wrong.

Second, we ask very broadly what business is about. We step away from the most popular views expounded by economists, sociologists, and other social scientists when we claim that business in general, not just business today, is about creating good lives for owners, customers, employees, and other stakeholders. Working out that answer convincingly, which will take the course of the book, explains the importance of turning businesses into masterpieces.

Third, we can ask and answer the question "What makes masterpieces admirable?" It is their moral distinctiveness and their capacity to supply wonder and admirable, good lives to many of those associated with them. Masterpieces exist in an economy of admiration, which, as we argue at the end of this book, rests on a deeper economy of gratitude.

Fourth, we can discerningly explore what makes our postmodern times morally distinctive and different from our ancestors' times. Drawing on

Nietzsche and his interpreters, we argue that in postmodernity humans find nothing above criticism. We cannot simply believe in anything for long with our full hearts and full conviction. In this regard, we are, in the philosopher Ludwig Wittgenstein's terms, a different form of life from our ancestors. They could be various kinds of fundamentalists; unless we actively hobble ourselves, we cannot be. That does not mean that we cannot live in and burnish our ancestors' traditions, but we do not do it in the same way. Yes, we lack the resonating, total embedding in a single tradition that our ancestors had, but we have a freedom for wonder that our ancestors never had.

Fifth, based on our understanding of postmodernity, we search for the types of good lives today. We draw again on Nietzsche, who finds four significantly different, incompatible good lives: cultivating a distinct moral and aesthetic style, living one brief story after another (brief habits), taking risks, and improvising so that our mistakes become acts of moral and aesthetic beauty. These lives enable us to feel wonder and admiration while leaving our resonating embeddedness in a tradition relatively weak. These are the lives that today's masterpieces must enable.

Sixth, we ask whether business has the capacity to produce the wonder needed for good lives and answer affirmatively by looking back to the radical, liberating commercial exchange invented in ancient Rome and bequeathed to us over the centuries, even if most of us have forgotten it.

Seventh, we ask how business enables postmodern good lives for customers. It is not enough to deliver heartfelt goods. Customers can purchase them but still remain in the go-with-the-flow herd of nondistinct animals. Good lives require moral, aesthetic, and economic distinctiveness. Customers need a way to glamorize their distinctiveness; businesses do that by enabling them to become opinion leaders.

Eighth, we ask, What will happen if business leaders do not start focusing on making masterpieces? Is there an alternative postmodernity? What is it? It is possible, we argue, even likely, for there to arise a postmodernity in which one new herdlike normal follows after another, eternally providing more convenience and more flexibility. That is what masterpiece creation stands against, and that is why we consider it important to cultivate the skills and desire for building masterpieces.

Ninth, drawing on the classical tradition of oratory, we feel obliged to add and will add a *refutatio*, where we take on the objections that will likely arise and give our responses. These nine aims are the subjects of the sections in store in this chapter. We hope you find them distinctive both aesthetically and morally.

Where We Stand: A Small Band of Scholars

So, if our masterpiece-creating leaders dwell in the tradition of Machiavelli's masterpiece-creating princes, do we, as authors of this book about creating masterpieces, also dwell in Machiavelli's tradition? We do, but in a way that might seem counterintuitive. After all, we are explicitly drawing on the humanities, and the Renaissance humanists were Machiavelli's primary enemies.[3] Renaissance humanists stood for the classical virtues, not for Machiavelli's virtù, aggressive effectiveness or, as Bernard Crick glosses the term in Machiavelli's *Discourses*, "'civic spirit' . . . if by 'spirit' one means spirited action."[4] As James Hankins shows in his magisterial work *Virtue Politics*, the Italian Renaissance humanists believed that "virtue and wisdom . . . would impart charisma to a ruler and cause his subjects to bestow upon him their willing obedience."[5] Today's leadership analysts are much like their Renaissance humanist ancestors in basing leadership on soft virtues: empathy, vulnerability, psychological safety, authenticity, the ability to bring out the genius in everyone, and so forth. The unspoken premise is that all of us are mostly good. Favoring the humanists over Machiavelli, Hankins gives us the remarkably similar humanist picture that is plain about its premise:

> Human beings [have] a natural desire for goodness and wisdom that could be cultivated through education and encouraged through a variety of social technologies, including public eloquence, historical writing, and the arts. Like most ancient philosophers, they believed there was a divine element in human nature giving it access to an intelligible moral order in nature. . . . Divine rationality could order the souls of rulers and, through them, civil society. Human beings in society had a natural desire for good rulers and would willingly obey those who ruled with justice and promoted the common good. . . . Most humanists were well aware of the large gap between ideals and practice in the ancient world, but they valued classical ideals as articulating aspirations for political leadership they felt were missing in their own time: virtue, nobility, equality (rightly understood), and wisdom. . . . They believed that the study of classical literature and philosophy written in Latin and Greek could rekindle a love of lost ideals and lost greatness.[6]

Thus, we have a paean to leading through rational persuasion. Machiavelli, however, begged to differ. He thought that in general only virtù could yield prosperous, glorious states and that the classical virtues cultivated in leisure were a danger if left without the active lives created through virtù. We say much the same for moral risk-taking.[7]

Moreover, in Machiavelli's time humanists had taken over the universities and elite government posts. Indeed, Machiavelli could only rise to second chancellor rather than principal chancellor "since that position . . . had ordinarily required great distinction in Latin literature and an international reputation," which he did not have.[8] We find ourselves similarly placed. The humanities now include Machiavelli, but many business books still draw on the humanities in the pre-Machiavellian humanist sense. Consider, to name a few, Joseph L. Badaracco Jr.'s *Managing in the Gray*, Gary Saul Morson and Morton Schapiro's *Cents and Sensibility*, Robert Solomon's *A Better Way to Think about Business*, and Oliver F. Williams's *The Moral Imagination*.[9] Although such books are erudite and insightful in their own ways, the problem we see with them is that they are, like the Renaissance humanists, too respectful of the business pieties we oppose. They end up seeking to tame the humanities to offer what we think are simplistic admonitions for humble, empathetic, authentic, team-playing leaders who set up psychologically safe spaces.[10]

We hope we will not be misunderstood. We do accept that the commonly noted virtues are useful for leaders, but we do not think these virtues are the *defining* features of successful leadership. It would be nice if they were! We are among the very few, after Philip Selznick and his immediate successors, who see that implanting new moral values is an essential part of leadership.[11] But most of Selznick's successors think that leaders establish new moral norms through rational persuasion, not by shocking moral risk-taking. Accordingly, a great deal of the literature focuses primarily on reviving old values, especially under the heading of spiritual, ethical, charismatic, or transformational leadership.[12] However, we find Machiavelli's way of thinking more insightful because he does not turn his eyes away from the "crooked timber of humanity."[13]

Just as Machiavelli sought to bring to life the exercise of virtù to maintain an order in which the other virtues could exist, so we are bringing moral risk-taking (in the face of moral anomalies) to establish moral orders in which some of today's recommended virtues may find a place within a masterpiece organization.[14] Likewise, just as Machiavelli claimed that without virtù leaders would fail when faced with difficult necessities, so we, along with Christopher Michaelson and Patrick Taylor Smith, claim that without moral risk-taking, leaders will fail when facing moral anomalies.[15] However, unlike Machiavelli, we claim that in bringing moral risk-taking and morally distinctive masterpieces to light, we are also bringing the thinking of the humanities to organizational and leadership thinking. In viewing our contribution in this light, we might say that we bring realpolitik to the tradition of virtue ethics, out of which our own thinking grows. In this, we are also successors to and go beyond Steven Sample's *The Contrarian's Guide to Leadership*. Like us inspired by Machiavelli, Sample breaks free of the wisdom of the herd, focuses on listening and truth seeking, and recognizes *moral* diversity and the necessity of taking morally risky actions. However, he does not include the presence of moral anomalies or explain how moral risk-taking changes moral orders.[16]

Our thinking about businesses as masterpieces also has as one of its ancestors the famous Victorian, humanist, aesthetic, and moral philosopher John Ruskin.[17] Ruskin esteemed businesspeople ("merchants," he called them) as having careers as worthy as the most distinguished professionals because merchants, like the professionals, would die for something. According to Ruskin, the soldier would die rather than "leave his post in battle"; the physician would rather die "than leave his post in plague"; the pastor rather than "teach falsehood"; the lawyer rather than "countenance injustice." And the merchants would die to provide goods for their nations (we could extend that to customers generally). Of course, in our postmodern world we are too critical of everything—even our own masterpieces—to speak of dying for them, though we frequently give our lives over to them. However, it is not so much the to-die-for commitment that makes Ruskin's thinking like ours. Merchants, Ruskin says, would die for the organization that provides goods to the nation because their organizations fulfill "the responsibility for [providing] the kind of life [those working in the organization] lead."[18] For Ruskin, business leaders design organizations that make the lives of those working in them worthwhile; those organizations are precisely what we call "masterpiece organizations." Though we are a lonely band of scholars and consultants, we explore lands that Machiavelli and Ruskin discovered. We turn now to look at what it means to create good lives today.

What Is Commerce About?

Many economists think that commerce is about the production and exchange of goods to satisfy needs and desires. Some social scientists such as Abraham Maslow (as commonly received) are like the economists in that they start with basic needs and develop a hierarchy reaching up to spiritual needs.[19] Various businesses respond to various levels of need. More generally, social scientists tend to follow the tradition of the sociologist Max Weber, wherein organizations are "iron cages" (systems focused on rational calculation, control, and efficiency). Such organizations satisfy needs within a strict cost-and-benefit analysis. Philosophers have mostly concurred and gone along with that general sense of commerce as managing necessity and in thinking that, in contrast, designing a state and creating works of art or thought are the genuine acts of creative freedom. We claim, however, that doing business is every bit as free and creative as designing and running a state, engaging in breakthrough thinking, or writing an epic poem. Business leaders create masterpieces, and they have for centuries. Business leaders operate between necessity and freedom; they do not simply supply goods. When they are in good form, they also supply *good lives* for customers, themselves, employees, and others.

Philosophers and other academics are not the only ones to see business as submerged in needs. We are surprised with the conceptual attachment that management consultants have to animal needs when describing both management and business. We find numerous consultants pointing out that leaders and others in organizations need to manage their animal impulses to flee, freeze, or fight.[20] Yes, animal impulses sometimes take over and drive us. If we are swept up into an ocean wave, we might feel ourselves drowning and panic. Likewise, if a criminal attacks us, we might flee, freeze, or fight. In such cases, animal impulses hold sway. But those moments are rare. We side with Aristotle in seeing that the cultivated second nature of human beings—habit—for the most part rules. Habits give us an accultured nature that pervades, refines, and ceaselessly alters our animal or other needs. Without noticing it, most people are, mostly unconsciously, cultivating this second nature with all the ordinary activities they undertake— conversations they open, postures they assume, the food they eat, courses they take, books they read, trips they make, initiatives they support, blogs and podcasts they post, things they buy, the work they pursue, and so forth. Thus, people are looking for goods that suit their habits and the good lives they cultivate. What does it look like for businesses to do this? How can a business honor its customers in that way?

Companies design products around use cases so that they can make the product part of a life. Are they making it part of a good life? Not always. To do so demands more from the use case than is ordinary. Create a use case where the user is likely to say after a while, "How did I live without this?" From mobile phones and laptops to cars and banking services, many companies have done that.

Of course, when products or services involve high levels of artisanship and personalization, one can easily see how to create a use case that ends with the user unable to imagine doing without the product. But even if you are selling commodities, you also sell the dignity of the workers who enable their production. You also sell the solidarity of your customers with the workers. Loggers, fishers, and miners risk their lives more than most of us. (Consider the deaths per 100,000 among these groups.) If you sell lumber or extracted material, let your customers know that they are purchasing the courage of your workers. Honoring courage is part of a good life. If your workers must toil, we suggest selling the dignity of hard work. Honoring hard work is part of a good life. Obviously, in looking at the culture of your organization, you will want to apply the same lessons. How will you enable your employees to see that what they are doing is making for others and themselves good lives? Think about the good lives your products and services enable, and market them. In general, because we are our second natures, commerce is about creating good lives. But lives that were good in the past—for instance, simply maintaining a family—need something more to be good lives now in our postmodern world. What sort of good lives does postmodernity allow?

Our Postmodern Condition

> If you're lost, you can look and you will find me
> Time after time
> If you fall, I will catch you, I'll be waiting
> Time after time
> —Cyndi Lauper and Robert Hyman, "Time after Time"

To understand our age, we turn to Friedrich Nietzsche, the philosopher who gave us the constituting account of postmodernity (the account that crystallized the postmodern trends to make them dominant in our lives) and did so, by our calculation, in 1882 with his first edition of *The Gay Science*. In defining the age, he did so with such penetrating articulateness that he made it so. Nietzsche boldly told us: "God is dead. God remains dead. And we have killed him."[21] How did we manage to kill God? This is not merely an academic question. Answering it reveals much about our situation today.

According to Nietzsche, we honed our skill of criticism until we could no longer take fully seriously any belief we had. We can criticize everything, and that leaves us with no genuine piety, at least no piety as devout as our ancestors'.[22] Without piety and reverence, we can make sense of the *idea* of a god, but we can have no robust experience of the divine. That is how we killed God in Nietzsche's sense. Of course, we can still act passionately about this or that injustice—#younameit—but a fanatical sentiment is too hyped up to ground a good life or for us to believe in for long. No matter how grounded we are in a tradition, whether the tradition of social justice or an Abrahamic religion, we must acknowledge that we experience the power of acidic criticism. It starts burning through others' beliefs, then burns through our own most closely held beliefs, and, finally, burns through itself, leaving us with only precarious belief and no contentment. We face a stark choice: either we dim our critical moral wits down with a dogmatic fanaticism about something we insist is uncriticizable, or we sharpen them by constantly seeking better reasons for our fundamental beliefs.[23] Fanaticism, especially tribal fanaticism, is, of course, widespread, and its self-righteousness stands against the sensitivity of moral risk-taking, which genuine leaders, creatives, and truth sayers need.

Nietzsche also gave us the thought experiment that, even if we have not heard it, captivates our age and will do so until postmodernity ends. Nietzsche called it the "eternal recurrence," and it is based on an old Stoic thought experiment.[24] Stoics engaged in it when contemplating suicide. Imagine that the universe will repeat itself exactly the same over and over again, and, with it, you with your life are repeated over and over again— each small pain, each shame, each triumph, every blissful moment, even this moment, all in the same order, all over and over again.[25] Can you imagine that? Yes. We surely can. Though the notion is challenged today, the mathematical physicist Henri Poincaré took it beyond a thought experiment and showed its mathematical likelihood. In Nietzsche's day, the physicists Eduard von Hartmann and Louis Auguste Blanqui proposed it as a scientific theory. But if you imagine it, then you have imagined a world where you cannot take seriously any accomplishment or defeat. The endless repetition strips either of any meaningful consequence. Accomplishments and defeats become equally meaningless in a world where they are just mechanically repeated over and over again; pains and joys are just noise. In Nietzsche's hands, the question is not the hopeless regret of the ineffectual but rings (and we think has rung) just as truly in the hearts of Mandela, Bezos, Roddick, Winfrey, or any of our postmodern masterpiece creators. No doubt we all have raised and faced this possibility, "What if all the differences I have made don't make a difference? What if nothing matters, and I can't make anything matter?" What if, as Macbeth says:

> Life's but a walking shadow, a poor player,
> That struts and frets his hour upon the stage,
> And then is heard no more. It is a tale
> Told by an idiot, full of sound and fury,
> Signifying nothing[?][26]

We will see that each successful way of facing this possibility has the contours of one of Nietzsche's good lives. And that will mean that someplace in your soul you have already heard the snap of Nietzsche's final question at the end of the eternal-recurrence speculation: Can you affirm life in its meaninglessness (we prefer "meaning poverty")? Can you *affirm* your life with all its shames and triumphs, large and small, even if you cannot affirm it as meaningful? Can you follow Nietzsche and affirm it as admirable, the way a monumental building such as the Parthenon can be admirable aesthetically and morally in its grandeur, nobility, and testimony to work and imagination? Consider Venice's gilded palaces lining the canals. While looking at these monuments, we can see the beauty and feel a powerful moral force behind their creation.[27] We may not be able to see the builders' good and bad lives, but with a little dramatic imagination and realism we can see in the assertiveness of these masterpieces the moral risks that the owners took; we cannot help but imagine the civic or family conflicts and the trials in the lives of such masterpiece creators. We can admire and thus affirm them. Once we have laid out our lives in such detail, we find that we are already burnishing them, already noticing the breaks from the past, already seeing the risks undertaken and lost, already seeing our improvisations among the rest of the trash of life, and, yes, we can affirm our lives as well. Setting our lives out is an act of affirmation. Within the eternal recurrence, we cannot call it a meaningful life, one that has contributed to a wider purpose. We might even despair of making it so. After all, we no longer have the Stoic confidence that the gods care for the virtuous by testing them and enabling them to show their virtues. We do not hold with the Stoics that a life of ease shows the gods' lack of care.[28] But after laying out our own lives, we can affirm their aesthetic and moral distinctiveness, and that is our postmodern start toward admiration.

When we see ourselves as such, postmodernity opens before us as a wonderland of multiple perspectives and ways of acting, soliciting us to see and explore their beauty and moral awe, to burnish, toy with, or leave and discard. Find and admire and glamorize whatever provokes wonder. You do not have to decide if your life is "a tale / Told by an idiot." It is in any case a tale to burnish, and within that frame of reference you can, through the wonder that comes with daily burnishing and practicing, find a nonfanatical devotion to, say, social justice, Abrahamic religion, or, for our immediate purposes, an organization. You need not be so grand to have a good life. You can devote yourself to the traditional homely goods that Herman Melville called "attainable felicities" in *Moby-Dick*: "the wife, the heart, the bed, the table, the saddle, the fireside, the country."[29] That is a different kind of good life, but it, like the grander version, looks to the wonder of temporary joys. Nevertheless, with any of these lives you also live with the knowledge that your life *might* be "a tale / Told by an idiot," and so you affirm it by burnishing it all the more intensely and creatively for your own admiration, an admiration like the one you feel for the palaces along Venice's canals. Making our longings and selves admirable in our multiperspectival and ever-critical age requires admiration received from others, including at least some others quite different from us. (Admiration received from only the like-minded is like admiration from your parents. It is not the real thing.[30]) Why make ourselves admirable? Admirability replaces heartfelt meaning. If you are a leader, admirability gives you the necessary power to lead, the moral authority to have others do as you would want them to when you are not directing them.

Within our hypercritical and therefore meaning-poor postmodern world (where no meaning or tradition has an uncriticizable hold over us), Nietzsche found four distinct types of lives we could find admirable. The key is that we feel they are admirable, as the palaces are, even if there is no resonant meaning or purpose in which we can dwell. These lives provide wonder and generate admiration.

Four Good, Postmodern Lives

The first and for leaders the most important is a life where we cultivate our natures, dispositions, skills, actions and interactions, and aspirations according to a *style*. In seeking beauty in our lives, we treat ourselves like a work of art. We revise and revise. Every day we have a new inspiration about what will make ourselves bespeak our distinct style. Every day, then, has its wonder even if we cannot say that the style is widely important and meaningful. Nietzsche explains:

> *One thing is needful.*—To "give style" to one's character—a great and rare art! It is practiced by those who survey all the strengths and weaknesses of their nature and then fit them into an artistic plan until every one of them appears as art and reason and even weaknesses delight the eye. Here a large mass of second nature has been added; there a piece of original nature has been removed—both times through long practice and daily work at it. Here the ugly that could not be removed is concealed; there it has been reinterpreted and made sublime. . . . In the end, when the work is finished, it becomes evident how the constraint of a single taste governed and formed everything large and small.[31]

Though the description of this good life has an aesthetic bent, as do all of Nietzsche's descriptions, he is clearly writing about changes in behavior. Adding a large mass of second nature is adding a new cluster of behaviors, say, courageous or wise ones. When he writes of the ugly made sublime, he again has in mind behavior. In one coaching engagement, we helped a CEO full of anger learn how to mute it so that its intensity came out as profound but quieted in a way that enabled his subordinates to hear it. This change is a moral change even if we see it as like Miles Davis muting his trumpet (as he did his anger) to play "Someday My Prince Will Come." Because this way of creating a good life is most suited to leadership, in chapter 9 we describe in detail how to live it with an extended example of a person we coached.

Nietzsche calls his second case of a good life *brief habits*.[32] It is a life of short stories where one fully and delightedly engages with an organization or group of people until one finds oneself soon pleasantly sated, at which point that story is over. But at the door is a delightful new engagement.

Clearly, this life likely has no single unifying style because each brief habit is independently captivating in its wonder. That one could become sated with a current story and then fall in love with a new life makes best sense if these different lives or habits, as Nietzsche puts it, are moral habits with different moral orders. Moving from one story to another with the same moral order is less likely to produce wonder than moving to one with a different moral order. Gig economy workers and consultants might live such lives. Video game developers chase the fun in different games as these developers move from studio to studio. One could also move among Melville's attainable felicities. But we think masterpiece-creating leaders identify themselves too completely with their organizations to live this good life of brief habits. Even Silicon Valley's serial entrepreneurs develop a style. As we shall see in chapter 8, Julia Robertson consciously tries to give such lives to her temporary workers.

In Nietzsche's third case of a good life, one ceaselessly *tests* oneself with high risks and more often fails than succeeds: "I know more about life because I have so often been on the verge of losing it; and precisely for that reason I get more out of life than any of you."[33] Nietzsche is clear that it is a good life whether you win or lose because of the depth of the risks you take. This life suits the moral risk-taking of masterpiece-creating leaders, but we believe it has much too much a derring-do way of being for many to have succeeded as leaders with it. Perhaps Richard Branson has found a way to do it. With each business he creates, he finds someone who has a genius for delivering the product and service, while he takes the risks in the business and in his private life.[34] When leaders take moral risks in the face of genuine anomalies and fail, these leaders may recover a good life in this manner. Arguably, Andrew Fastow, Enron's former chief financial officer, lives this way now as he seeks to redeem himself.[35] We will see more about this type of life in chapter 8.

Nietzsche's fourth good life is that of an *"improviser of life* who amazes even the subtlest observer."[36] The improviser is ready at any moment to incorporate any mistakes into the thematic order of the moment and make these mistakes part of the overall beauty. This life does not devote itself to a consistent style but remains open to the solicitations and exigencies of the moment and creates beauty out of them. Again, its wonder comes from its responses to chance. Two visionary consultants we respect, Fernando Flores and B. Scot Rousse, describe what we take to be this life as the life of navigation.[37] Others describe it as constantly being present.[38] Fictional characters impressively portray such lives in art and films.[39] Han Solo, Luke Skywalker, Princess Leia, and Chewbacca form a brilliant improvisatory team: "How are we doing?" "The same as always." "That bad, huh?" In our consulting practice, we coach many senior team leaders who are followers of the CEO and improvise to keep the organization's defining practices—we will call them signature practices in chapter 7—working. Such people are seen as political in a good sense, and in coaching them we say that we are helping them become even more political. Because they do not hold to a single style, they can and do make subtle, improvisational adjustments to practices and positions that others find attractive—beautiful—and that most often preserve the general moral order of the improvisers' organizations. In this book, Anita Roddick's husband, Gordon Roddick, exemplifies this good life and, as we shall see in chapter 8, saves the day. W. L. Gore and Associates and Morning Star are companies widely reputed to have managers who live such lives. We genuinely wonder if their top leaders can be improvisers as well.[40]

When we say that a masterpiece is admirable, it is so because it gives a wide number of people associated with it one of these four good, postmodern lives. Are there other good postmodern lives? There is no reason there could not be, either now or in the future. But it remains a wonderful part of Nietzsche's genius that he could find four distinct, mostly incompatible good lives. They resist blending, and to those leading or trying to lead one of these lives, some aspects of the other lives remain essentially mysterious. Yet despite their differences, all these lives provide wonder without deeply hooking people on resonant meaningful purpose. In all these good lives, one must find wonder daily. If we want an organization to help generate that wonder, then we will need to identify the deep well of wonder in business. We turn next to that goal, and as we shall see, that wonder, as is its wont, comes from the most unexpected place.

What Is the Wonder of Commerce That We Need to Revive Every Day?

> I want you to come on, come on, come on, come on and take it
> Take another little piece of my heart now, baby (whoa, break it)
> Break another little bit of my heart now, darling, yeah, yeah, yeah (whoa, have a)
> Have another little piece of my heart now, baby
> You know you got it if it makes you feel good.
> —Jerry Ragovoy and Bert Berns, "Piece of My Heart"

Students and clients tell us that the most frequent source of wonder in business is the invention of a clever competitive strategy. Clients feel wonder in the opportunistic cunning it takes to find an opening that their competitors miss; these clients also feel wonder over the invention of truly great products or services. Both answers show hearts in the right place. But these answers do not pull us far enough from the world of needs. Moreover, an organization does not need a cunning strategy or a novel product or service to create wonder daily. We claim that the wonder of commerce is more basic and lies in something that economic rationalizations of exchange cover up.

In economics and most business thinking, exchanges are simple transactions of something for something. Of course, MasterCard or PayPal might find a way to make them even more convenient. Block chain might make them more trustworthy. But the exchanges are still transactions, hardly worth thinking about. A small dose of philosophy mixed with a little history will challenge such suppositions.

Let us go back to Roman times and earlier. Yes, back then you could exchange grain or arrows in a transactional manner. But what about the estate whose paths you and your family walked for generations, whose beauties you habitually sought, whose fields you planted and nourished? What about the horse you trained to follow your every whim? To these examples, Romans would have added their slaves and children, who were intimate parts of their lives. For many ancient cultures, you simply could not sell your estate or children, and conventionally you held on to those others. They were too much a part of you to sell. The Romans did something revolutionary. They invented a second form of exchange called *mancipio*, which is the root of English term *emancipation*. Indeed, these exchanges were cases of liberation from a web of habituations. In the Roman rituals of emancipation, the buyer, seller, and neighbors had to give witness to the reality of this extraordinary, wonder-creating act. They understood that in this transaction the buyer and seller were not simply exchanging value for value but exchanging something that carried a piece of the owner's heart with it, and that piece of the heart would be reincorporated into the purchaser's life.[41] The Romans invented and bequeathed to us a kind of exchange that is, metaphorically speaking, heart transplantation.[42]

Do we have transactions today like those Roman transactions? At first glance, it seems we do not. After all, we abhor slavery and the thought of selling our children. Most do not have land that their families have enjoyed for generations. Work animals are rare. Yet we nevertheless do have such transactions today. Consider the founder selling her company. Consider the artist selling the rights to her artwork. Consider the inventor giving or selling the patent that she earned by laboring night and day for more than a decade. Consider the simple householders selling the home that still has the marks that came with raising their children. Consider the craftsperson selling the best piece she ever created. In our contemporary way, we designate these transactions "emotional" or "troubled" sales that require additional handholding. We see an added complication to the pure transaction, and so we miss the point.

The point is that these emotional or troubled sales are the kinds of sales that express the greatness of exchange, a greatness that the Romans brought to our civilization: we can exchange goods wedded to our hearts. The idea that we reserve exchanging hearts for marriage is a stultifying, dangerous myth. Steve Jobs was on to this. We all know that he designed every detail of Apple's products with absolute devotion. Though he had not studied history, he knew that he was not exchanging value for value but was instead emancipating something, and that is why Apple stores look the way they look and why Apple packaging suggests that each Apple product is a jewel. Jeff Bezos, too, knows this. He surrounds goods with heartfelt reviews and his own promises for quick delivery and easy return. He sells like an artist troubled that you will not appreciate the art. If the product does not fulfill your heart, send it back right away. Bezos exhorts his team, "Wake up every morning terrified. Not of our competition, but of our customers."[43] Anita Roddick knew that her stores were not simply about exchange. They were about bringing joy into the lives of her customers. She sold goods she lovingly prepared or lovingly searched for. Her celebration of trade was, in our eyes, a celebration of Roman emancipation. Roddick heaped scorn on purely transactional exchange.[44]

In our work with clients, we try to bring back as much as possible the selling of a piece of your heart, even in the humblest of circumstances. Consider the gas or electric repair person offering the homeowner, whose power is off, a cup of hot tea from the van or some other token to increase comfort while the gas or electric power gets reconnected. Imagine the bank selling you a carefully crafted (although still mass-market) mortgage that takes account of your worries about debt. Imagine the brilliant, analytical, insurance underwriter treating you in her heart as a friend and designing a friend-worthy deal. Imagine a banker who gives you the keys to the bank so you can have an extended meeting to keep your own business going. Umpqua Bank managers famously did this. Consultants generalize such behavior as going the extra mile. It *is* going the extra mile. It is not simply working a few extra hours to get a report done on time; rather, it is working a few extra hours to create and sell something you love.

The wonder of commerce is the transaction as *mancipio*, emancipation—a heartfelt transaction. If wonder comes from the transaction made into a heartfelt liberation, then the well of wonder in business is nearly infinite.

How Do We Give Our Customers Good Lives?

So far we have said that you can help your customers to good lives by creating use cases that drive them to say, "How did I live before I had this product or service?" After looking at exchange, we added that you can build such use cases when you are selling something you love or when you draw on admirable capacities of your teams, such as the courage of your fishers and miners. The point is to create a product or a service that is so much a part of who your team is that the sale is like an emancipation in the old Roman sense. Here we are asking the harder questions: How do you get people to go beyond incorporating this product or service into their lives? How do you get them to transform their herd-following, going-along-with-the-flow lives into one of the four morally distinctive good lives: (a) the life of (moral-aesthetic-economic) style cultivation, (b) the life of absorption in discontinuous short stories, (c) the life of testing oneself morally, aesthetically, and economically with risky ventures, or (d) the life of improvisation—taking chance events, even mistakes, and making them morally, aesthetically, and economically beautiful?

Unlike the lives of merely adjusting to and fitting in with a new normal, the good lives Nietzsche sets out require us to glamorize our lives so that others admire them and so that we ourselves can admire them more intensely. Such lives require greater inventiveness than one finds in conventional lives. The person manifesting a distinctive style is living like a writer revising her work every day. Others must be able to sense a change even if the precise difference remains carefully hidden. The life of brief habits is much the same. In going from one beloved life to the next, from one gig to the next, people must show themselves fully absorbed in each.

People leading this good life must throw themselves wholly in, even if they know the commitment is—looked at from a lifetime as a whole—temporary. Improvisation cannot get along simply by clever covering of mistakes. It must appear subtle, sly, arch, and in its archness, it glamorizes itself. Businesses help their customers live postmodern good lives by helping with this glamorizing.

Once a business produces a product or service that brings admiration or wonder to its customers' lives, then the business can offer a platform for the customer to express, promote, or remark on the product or service and on its role in the customer's life. Enable your customers to become opinion leaders and talk, write, or act themselves into good lives. Recording companies took the lead in making this offering, but Amazon and other successful companies are not far behind.[45] Recording companies realized that they had to take the star-making abilities they brought to their performing artists and apply them to fans who in their own turn sought to promote artists (and themselves) with intelligence, verve, boldness, and wit. Such customers need attractive sites and publishing capabilities from which to speak. They need, for instance, to be able to play clips from the performing artists' shows. They need to be able to see clips of their own interactions with the product. Jeff Bezos realized very quickly that enabling and encouraging his customers to write reviews would give him an advantage over other online retailers.[46] Amazon even promotes active reviewers. Airbnb and Uber have made reviewers a key part of their business models. Yelp is customer reviews.

There is still much mystery in transforming customers into opinion leaders. Most organizations are simply trying to find those already inclined to act as opinion leaders and mavens. For these organizations, the basics are obvious and clear: Send the email requesting feedback. Provide a great stage (writing tools, visual tools, word-count limitations). Ask some questions about the experience and product to prompt thought. Attractively show what others are saying. Experiment to find just the right amount of interaction to promote among your customers.

We advise businesses to go beyond the basics; opinion leaders are not just influencers. Opinion leaders take reputational risks with their strongest and best opinions, and if the opinion leaders are sufficiently creative, they may even take moral risks in breaking with conventions. Our clients tend to worry about offensive opinions. But when our organizations are masterpieces, the leaders want their customers to take such risks, and so leaders and their teams figure out ways to offer them platforms to do so. We do not have a well-trialed solution. We used to point to how on Martha Stewart's site her opinion leaders strove to sound like her and, amazingly, most succeeded. As we write, Elon Musk is trying to create on X, formerly Twitter, a platform of multiple nontoxic voices. Yes, it is hard. We suspect that, on sites where consumers become opinion leaders with multiple, non-toxic voices, deft curation will be king. The point will not be to curate in order to create a safe space but rather to curate in order to create a stage customers would want to stand on. Consider offering respectful thanks to all reviewers who are willing to put their reputations on the line in taking a strong stand. Then consider organizing reviews by different themes and line up pro and con pieces against each other. Imagine a curator saying what is distinctive about each side of a debate. It is easy to imagine this for Amazon, and artificial intelligence might be able to go a long way toward making the first cuts. Refine the current guidelines for nontoxic speech to bring out moral diversity. Such curators will look for a new civility.

Then go further: give a starring position to those reviewers who find a new or unusual use for the product or service. Those are your convention breakers and truest customers because they have taken a piece of your heart and made it theirs. When customers read these reviews written by conven-tion breakers, it opens the sense that each new customer is like the first per-son to purchase the product or service. Thus, you help customers become self-cultivators, short-story changers, risk-taking self-testers, or improvisers. Give them a curated stage in the appropriate brash or gracious style, add the voice of a leader of ceremonies, add awards, and customers are or will become opinion leaders. Let us be humble as well and see what Elon Musk comes up with.

If Not Masterpiece Creation, What?

For many who write business books, a business organization's end goal is to become like a Standard and Poor's 500 company, one that has revenue and a market cap in the billions, has global customers, and has a defensible competitive advantage that will last indefinitely. Jim Collins gives a descrip-tion that many leaders find compelling. Leaders create great companies, he says. They have a humble leader and a great team (all of whom are on the same bus); a basic, simple, bold product or service concept; a culture of zealous discipline; and then a set of processes (flywheels) that get better and better and better and faster and faster.[47] Don Sull is the visionary who goes beyond Jim Collins's view. It is not enough to have a cool product, a defensive moat, and an ever-efficient flywheel. Tomorrow's company will have a flywheel of constant innovation of product, service, organization, and business model, he notes.[48]

We admire Sull because he sees very clearly the future that will dawn so long as we do not become masterpiece creators. His postmodernity is an alternative to the one we seek. In his postmodernity, important, hierarchical distinctions—such as good and bad, male and female, spoken and written, private and public, and so forth—would, in the agile world of maneuver, become fluid. There is a new normal and then another new normal and then another new normal, and so on. It is a world of stimulating a new herd need, then swiftly creating mimetic desire (desire to desire what another desires), and then streamlining processes to get the product or service out quickly to achieve a new normal in the blink of an eye.[49] Sull captures how we are moving in our postmodernity. How long before we reach the tipping point (a herd concept) for a new normal with electric cars, autonomous cars, a cashless society, cyborgs, robot doctors, robot lawyers, robot professors, robot you name it? Stimulate a new herd need, use mimetic desire to have it catch on, and then gear up productive capacity. In this world, leaders might lead based on influence. After all, influence drives the all-important mimetic desire. The next new normal can come from finding the slice of genius in everyone.[50] Then do it again and again and again. This picture is where our postmodern technology left to itself leads us. We have more and more technological innovations that create more and more convenience, more and more distance from basic needs and thus from necessity, even the necessity of death. We have a version of Nietzsche's eternal recurrence but with Heidegger's addition, the eternal recurrence *of the same*: innovation repeatedly bringing us back to more of the same—more convenience and more freedom from the necessity, more freedom from the body (safety), more flexibility, and so forth.[51] The same moral norms get repeated, one new normal after another. We believe that this alternative postmodernity has people *accepting* the eternal recurrence or ultimate meaninglessness with the anxiety (maybe panic) that goes with fad following. People become members of a herd or tribe. In contrast, we argue masterpiece-making postmodernity recognizes the same ultimate meaning poverty but responds to it with the affirmation and wonder of good lives that engage in creating admirable moral diversity in masterpiece organizations and ways of living.

We can picture the two postmodernities as different moral aesthetics. Think of the rows of big-box companies in Silicon Valley, each trying to outdo the other with more convenience and more freedom. Is there much moral difference among them? Or are they mostly embellishments of Intel, HP, Google, or Meta? Nietzsche challenges us to picture, instead of the boxes, the palaces of Genoa. He writes about the autocratic ruling families of Renaissance Genoa, about the streets lined with beautiful palaces.

> I keep seeing the builders, their eyes resting on everything near and far that they have built, and also on the city, the sea, and the contours of the mountains, and there is violence and conquest in their eyes. All this they want to fit into *their* plan and ultimately make their *possession* by making it part of their plan. The whole region is overgrown with this magnificent, insatiable selfishness of the lust for possessions and spoils . . . and, thirsting for what was new, [each] placed a new world beside the old one, each rebelled against each at home, too, and found a way to express his personal infinity. Each once more conquered his homeland for himself by overwhelming it with his architectural ideas and refashioning it into a house that was a feast for his eyes.[52]

Those palaces, expressions of personal infinity, are the masterpieces we are seeking to help leaders make their businesses into. Such masterpieces do require desire and conquest, as Nietzsche would have it and as Madam Walker undertook. The palaces of Genoa stand out for us today in their aesthetic differences, but we can have little doubt that their owners had moral differences as well that revealed themselves in the aesthetic differences. And even if we doubt that was the case for Genoa, we should believe that the masterpiece business of today will have different organizational cultures based on diverse ways of treating customers and employees. They will aim to create products that require emancipation and then for customers who will use platforms to glamorize their ways of life with the products.

How do we get to this feast for the eyes, the array of beautiful businesses modeled on Genoa, with each leader's infinite ambition channeled for *admiration*: the moral and aesthetic sentiment of respect, approval, and esteem with wonder? The rest of this book aims to show how.

For now, let us briefly consider two companies half in the postmodernity of masterpiece creation and half in the world of the technological eternal return of the same. We look at their masterpiece sides. Apple transformed its industry, and Amazon transformed retail. In each case, they are helping customers make good lives and feel emancipation in the goods sold either through the gift-box design or through the speed and ease of delivery. Their customers become great promoters, members of genius bar teams, or famous reviewers. These genius bar people and reviewers speak and write as though they were the first ever to get the product and about how to make it part of a good life. Their excitement is palpable. Of course, these geniuses and reviewers say that some products are poor, but each genius's or reviewer's personal style comes across; their styles stand out from the herd and inspire us to do the same.

Apple and Amazon are also known for their tough leaders who have singular visions, take difficult decisions and risks, and stand for their organization's greatness. Jobs was a perfectionist who frequently set impossible deadlines and berated people sometimes for reasons no one could understand. People at Apple spoke of Jobs's reality-distortion field.[53] Bezos fiercely holds to his rule that every new hire must be better than the previous one and insists that as job descriptions become more demanding, people must retire. He famously retired Amazon's founding employee, who created the first Amazon site.[54] Each time these leaders made these decisions, they took moral risks. If they had not produced masterpieces, they would have faced scorn. We think it is easy to see Nietzsche's description in them. There is passion and conquest in their eyes. Both leaders make the world part of their plan: Jobs in creating friendly, humanistic technology and Bezos in taming the internet from its wild early days for the sake of stable retail. They take possession of our world. These are glorious cases, and we chose them for that reason. They let us see glories clearly. But the two Upper East Side hardware stores with different visions of selling hardware, treating customers, managing employees, and caring for suppliers are distinctive moral beauties as well. Masterpieces come in every size.

Is masterpiece creation for you? Are you willing to focus on something other than productivity, profitability, and revenue to create your masterpiece? Or are we perhaps naively idealistic? Normally, masterpiece creators achieve the traditional measures of success because an organization needs to receive admiration from diverse groups simply to be considered a masterpiece. Masterpieces generally succeed morally, aesthetically, and economically. We can promise that in creating and leading your masterpiece, your wits will grow sharper; your employees will have more vitality; your customers will see their lives differently and become opinion leaders. You might maximize profits. Or you might not. But you will create a good life. If your masterpiece requires a rarefied taste and therefore persistent educating of palates, go for it. Yes, you may take a temporary financial hit, but what a monument you will create and leave behind! Leaving such a monument behind is certainly a vital way to face death. We all face death. Ancient philosophers were known for thinking that facing death well was the point of philosophy. Masterpiece creators are like those philosophers. They seek, as Nietzsche said, to embody their infinite desire in something finite that will outlive them.

In our search for a way to avoid death, technology, with its drive toward infinite safety, is our attempt to free ourselves of the necessity that grounds both meaning and admiration. How are you facing death? Peter Pans do not create masterpieces. Peter Pans live in the economy of infinite possibility, where they want it all, where they are constantly looking for the next leadership position and following fads that promise no more than new fads. Masterpiece creators have infinite passion for finite masterpieces: oneself and one's intensely distinctive organization. Masterpieces do not have flywheels that make them perpetual motion machines. Masterpiece creators fulfill a destiny and then are no more. The works they create live on, but they too will die. It is in the face of the infinite loss of death that leaders have an infinite passion to create a finite masterpiece. Only in the face of death—making it bearable—can we see the infinite passion. "Et in Arcadia ego," Death says: "I am even in Arcadia." As they created their Arcadias, Jobs and Bezos certainly knew that death was there. As we sing our praises of masterpiece creation in business, we are aware that many sensible people do not like the music, and we want to anticipate their objections and give our answers here. At the very least, we hope to reduce the background noise produced by the "what ifs" and "did they considers" that our book will stir up. We know we cannot dampen all the noise, but we at least want to provide as much as possible a quiet concert hall for our song.

Why Do Sensible People Disagree with Us, and How Do We Respond?

Here we examine seven objections that reasonable, experienced leaders and scholars have raised and provide our short answers.

First, there is a strong reaction against heroic or strong leaders. Many consider such leaders, no matter their biology or gender, patriarchal. They privilege strife over sympathetic engagement. As such, their form of leadership works against diversity, equity, and inclusion. Moreover, this book reads like "Harold Bloom on Management and Leadership." It draws insights from the Western canon, which is already noninclusive and nondiverse. In short, it promotes a narrow, elitist form of leadership.

Our response: In the preface, we have already described the diverse leaders we have worked with, but our general response is that masterpiece leaders, with Madam C. J. Walker as typical, are a blend of gendered skills and virtues. Let us start with a common way of understanding nonpatriarchal leadership. It arises from deconstructing the given cultural, binary distinction of leader and follower by discovering that the truly effective leader follows cues and insights from others. In short, the heart of leadership is followership. In a sense, we agree with the claim about listening to cues and others and doing so even more insistently than deconstructive thinkers do. Our masterpiece leader listens not just to cues but also for difference in others that challenges her or him profoundly (see chapter 4). Our leader remains sensitive to moral anomalies and "stays with" them until a resolution appears.[55] Our leader understands that moods open diverse ways in which things matter and works with them and intervenes in others' moods to get a more workable grip on the world (see chapter 3). Our leader understands that practices more than beliefs create cultures and so engages with changing practices (see chapter 7) rather than simply declaring new values. Masterpiece leaders promote an economy of gratitude within their organizations and communities rather than an economy of obedience (see chapter 10). Such leaders have apt followers because the followers are grateful, not because they are obedient. These virtues are generally seen as nonpatriarchal and nonheroic. Our masterpiece leader also seeks truth, speaks it to power both wisely and courageously, and takes moral risks (see chapter 5). Though normally seen as patriarchal, there is nothing exclusively patriarchal in truth telling and moral risk-taking, as several examples show: from Hypatia, who famously died for telling truth to power in 415 CE, to the suffragettes who fought for women's right to vote in the United Kingdom in the early twentieth century. For recent cases, consider such courageous journalists as Anna Politkovskaya and Daphne Caruana Galizia, who were murdered for researching and reporting on the Russian war in Chechnya and on political corruption, respectively. Let us not forget Sherron Watkins, who boldly blew the whistle on Enron. We claim that the masterpiece leader is a blend of patriarchal and nonpatriarchal virtues, a blend of remaining open and engaging in strife.

But what of our use of the Western canon? Yes, we are steeped in it and find it fascinating, despite its limitations. As Alasdair MacIntyre notes with respect to his adherence to the Augustinian-Aristotelian tradition, for us to speak for other traditions would be disingenuous.[56] The critical question is not what tradition one is embedded in but whether one's tradition makes room for others. In this book, we use the Western canon against the nondiverse and noninclusive uses it has historically often been put to. Drawing on it shows that leading organizations is a poetic act. As artists, leaders create masterpieces. They need the artist's skills of receptivity, moral sense, and moral imagination. The end goal of helping leaders to create morally distinctive masterpieces is to create a world of moral diversity, most of which we can admire if not embrace. Such diversity allies well with all the other forms of diversity. Moreover, we do not think intellectual-cultural masterpieces belong solely to one culture or tradition. They find ways to cross cultures. As Yuval Harari aptly notes, "Tolstoy isn't the exclusive property of Russians. . . . Tolstoy speaks of feelings, questions, and insights that are relevant to the inhabitants of Durban and Johannesburg no less than those of Moscow and St. Petersburg."[57]

Second, some claim that moral change *should* properly be left to democratic institutions, certainly not to business.

Our response: Within a liberal democracy, businesses, just like other organizations or, for that matter, like other individuals, drive moral change. Think of tobacco companies' aggressive push of smoking among women in the 1950s and 1960s as a sign of self-defining personal style. Think of the Body Shop's environmental activism. Think of Meta's stance on determining what content is worthy of sharing or rejecting. Or think of Starbucks, Tesla, Airbnb, Microsoft, Netflix, Levi Strauss, PayPal, Amazon, Reddit, and other US companies that have committed to helping their employees get access to reproductive care in the aftermath of the Supreme Court's decision to end the federal protection of abortion rights. Are these not examples of business-driven moral stands? In a liberal-democratic framework, individuals and organizations engage in shifting moral norms when they believe it is the right thing to do. Doing the right thing vis-à-vis employees, customers, local communities, the environment, and so forth is not something a company can avoid addressing, especially now in a connected world of instant and ubiquitous communication. In conditions of postmodernity, just as companies expect employees to bring themselves fully to work, companies cannot escape being corporate citizens. They do not do well becoming mere economic machines.[58] As we have seen with the corporate response to the Russian invasion of Ukraine, avoiding taking a stand looks like a moral dodge. Business organizations, willingly or not, drive moral change. The point is to do it wisely and not just as a matter of following the herd.

Third, related to the previous point, some still think—though less commonly today because of climate and social justice concerns—that business leaders should work primarily in the realm of convention and prudence and therefore not try to *change* moral norms. They can respond to changing moral norms but not lead the change.

Our response: Because many small and mold-breaking businesses distinguish themselves morally, and because many leaders are trying to do the right thing (following their own lights, not necessarily a given code), we, as educators and consultants, would do well to give leaders tools to deal with this moral dimension of their organizations. It is not as though they will not try to work in the moral dimension if we do not say anything about it. Mere prudence might well advise against any moral risk-taking, but courageous leaders who face moral anomalies are going to try to answer the anomalies, and they deserve the necessary tools: intervening in moods, building trust by cultivating virtues, listening for difference, seeking and telling truth to power, creating distinctive organizational cultures, developing strategies around moral risk-taking, and constantly cultivating and transforming themselves as needed for the sake of their masterpiece. Using those tools makes them far less likely to do evil.

Fourth, moral risk-taking is inherently risky. Leaders do not want and should not want to become tyrants: tomorrow's Maos, Hitlers, or Putins.

Our response: True enough. But sharpening the skills for finding and resolving genuine moral anomalies makes such autocratic or totalitarian outcomes less likely. In fact, autocratic or totalitarian rulers generally take moral risks for the sake of expediency, which we oppose. Our leaders take these risks for the sake of resolving moral anomalies, situations where there is no right thing to do that yields practical success. Blinding people to their own moral distinctiveness and the risks that they might take actually serves the Maos, Hitlers, and Putins. It does not serve people such as Václav Havel and Lech Wałęsa, who grew up in totalitarian moral orders but were not blind to moral anomalies. We will likely have better leaders if they understand that they will be called on to take moral risks and if they constantly try to develop conscience, practical wisdom, and what Rowan Williams, the former archbishop of Canterbury, aptly calls "a tragic imagination." "The tragic imagination," he notes, "insists that we remain alert to the possibility that we are already incubating seeds of destruction. Our habitual discourse with ourselves as well as with others may already have set us on a path that will consume us."[59] Of course, there are no guarantees that moral failure will not come about when leaders take moral risks. What is critical is that leaders answer the Socratic question posed by themselves and others in roles of governance: Am I (or are we) doing the right thing?

Fifth, some may think that we stand too much against psychological safety, and so they are suspicious of our claims.

Our response: We stress the importance of cultivating courage and the responsibility to seek truth and speak even unpleasant truths. We do not underestimate psychological safety, but neither do we exalt it. We seek proportion. Psychological safety is part of the overall rise of safety as a moral norm in postmodern societies, and this type of safety is primarily about getting people to share their views freely. This is laudable: people are more likely to speak their minds freely (an important value in liberal postmodernity) to the extent they feel safe. However, if they do not feel safe, within the code of psychological safety they are authorized to withhold what they believe to be true, even if withholding might have unfortunate consequences. According to this norm, you do not have to say it if you see it.

To bring together truth seeking and telling with psychological safety, we need to distinguish between the social psychological approach and the moral approach to speaking truth. The former concerns the conditions that will encourage truth seeking and truth telling in a group or organization, and a climate of psychological safety might help achieve that end if—and it is a huge *if*—sharing views turns into seeking the truth of views. The moral approach concerns the moral imperative of speaking one's mind in search for the truth (following the Socratic aphorism "the unexamined life is not worth living"), and speaking such truths as morally required always carries risk. Our worry is that overemphasizing psychological safety detracts from the moral act of truth seeking and telling, and that is why we stress the importance of cultivating courageous speaking. We certainly encourage enabling people to feel free to speak, and we believe that it is important for leaders to do so. We urge careful listening in order to hear challenging difference. Genuinely listening and courageously speaking are important moral qualities for leading a good life. Techniques for imparting psychological safety might get people to speak more freely, but they also impede the cultivation of these moral virtues.

We concede that even when companies such as Google have embraced psychological safety as a defining, signature practice, they can become masterpieces. Google is unquestionably a masterpiece with psychological safety as an important moral norm. How do we explain that contradiction? We still believe that courageously speaking truth will enable masterpiece creation and that failing at it will impede masterpiece creation. But moral norms such as "speaking truth" or "speaking truth only when safe" exist and have their meaning in moral orders, and in masterpieces these moral orders generally have discordia concors (inharmonious harmony). With that in mind, we explain Google as best we can. Psychological safety is an antiauthoritarian norm. Within its rule, no leader has the moral right to expect people will tell her the truth unless she makes them feel safe. A leader does not deserve the truth simply because she asks for it. We believe that this destabilizing of authority binds people at Google together. Because Google managers need to hear the truth as much as managers in any other masterpiece organization do, psychological safety requires and empowers them to look for and overcome micro-intimidations. Thus, we have a disharmony (needing truth and having no requirement to tell the truth) that Google harmonizes through vigilant attention to micro-intimidation and by lavishing other benefits. Consequently, we see Google as a case of wonderful moral acrobatics.

Sixth, leaders might say that they have followed the advice and findings of the leadership literature we oppose or move beyond and that they have done well financially and operationally.

Our response: We have little objection to a leader who really wants simply to create an operationally and financially successful business that makes most employees and customers happy. We concede that doing so is not an easy task. If the pious advice available from many sources (which we mention in passing and in our endnotes) helps achieve that success, we certainly accept that. But we believe that such success will put businesses merely on the path of seeking one new normal after another. Each new normal will very quickly become *normal* and not captivating or admirable. We do not insist that business leaders fix our deep, postmodern cultural problems. However, we invite them to. We are writing about how our most *truly admirable* businesses are and how our most *truly admired* business leaders are. These leaders create organizations that shift not only conventional norms but also moral norms. These leaders have led the creation of such contemporary masterpieces as Google, Amazon, Bridgewater, the Body Shop, Netflix, and (as we shall show) Impellam. Leaders of small neighborhood businesses do the same. We invite others to follow these leaders to create an admirable postmodern world of wonder and gratitude as opposed to the anxiety that comes from a never-ending series of new normals.

Seventh, suppose leaders follow our advice and create morally distinct organizations, each one admired by some but not others. Would this outcome not return us to a society of hostile tribes? What protection do we offer against that?

Our response: We take this objection seriously and do not have a fully worked out answer. As pluralists, we believe that a world of morally distinctive organizations is preferable to a world of the new normal repeating the same moral norms. We also acknowledge the risk of warring tribes. Pluralism always hangs in the balance. We will argue at the end of the book that the postmodern settlement we are promoting rests on an economy of gratitude, which runs against tribalism. Indeed, the very ethos of an economy of gratitude inclines us more to interconnectivity and mutuality and less to tribalism. We can sketch a picture of this economy here.

Let us start with the gratitude we feel toward masterpiece-creating leaders. We feel gratitude toward the leader who in morally tough (anomalous) circumstances acts in a morally shocking manner that brings to people in the leader's organization and perhaps the larger community a new moral order where some things that were previously immoral are now moral and vice versa. Because this new order resolves moral difficulties, we admire the leader for the risky action and the leader's organization for maintaining the new order. We admire both because we also feel gratitude for the risky action that the leader took and that the organization continues to support.

Fair enough. Why speak of an *economy* of gratitude? We believe that the leader's action is a riskier version of the way we create and exchange value for each other daily. We are so interconnected with each other that we are co-responsible for each other's actions. We swim in a sea of intended and unintended consequences of others' actions pushing us one way and then another. Our actions are not independent of all these currents pushing us. Likewise, in these waters we are regularly pushing people to act beyond what is habitual for them; in the usual cases, we do that to make their lives or our shared life better. We call such activity sales, management, teaching, healing, friendship, partnership, or marriage. We sometimes call it manipulation or bullying. But the point is that when we push others to be better, we are always left with the question of whether we pushed too hard, not enough, or just the right amount. But in this world of noncriminal, pushy micropractices, it is gratitude, not any other ethical concept, that determines the rightness of the action. The gratitude comes in two ways. If the person we pushed beyond her habits finds her life better, she feels and expresses gratitude to us for our micro-risk-taking. If she simply feels pushed to no good end (and perhaps manipulated), she likely gives us a pass for our effort, and we feel gratitude. (Obviously, we do not always receive a pass, and then we pay for damage, but that payment occurs mostly within an economy of gratitude, which limits the damages paid and which frequently leaves us grateful for recompense.) Gratitude is a basis for the value, respect, and admiration we pass back and forth. Because we live in the exchange of gratitude in matters of micro-risk-taking, we are inclined to make sense of leaders' macro-risk-taking in the same way.[60]

Of course, a doubter could point out that our everyday economy of gratitude takes place only among people who share the same moral order. Frequently, that is the case. So, the question becomes: Is moral risk-taking *in itself* admirable enough that many people might feel gratitude for the leader who creates a distinctive moral order, even one that those people cannot embrace? We concede that people do not generally admire moral risk-taking that much *yet*. We cannot promise they will tomorrow. However, we hope to have the moral luck that others who see the problem and value of admiring diverse moral risk-takers will share the burden of founding with us a new, subtle gratitude for moral orders that can be admired in their distinctiveness even if they are not widely embraced.[61] This book is that invitation.

3 The Unnatural Acts of Managing Moods on the Way to Creating Masterpieces

If music be the food of love, play on,
Give me excess of it; that surfeiting,
The appetite may sicken, and so die.
—William Shakespeare, *Twelfth Night, or What You Will*

One outcome of the COVID-19 pandemic is that everyone has had to engage in unnatural Zoom or Microsoft Teams acts as part of the new normal. A short while ago, people in business would shake hands, look directly into each other's eyes, and get a visceral sense of trust or otherwise. With continued remote working, we are missing the old intimacy. Many at McKinsey advise on how to thrive naturally in a new normal.[1] We are asking you to act unnaturally now *and forever* to turn your leadership style and your organization into a masterpiece. Creating masterpieces is surely an unnatural, highly artificial act. In this chapter, we focus on the unnatural workplace act of intervening in other individuals' moods.

Why manage others' moods? For years, we answered that question by pointing to elevated performance. When people are in a similar mood, things matter in similar ways, and people coordinate and communicate far more efficiently. Moods, moreover, are highly contagious. If you enter a room with people in a mood of fear, you will catch it and start seeing things as threatening. Bad and good moods get us listening to the same music. But bad moods tend also to make us standoffish; we disengage or engage only in superficial, manipulative, or hostile ways. Good moods get us to engage with genuine interest and thoughtfulness. With that kind of engagement, people are more productive. That used to be our answer for why we should manage moods. It is correct. We still stand by it. In our informal studies, we found that mood management, along with the honest speaking and promise making that goes with it, could alone raise individual and team productivity by 20 percent. But why do we advise managing moods now in this book about creating masterpiece organizations?

Every masterpiece has a mood—a way that things matter. Is your masterpiece organization going to change the world the way a high-tech or biotech company would by discovering something strikingly new and unexpected? If so, you want a mood of bright hope. You will fight to keep it from falling into burning resentment as certain groups of researchers have good fortune and others do not. Does your masterpiece exude admiration for customers, colleagues, or shareowners? Do people come to work to be with each other? Do people love going the extra mile to help customers and colleagues? If so, you want the mood of warm admiration, and you will fight against falling into a frigid mood of fear. Fear arises naturally as people make themselves more vulnerable to others and then feel betrayed. Or is your masterpiece one that gets things done well and efficiently? High performance matters more than anything else. Then, you will want a mood of zeal, and you will fight to keep your mood of zeal from falling into resignation as your organization faces a couple of defeats in a row. Perhaps you want your masterpiece to be one of brilliant teamwork as teams take ownership of their accomplishments and shoot for bold mastery? You then want joy like that of Christmas (or a similar generous, help-giving holiday), where people are looking for a way to do their share and then some. And you will fight against a mood of arrogance where people try to make themselves into kingpins.

Masterpiece creation requires managing moods, and any one of these typical good moods—hope, admiration, zeal, or joy—will also draw from stakeholders the moral sentiment of admiration. We feel obliged to use the same word with two different meanings. When we speak of the *mood* of admiration, we are speaking of the warm affection of love that employees feel for fellow employees and customers. Clients feel uncomfortable with the term *love*, so we use *admiration*. The general form of admiration that masterpieces elicit is far more a reflective, aesthetic judgment of an arresting sublime monument. The dominant mood you build into the organization will be under siege by its negative twin mood—resentment is the enemy twin of hope, fear of admiration, resignation of zeal, and arrogance of joy—and the media like supporting these enemy twins. As a leader, you are responsible for the mood and therefore need proficiency in the basic tools for changing individuals' moods in particular circumstances. In chapter 7, we focus on changing entire organizational moods. For now, let us consider individuals. In the first instance, consider the members of your leadership team.

Doing What Comes Unnaturally: Managing Moods

Most of us have enough emotional intelligence to manage our own moods much of the time, but we rarely manage other people's moods well. As artists creating a commercial-culture masterpiece, we need to do that. The virtual world challenges us to sharpen this skill more than the direct person-to-person world does. Recall the most recent virtual meeting you ran. The odds are that you started out in a can-do mood; then, as people started issuing reports to make their work look good, and others zoned out, the meeting's mood fell to boredom. You raised issues and asked for responses. You received extraordinarily polite, dutiful responses with just enough genuinely interested insight to make clear the robust conversation *you were missing*. But you found it hard to intervene when the tone was so polite. And as you neared the end, you felt a shared mood of irritation settle over the team. You might even have felt frustration or anger. You then politely listed commitments or action items; participants nodded without conviction. We all have had this happen. It even happens in face-to-face meetings. You end up a leader of zombies. Some virtual meetings are here to stay. Make them masterpieces as you would a face-to-face meeting.

Moral philosophers give us three successful ways to turn around such declining individual moods. But to take their lesson, we need to learn to direct attention to moods. We need to notice the moods that others are in or that we are in *and then call them out*. For many managers, that action is one of the most unnatural of the acts we advise. Sometimes we do it with family: "You sound depressed today." But it just seems too intimate for work. It should not be. You are not poking your nose in someone's business; rather, you are pointing out an emotional state that has high relevance to productivity. We recommend that the first time you see someone zoning out of a meeting and its can-do mood, you call it out: "What just happened? You seem to have gotten into a distant mood." Or "I feel as though I'm losing you." Or "Do people feel the mood of the meeting shifting?" It is critical to call out the moods of irritation or boredom at the first sign. If you wait, the mood normalizes itself. Others will think that mood is normal or at least normal for the person in it: "She is just generally cold. How could you ask her to change who she is, let alone ask her in a public meeting?" Or worse, the mood will take over the whole meeting, as frequently happens with virtual meetings, and when that happens, it seems impossible to snap people out of it. Noticing the shift in mood and calling it out is the first essential step to getting back to a positive mood. Do it in the way that suits your style. You could range from "You really help a lot when you bring your cheery mood" to "What just happened to your mood? Don't let it infect the meeting." It is even possible to bring out the mood by saying that something is off and that you want to go around the room and have each person say what mood each is in. Believe it or not, our clients over the years have frequently resorted to this approach. It works. Now, to the philosophers.

First, Martha Nussbaum, one of today's most brilliant philosophers, draws on one thousand years of Stoic thinking when she tells us that moods and other emotions (which she mostly focuses on) are not irrational; rather, they are "judgments in which people acknowledge the great importance, for their own flourishing, of things that they do not fully control."[2] In other words, when we think or speak about something we judge important and that we cannot control, our words necessarily carry emotions. According to Nussbaum, all who claim they can engage in unemotional, objective thought about important, uncontrollable things *are wrong*. Wow! We cannot be Mr. Spock! Thoughtful managers and scientists already know that emotion lives inside our judgments of important matters. The leading British statistician Sir David Spiegelhalter, chair of the Winton Centre for Risk and Evidence Communication at Cambridge University, said on BBC Radio 4: "I think it's very important that we have to acknowledge that we can never take an objective view about evidence. We always bring our, I think, personalities into it, and mine is unfortunately very optimistic, and that's why I'm very glad I'm not a government adviser."[3] In other words, facts do not speak; only people do, and people necessarily speak with the emotion that goes with their judgments.

For Nussbaum, any statement about something important has as part of its meaning an emotional content. When I say, "*My* newspaper is missing," the statement carries anger, and if it does not, it means something different. Nussbaum proves the point of how rational emotions are by noting that if someone challenges the newspaper proposition effectively, the emotion disappears. Your spouse says, "It's not missing; you left it in the bedroom." The anger is gone. Because the original proposition is empirically false, the emotion involved in the statement shifts. Such shifts can happen with most judgments, in particular ones revolving around work. "The root cause of our accidents is our insufficient training of drivers," says a speaker in resignation about having to change a whole training regimen. Look now what happens with this response: "I just ran a test where I changed the design of the mirrors, and accidents were way down. We do not have to change our whole training regimen." From resignation emerges relief. So the lesson from Martha Nussbaum is to find the judgment—often a tacit assumption—that is driving the mood and then change it. Get into the details of the judgment rather than just some vague expression of it. Change the detailed judgment and change the mood.

Let us look at the hypothetical virtual meeting and what a Nussbaum-style intervention would look like. When a team member says honestly, "You're right; I zoned out of the meeting because we have faced this problem a dozen times before, never resolved it, and are unlikely to this time." You can respond, "Well, this time we are going to listen to reasonable solutions, and then you and I will select one to trial. It is time to get our hands dirty." Vary responses according to your leaderly style. But change the assumption.

Let us turn to William James's insight on moods. William James, the great American pragmatist philosopher and philosophical psychologist of the late nineteenth and early twentieth centuries, tells us that we can change our moods and other emotions by challenging the claim that we should be true to our emotions—the claim of authenticity. Normally, if our manager tells us to do something crazy, we remain true to our anger, even though we stifle our expression of it. Why? If we do not stay true to our feelings, we fear losing ourselves. Could that be right? The English poet William Wordsworth thought it was. Since William James takes such a strong stand against remaining true to one's feelings, it is worth taking a moment now to examine the authenticity that is a matter of remaining true to one's *self*.[4] Authenticity became a moral virtue at the hands of Jean-Jacques Rousseau, William Wordsworth, and Walt Whitman. For English-speaking people, Wordsworth was critical to the adoption of this notion.

Wordsworth's poem "Michael" set the course for authenticity. In it, Michael, a sturdy, active, vigorous shepherd, loses his son to urban dissipation. Wordsworth celebrates Michael's spending the last seven years of his life in despair as he tries to complete the sheepfold that he and his son started before his son left for the city. The poem makes us feel respect for Michael's broken heart and honor his fidelity to it and to his memory of his son.[5] It is certainly true that the loss of a son can be devastating, and there is virtue in honoring and expressing that devastation. It is certainly better than denying it or narcissistically ignoring it. Lionel Trilling, the famous Wordsworth scholar and theorist of authenticity, points out that earlier forms of being true to oneself, such as when Polonius admonishes Laertes in *Hamlet*, reach to sincerity but not to authenticity. In contrast, Wordsworth's Michael is his grief, and the poetry impels us to respect that forthright honest emotional stand and put a high moral valuation on it.[6] That form of authenticity is indeed now part of our culture today.

We propose that anyone who thinks seriously about this Romantic moral value will find it lacking, as ultimately did Trilling. It leaves us too absorbed in ourselves, in our life stories, and not creative enough. The great existential philosophers of authenticity, Kierkegaard, Heidegger, and Jean-Paul Sartre, reformed the Romantic notion of authenticity. When they used the term, they meant being true to the *human way of being*, not being true to *one's self*. Those philosophers understood that an essential part of being human is precisely that we can be different from who we are; we can develop ourselves. Thus, being your*self* is not necessarily a human virtue.[7] It elevates "who I am" at the expense of "who I can or should be." What if, for example, I experience feelings of envy, racial contempt, or vindictiveness? Would Wordsworth counsel that I hang on to them to maintain my authenticity? Could I admire myself if I did? The existentialist thinkers see working on and changing oneself as being true not to this or that self but as being true to human stand taking.

Because the Romantic sense of authenticity has such a hold on our hearts, it is worthwhile to attend more closely to the existential philosophers' antidote and get a picture of how they see our engagement with the world. The existential philosophers start from the position that my authenticity is not so much remaining true to myself as availing myself of what my culture, tradition, or practice affords me to pursue lucidly, resolutely, and with a sense of ownership. For the existentialists, neither cultural practices nor traditions are monolithic. They have conflicts. They have dominant and marginal practices. The freedom to which existential philosophers would have me be true is seeing what the situation calls on me, as a person having distinctive skills and dispositions, to do with resolution.

The practices in which we dwell are always evolving, so it is unlikely that they would call a person to all-consuming grief for seven years. For the existentialists, who see freedom as adjusting to changing practices and traditions, Michael's long grief would be a case of heroically giving up freedom and becoming a stereotype.[8] Thus viewed, the existentially authentic person cannot have the self-absorption Wordsworth endorses.[9] On a personal level, I cannot get caught up in just being the selfsame person. In my authentic resoluteness I am dealing with the conflicted traditions in which I am embedded. Drawing on those traditions, I take a stand for a certain distinctive course of action and experience the agony of carving that path amid the uncertainty and possible risks I may be undertaking. On a social level, through my authentic action, I carve out a distinctive way to act that contributes to the world, evolves traditions, and requires involving others. So, attention to the social, tradition-affirming and disaffirming details of the situation keeps me from self-absorption (whereby I am all that matters). Attending to the social effects of my action prevents blind conformity (whereby I count for nothing).

Accordingly, we are advising against seeing yourself as Wordsworth and the Romantic poets encouraged. Admire that moral order but do not embrace it. The shift you should make is from telling yourself who you are and being that person to conversing with others to see who you could be. Others in our social situation shape (although they do not determine) what we think and do. We experience this self-making in productive dialogues and conversations, where "egos fall away and are replaced by something much more important: the matter that matters."[10] In such conversations, we put away our preoccupation with self-aggrandizement to experience ourselves as "participants in a shared event that is greater than ourselves."[11] The question, therefore, is not what we get for ourselves in a situation (such as the satisfaction of being right in a meeting) but what we lucidly and resolutely contribute to the situation, the organization, or the masterpiece (for instance, by asking, "How do my actions contribute to making this a good meeting?").

Thus, starting with the existentialists, we end up again with Nietzsche, the great philosopher of masterpiece production. We seek to make ourselves admirable both to ourselves and to others. He tells us not to be true to our disappointments and blemishes but rather to erase or sublimate them. How, though? How do we change ourselves and our moods? We turn back to the pragmatist philosopher William James for the simplest, most direct approach. He writes: "If we wish to conquer undesirable emotional tendencies in ourselves, we must assiduously, and in the first instance cold-bloodedly, go through the outward motions of those contrary dispositions we prefer."[12]

The contemporary management thinker Herminia Ibarra makes the same point in her study of leaders. She notes the difficulty with authenticity. So far as it emphasizes the importance of "being yourself," authenticity can easily become an excuse for personal inertia, a reason to prefer the comfort zone of the familiar self. "The trick is," notes Ibarra, "to work toward a future version of your authentic self by doing just the opposite: stretching way outside the boundaries of who you are today."[13] With her notion of being true to one's *future self*, she tries to capture the Romantic sense of self while absorbing the existentialists' and James's understandings.[14]

What follows? Let us return to the meeting where we call out someone who has slipped into a mood of resignation, frustration, or anger. Suppose when we call the person out on the mood, she says, "I checked out because I don't think we will get anywhere." Standing on the shoulders of William James, we respond: "Will you start acting as though we can do it? We surely won't if you don't." Or if your leadership style will not allow a response like that, you could try: "You might be right, but let us put up a braver face for the rest of the meeting. It will do all our hearts good, and we might see something we have not seen before." Or if you like a more down-to-earth style: "Shifting a mood is like any other hard thing; all of us have to fake it until we make it." Find your own version.

We recommend following James's wisdom in dealing with your own moods, particularly in an era of wearying virtual meetings. Give yourself a good talking to: "I am weary, and so are others. I will act as though I am full of energy. Let me see what that does for the others." Know that you have one of the world's greatest philosophers by your side; act with zeal and artistry to create your cultural masterpiece. We find it fascinating that James tells us that such action must be "cold-blooded." In our experience, he is absolutely right. You must be uncompromising with yourself and with others when it comes to managing moods. Anything else is what Aristotle called *akrasia* (weakness of the will), and it prevents the necessary discordia concors (inharmonious harmony), which is the aesthetic and moral principle of masterpieces. Acting out of the mood that is to come *before* it arises is a simple personal case of discordia concors; it always has beauty. Paradoxically, you experientially affirm and behaviorally deny the mood at the same time: "Yes, I understand your weariness, and I am feeling it too. But I will act as if I am not weary for the rest of the meeting and hope that you will too."

We turn now to a more complex means of changing moods. We follow the thinking and advice given by Richard Wollheim in *On the Emotions*.[15] His account of emotions builds on the others we have discussed and draws on Sigmund Freud as well. We can use it for ourselves and for coaching others. Freud believed that our emotional sets arise from stories we developed (mostly when very young) to explain traumatic moments. Like Nussbaum, Wollheim thinks of emotions in cognitive terms, but he focuses on stories instead of on assertions. He is also like James in that, as Freud perceptively noted, if we could force ourselves to relive the experience behind the story with the wisdom of accumulated years, we would naturally change the story and our *entire* emotional set. Wollheim and Freud tell us people really can change, but people must try to do so.

How does this change work? It works by getting clear about the story we are telling ourselves about ourselves and then looking at it as though we were script doctors who are fixing what does not seem believable, what is boring and trivial, and what is ponderous. The point is to develop a new, richer, more compelling story about what is happening, a story that brings more clarity about our own and others' motivations and desires. In developing this new story, new options for action will appear. In filling in the details based on our observations, we will create the motivation to act on the new story.

So how do you go about becoming the script doctor of your life? When you are facing your weariness toward the end of the day, ask yourself: "What would the story of my career be if this were its end? How could the story of my past triumphs make sense if they led only here? If the triumphs do not make sense of this moment, can my vices have brought me so low? How did they do that? How have I handled my vices in the past?"

Precisely because we always can be other than who we are, once we start asking the script-doctor questions, we will find ourselves rebelling against the weariness, sadness, sorrow, or even anger defining our lives. And even if we are Michael-like and believe that poorly managing things in the past, letting things go, acting on empty hope, or not thinking hard enough has landed us in an insurmountable muddle of our own desert, just filling out the story's details forces us to ask about context: "What kind of world is it?" We can now ask about the motivations of the various characters in the story: "What exactly did they say? Why did they say what they said? Why did they do what they did?" As we tell the story, we can ask about others' interpretations of what we said and did: "Did they interpret my actions morally? Did they interpret my actions as calculated moves to achieve some larger, hidden goal? Did they interpret my actions and words as reflex reactions?" Then we can ask how clear we were about what our motivations were for what we did and said.

Such questions in search of details might include: "What is my board or my CEO or my team saying that makes me feel so weary? Why are they saying what they are saying? Are they simply in an unimaginative funk? Are they responding with worries of their own? Are they making moral judgments or calculating predictions? Have they interpreted my actions as weak and craven or as simple miscalculations? Are they impatiently waiting for me to come up with the decision? Are they resigned to going along without hearing my inspiring thought? Do I, against my better judgment, actually enjoy the dilemma I am in? Am I just biding time? Am I wallowing? Is there a Gordian knot I can simply cut through?" Once you start eliciting the details and putting them in context, other questions emerge. Suspect your suspicions. Look at things from different perspectives. Do it with James's cold-bloodedness. As you start answering these questions, you will find yourself altering your account of your situation. In some ways, you might find it to be more dire. But then unseen resources will appear: new weaknesses in your antagonists show up; an enemy of your enemy is ready to become an ally.

In asking yourself these questions, remember that we tend to think that people who speak to us are speaking in a confessional, where they are trying as hard as they can to tell the truth. That is almost never the case. "When that board member told me that I had six months to turn things around, was she trying to issue a tough threat, give the warning of a concerned friend, rehearse what she would say to the investor she represents, cover up her own lack of clarity, or something else?" "Why would my team members want me to think that they saw no way to close the £10 million gap? Are they simply responding to panic and seeking to run away? Do they want to get off the hook and put me on it? Do they want me to work a miracle? Do they want me to squirm in front of the CEO? Do they want me to have difficult conversations with customers?"

When we start looking at the possible motivations behind our colleagues' assertions, we will find that the mood in which we started out loses its hold over us as we become engaged in figuring out just what the situation is. What is really going on? What are the interpretations others are coming up with and responding to? Where are they coming from? The mood for asking these questions is curiosity or wonder. That new mood gets stronger as we try to get to the best account, the one that best fits with the actors' characters and most clearly explains most of the details. We then start coming up with responses to the situation: "Since the board member was doing X, I would want to respond with Y." In short, by working as script doctors trying to make out a compelling story, we will find ourselves back in the masterpiece-creation business.

When coaching others, do the same thing. And always suspect your and their assumptions. "What if he was motivated by envy or grandstanding or practicing lines for another audience instead of saying the truth?" "What if he hadn't really worked out a plan but simply wanted to say something to feel good?" Asking these questions frees the person you are coaching from her or his all-too-ready, normal interpretations. It stops the coached person from thinking of people as having settled states and fixed conditions and moves the individual to seeing people as mysterious, changeable, and acting in a drama. The coached person will come to see the situation as one where all involved are in the act of developing themselves and their views and exploring positions rather than speaking certainties.

As a leader creating a masterpiece of your leadership style and of your organization, you are responsible for drawing people into admirable accounts of themselves and of you. You will want to shift emotions to a particular mood, most likely joy, hope, admiration, or zeal. But in the nitty-gritty of daily mood management, you cannot always do that. It is enough to move people to any positive mood. If you impute motives to people that they find exciting, interesting, even captivating, they take on the story and practice it until they start living it. They might not have to force themselves cold-bloodedly. They might become captivated by the story. Though shifting stories is the most difficult of the three techniques for shifting moods, it is the most important and plays a role in a leader's cultivation of her or his leadership style and that of the leadership team. Cultivating a beautiful, positive mood is the first, big step in turning a leadership style and an organization into a masterpiece.

From Mood Manager to Masterpiece Creator

Many managers we meet love the ethos described in Jim Collins's book *Good to Great*. They want to start with personal humility, get a great team on the bus, look at the brutal facts, and develop a truly audacious business proposition based on the team and facts. They seek to develop a missionary zeal, clear policies, and processes that create momentum the way a flywheel does.[16] In short, they want to create high-performance perpetual-motion machines from which they can stand back humbly and give others the credit. Even these machines require zeal, though, and are therefore unlikely to run on their own. Moods need constant management. Even good to great companies require that. Leaders who make masterpieces never put down their paintbrushes. They are always bringing people and themselves along. There are no flywheels for maintaining a mood for very long. For that reason, mood management is a great introduction to developing the skills and habits of a masterpiece creator. No matter how steeped your company comes to be in moods of hope, admiration, zeal, joy (or any other great mood), the enemy twin moods of resentment, fear, resignation, and arrogance will not be far offstage and will be calculating their entrance. A weak moment in hope inspires resentment; a self-doubt in admiration beckons fear; a defeat in zeal makes resignation a nighttime partner; a felt betrayal to joy breeds arrogance. That is why you will always have your masterpiece-creating paintbrush in your hand.

There is always room to manage emotions more artfully for better lives and better business results. Shift from negative to positive emotions, and the burdens are lighter, our feet faster, our hands busier, and our minds sharper. We believe that the same is true of all business processes and operating models, but managing emotions is exemplary. Anyone who thinks otherwise probably thinks that there is an emotionless way to be rational or that you lose yourself if you are not true to your feelings or, cynically, that people just do not change much. Fortunately, the COVID-19 pandemic has had us all changing. Thus, we can see that we do not need to find a new *normal*. We have an opportunity to create a masterpiece. Start by mastering moods. If that seems hard, think how much of a wonder it is that we have so many various moods and can fall *into* them and pull ourselves *out* of them. Is it not amazing that we have joy and love as well as, yes, anger and hatred?

4   Trust at First Sight and Listening for Difference

All lies and jest
Still, a man hears what he wants to hear
And disregards the rest
—Paul Simon and Art Garfunkel, "The Boxer"

Virtues

Like believing in love at first sight, believing in trust at first sight is not very fashionable.[1] We prefer to believe that trust comes from repeated, reliable performance. Today's pieties claim that trust is hard to gain, easy to lose, and, once lost, extremely hard to regain. Shakespeare knew better. Some of his evil and pompous characters express such conventional sentiments, but the plots of the plays from *Richard III* through *The Tempest* show just the opposite. Trust is not so hard to gain nor so easy to lose or gain back. Shakespeare is not the only one who saw through convention.

We all have experienced on our first encounter the compelling sense that certain people and organizations are worthy of our trust. It is not because their reputations preceded them but because something just clicked. Today's intellectual fashion dictates that when we trust without repeated justification, we are suffering from a cognitive bias. This suspicion of our quick judgments of trustworthiness is wrong. We do trust at first sight. To be precise, we trust at first sight people and organizations who exhibit virtues we admire. Though it is also not fashionable to think in terms of virtues, we are nevertheless at least dimly aware of them. Without naming them to ourselves or consciously going through any reasoning about virtues—though we can conduct such reasoning—we just see the wise person straightaway and, likewise, the courageous, the just, the hope-ful, the loving.[2] Of course, we are sometimes deceived. We would not be finitely rational beings otherwise.

How frequently do we trust at first sight? Have you ever walked into a store for the first time and found it feels great? Consider those retailers such as the Body Shop and Sephora that encourage customers to try on the products or have showrooms for testing them. Consider other retailers whose employees are clearly having a fun time when you walk into the store. In the first case, the retailer appeals to the virtue of exploration. If you admire this virtue, you trust the store. In the second, the virtues on display are those of an entertaining host or hostess. As these two exam-ples suggest, there are many more virtues than the traditional seven: the four classic virtues of courage, prudence, justice, and temperance, along with the three Christian virtues of hope, faith, and love. Wit, generosity, responsiveness, resourcefulness, initiative, creativity, strength, athleticism, speed, productivity, precision, carefulness, and pragmatism are virtues, too. Cunning, commercial sense, agility, resilience, daring, storytelling, and self-confidence can equally be virtues. Machiavelli's virtù (aggressive effective-ness) is a virtue today. Virtues are excellences that lead to a good life.

As shorthand, ask yourself what you and others find admirable about your leadership, and more importantly, ask what makes your organiza-tion admirable to you and others when it is. The answers will name one or more virtues: "We are incredibly productive"; "Our workers love our cus-tomers"; "People are proud to work here." Or the answers will be one step away from virtues: "We are admirable because our profits grow at a steady pace." Ask then what the key virtues behind that achievement are: Brilliant planning for profit growth? Clever use of financial instruments? Flexibil-ity in responding to circumstances? Inventive product refreshes? Emotion-ally sensitive customer outreach? The virtues—brilliance, inventiveness, sensitivity—are there. If you want your organization to become trustwor-thy, your team members all the way down to your frontline employees need to cultivate admirable virtues in themselves. You will want them to express those virtues every day in their interactions. (We will not say much here about virtue signaling, although it is a common topic today. As we see virtue signaling, it does not manifest a virtue in action but shows a moral-izing approval of a stereotypical virtue.[3] It draws on stereotypes of virtues, and such activity ruins a masterpiece.)

Anticipating Anxiety

In addition to manifesting admired virtues, building customer trust is also about anticipating customer anxiety. The best organizations are exceptionally good at anticipating the anxiety they produce (even when they are at their best) and then doing everything they can to remove it. Take Amazon. It is an online, everything store. You can find anything there, and because it is online and can buy in bulk, it passes low costs along as low prices. But while that is fine if you want to buy books or download videos, it is not so good if you are buying clothes or diamond necklaces. You want to try the clothes on or see the sparkle of the jewelry in person. The inability to do so creates anxiety—an anxiety that springs directly from successful elements of the business model. (As of this writing, Jeff Bezos's heir, Andy Jassy, does not want to change Amazon's online business model.[4]) That is what made Amazon both possible and wildly successful. But the company does want to remove the anxiety. So Jassy and Bezos spend a significant effort making sure that products get to customers very quickly, that communication is strong, and that everything is easy to return.

We have polled clients, colleagues, and students by asking them: "What do you find cool about Amazon?" They point to the speed of delivery and the convenience with which they can return things. That response is weird, but we confirm it frequently. Amazon has a vast selection of products at low prices and exhibits the virtues of exactitude in process, magnificence in its ranges of offerings, appreciation of customers in offering them a platform to become opinion leaders, and in its low prices sensitivity to how hard customers work for their money. Those are the reasons we started using and trusting Amazon. But Amazon becomes truly memorable and distinctive when it mitigates the anxiety that it creates with its own brilliant business model and virtuous execution. Such self-awareness and the creative response to it produces outsize trust and admiration.

Consider self-awareness. Jeff Bezos's techies probably wanted early customers to love the variety, prices, and technical coolness of an online, everything store. They probably thought that customers should—and would—hardly notice the trade-off of the delivery delays in the face of the technological wonder that the techies loved. In fact, customers willingly made the compromise but never stopped experiencing it as such. Noticing that the sense of trade-off never abated comes from listening for difference.

It is the ability first to see and understand how others—your customers, employees, suppliers, owners, or community—understand things very differently in important ways from the way you do and second to have the courage to look at that fact sympathetically. That is what Bezos and his Amazon team did. Let us take another case where the details are clearer.

Mexicans and Cement

In the past, one of us worked with CEMEX, then the third-largest cement company in the world. In the 1990s, CEMEX wanted to sell more cement to lower-income Mexicans living in the gray economy. These Mexicans generally did not have enough money to purchase large bags of cement. The obvious idea was to extend credit to them, but that did not work because these lower-income Mexicans did not feel obliged to pay the money back to a large company. Yet they already had a neighborhood custom of forming groups of neighbors, pooling their money, and then letting one and then another have the whole pot of money for the week or month to make a large purchase. That sharing and discipline created a bond, and everyone in the group felt honor bound to pay (or ashamed of not paying) her or his share. Sometimes the purchase was a bag of cement to add a room to a home.

By listening to how these Mexicans saw the world differently and how they tried to cope with a middle-class world, the team found a solid bridge in a revised version of the group's money-pooling practice. In addition to setting up a money-pooling association strictly for cement purchases, we added more. Because these lower-income Mexicans did not plan carefully— thinking it arrogant and sinful—and consequently ended up leaving bags of cement outside to harden, we gave the option of having CEMEX deliver the cement just when needed. Because these Mexicans were not accustomed to planning their rooms, we gave standard designs. The bridge worked extremely well by most criteria. CEMEX sold two to three times more cement depending on the region, and the customers were happy because they were adding rooms to their houses in about one-third of the time and at a 20 percent lower cost.

Let us look a little deeper into what made this approach successful. Information, wrote Gregory Bateson, the great anthropologist and cybernetician, is "a difference that makes a difference."[5] When we come across something that is different from what we are familiar with, it potentially triggers action; at minimum, we try to understand it. Understanding frequently leads to clever accommodation.

We turn now to our case. We had to understand lower-income Mexican customers in their difference from us and from middle-class Mexicans. These lower-income Mexicans believe that the love of family and neighbors is the source of a good life. Working hard with discipline is not. Getting ahead on your own shows that you are taking something unfairly from the neighborhood. Moreover, God or fate determines what will happen to you, so long-term planning is either sinful or arrogant. Large companies from whom you buy products are patrons. You honor a patron by staying loyal, not by paying bills. Patrons overlook missed payments so long as loyalty remains.[6] Accepting such difference and looking it in the face are key to building trust and a good bridge.

If you are like *middle-class* Mexicans, you will find the moral norms of the lower-income Mexicans quite unappealing. You want people to plan and take responsibility for their fates. You want them to treat commercial organizations as providers of products and services who deserve payment for their products and services.

So how can middle-class people start seeing the lower-income Mexicans' moral norms as anything other than mistakes or outright evils? First, try looking at the living masterpieces the lower-income Mexicans were trying to build. We saw that these builders and their families were constantly reconstructing their homes to take account of changes in their families. No home was ever complete. If you have a new daughter-in-law, you construct a new room. These Mexicans' masterpiece is a distinctive family-oriented dwelling inside a tightly interconnected neighborhood that celebrates families. Even if your masterpiece—as was CEMEX's—was as different as bringing US financial practices to Mexico, it becomes possible to see that CEMEX and the lower-income Mexicans were working to create quite different, even opposing masterpieces, but masterpieces nevertheless. Second, do not try to bridge the difference by doing what makes sense within your own masterpiece. In CEMEX's case, there seemed to be an obvious solution to the problems in the lower-income Mexicans' way of life. For instance, these builders found it hard to afford a whole bag of cement, and when they got the money to purchase one, they could not use it in a disciplined way, and it was ruined in the weather. The obvious, responsible solution was to sell smaller bags, but CEMEX was unaware that it was a point of neighborly and family pride to display in front of one's home the big bag of cement. A small bag was humiliating. (At least, just-in-time delivery did not humiliate.) Third, find a bridge practice that achieves practical ends, suits the other's masterpiece, and then amend it to suit your own. CEMEX built on the indigenous money-pooling practice it found to turn it into one focused on cement, which included plans for rooms and cement bags delivered to stand in front of the house exactly when needed. The bridge worked for a while, but then it nearly failed. Neighbors were suspicious of neighbors who got ahead, so CEMEX had to add neighborhood parties to celebrate finished rooms. To keep things working, listening for difference must go on, but it is a hard skill to cultivate.

"The Franklin's Tale"

How does a leader cultivate listening for difference? Of course, the best way would be for all leaders to have the time to develop an anthropologist's skills: embedding oneself in the customers' culture, finding reliable informants from inside the culture, taking careful notes about what seems odd, and developing a big picture in which small, unusual acts make sense. Few leaders can do that.[7] We have a way for you to sharpen this skill during downtime. Read literature from moments in history when people were quite different from us. Pay attention to the statements or pictures that do not make good sense to you, moments where you want to say, "That can't be right." Charles Spinosa remembers having students read Chaucer's "The Franklin's Tale." In the story, a knight falls in love with a lady, and she puts him through various courtship ordeals to prove his love. Charles would then ask students: "Why, ultimately, did she marry him? What was her love like?" Students would say: "Well, the guy was doing all these things for her, and she saw he would make a good, generous partner. Beyond that, she thought that because he underwent the ordeals, he must deep-down-deep have loved her."

Chaucer thought otherwise. The narrator says she fell in love with the knight because she "pitied" him. Here is Chaucer's version:

And namely for his meke obeysaunce,
Hath swich a pitee caught of his penaunce
That pryvely she fil of his accord
To take hym for hir housbonde and hir lord.[8]

Here is a modern translation: "At last she took pity upon his pains, because of his worthiness and chiefest for his humble attentiveness, that privily she agreed to take him for husband and lord."[9] Charles would point out the line, and the students would say: "You can't take that line seriously. That is not what love is about. People do not marry people they pity." Now comes listening for difference. "What if you take that as the most serious line in the story? What if you think that there is now a dramatic difference between how we see and feel love and how people did in the Middle Ages?" Then you begin to see that love in the Middle Ages was radically different from what we have today. Romantic love was much more closely affiliated with Christian charity. It had little sense of partnership about it. A man showed his devotion to his beloved. Love was like a captivating religious devotion. The man was humble in his kindness. Knowing her lover to be finite and weak, the beloved in the tale pities the lover in a weak imitation of God's love for humankind and extends mercy.

Cultivating Listening for Difference

You do not need to be a scholar of the Middle Ages to fill in the blanks in "The Franklin's Tale." Once you take seriously the odd line about the lady pitying the knight, then you will note that the tale is full of concern with pity. We see the knight describing himself and the narrator describing him as piteous. There are plenty of hints, too, of the religious overtones of love and of how that makes the ordeals acts of pious devotion. Suddenly, the tale shines in giving its reader a view of a hidden world. To get a better grip on the world, you ask, "Do I see any vestiges of this love left in our world today, filled as it is with partnership lovers, companionate lovers, convenience lovers?"

Vestiges remain. Consider the sound of love from the Middle Ages in these half dozen or so of lines from Cole Porter's song, "I've Got You under My Skin":

I'd sacrifice anything, come what might
For the sake of having you near
In spite of a warning voice that comes in the night
And repeats and repeats in my ear
"Don't you know, silly fool, you never can win
Use your mentality? Step up, wake up to reality"
But each time I do, just the thought of you
Makes me stop before I begin.[10]

In the song, there is little question but that the lover is a fated, silly fool because of the willingness to suffer, out of devotion for the beloved. The song still has vestigial meaning for some of us today. If you see the vestiges and you have an organization that sells to lovers—real estate, holiday rentals, fine meals, jewelry, financial products, and so forth—you may want to build a bridge to that retro-medieval segment. How can your product or service glamorize the humbling power of such romantic love while keeping it sweet and pious? Would the silly fool marry the beloved because she pitied him? Of course. How can your product or service enhance that feeling? Try reading and listening for difference. Find the bridge.

If there are vestiges of medieval romantic love left in our world today and if you serve such customers, building a bridge will have enormous rewards, but only if it fits with your masterpiece. There is much more literature to read to sharpen your ability to listen for difference. There are also many more customer segments than the retro-medieval romantic lovers. To sharpen your listening for difference: Read texts or watch films from other cultures or periods (the 1960s or earlier). Interview previous leaders, young new hires, and especially customers unlike you. Engage in five critical acts of thought.

First, listen to capture the difference. Notice all the things that the author or person you are speaking with says that *do not make good sense to you*. If you find nothing, then you are not listening. We live in a world filled with ethical, political, social, gender, race, and cultural differences. Consider your salespeople and your analysts. Salespeople are different from analysts. They inhabit different worlds. They speak different languages. In short, salespeople tend toward being lovers who want to receive love. Analysts tend to be truth seekers who want to be right. The salesperson and analyst misunderstand each other's gestures and even explicit requests. If you think you know the other's language, be suspicious. To build a bridge, you will need to learn that language.

Second, form an interpretation about what the author or speaker might believe or might be saying that makes genuine sense of those weird things. Get into the other's world. Consider the salespeople and the analysts. What makes sense to them? Feeling good in being together or solving a puzzle? What do they find obvious or obnoxious? Saying things to feel good or saying things to understand the facts? What drives them: being loved or being right? Take the difference seriously. Ask, "What if the person to whom I am listening really disagrees with something I take as obvious? What experience could have triggered that disagreement?" It is essential to think in wonder. You will find that your sense of the obvious and acceptable will lead you to judge your interlocutor negatively, just as middle-class Mexicans judged lower-income ones. That judgment is inevitable but try to check it. What is important is to find the difference and not lose sight of it. Elevate it.

Third, ask yourself what traces of the other's view of the world you might find in your own world. If you are listening to a contemporary saying something odd, try to understand the contemporary's particular world, and then ask, "Who else do I know who might believe the same? Who else acts the same?" The middle-class Mexicans could understand neighborhood parties, and that was the beginning of finding the bridge.

Fourth, turn your inquisitive mind toward yourself and ask, "How am I fundamentally different from the person or work of art I am questioning?" The self-awareness that will emerge will sharpen your understanding of difference. And now, equipped with that understanding, you may find a bridge across your moral differences. Remember Bateson's definition of information: the difference that makes a difference.

Fifth, to find the bridge, ask, "How am I already dealing with this person across our differences? How is the person coping with me? What are the trade-offs I am making to deal with the difference?" The trade-off could be as simple as playing down pity whenever you see it. It could be as complicated as an alternative form of saving money. In the answers to those questions are the foundation blocks of a bridge if you want to build it. In going through these five investigative cognitive steps, you will find something amazing that might oppose your masterpiece and might also be worth building a bridge to. When you do that, you will also build trust. The bridge can be as simple as teaching your analysts a few techniques for friendly conversation with the sales team. It could be as complicated as a new business line or Amazon's logistical virtuosity.

So, to sum up, how do you build trust at first sight and then keep it? Identify, cultivate, and manifest your own and your organization's virtues. Respond to the anxiety such virtues (embodied in your masterpiece) produce; there will always be some anxiety—remember Amazon. Listen for difference. Build bridges. Those bridges will, if built well, show admiration of the virtues of others, which will add to and keep the trust. Last, we very seldom trust people who do not trust us. If we extend trust and genuine admiration, we are highly likely to become admired for admiring and trusted for trusting.

5 Truth First

Truth has had to be fought for every step of the way, almost everything else dear to our hearts, on which our love and our trust in life depend, has had to be sacrificed to it. Greatness of soul is needed for it: the service of truth is the hardest service.—For what does it mean to be *honest* in intellectual things? That one is stern towards one's heart, that one despises "fine feelings," that one makes every Yes and No a question of conscience!
—Friedrich Nietzsche, *The Anti-Christ*

May you grow up to be righteous
May you grow up to be true
May you always know the truth
And see the lights surrounding you.
—Bob Dylan, "Forever Young"

Today, consultants and academics advise leaders to be compassionate, authentic, and empowering consensus builders who admire and cultivate diversity.[1] They advise leaders to coach and inspire their teams and to do so with candor and honesty. Who would object to such advice? However, the reality is a little more complicated than those pious pieces of advice allow for. Truth seeking and saying is not high on the list of things for leaders to do today. Indeed, leading advisers would have leaders skirt around the issue of truth. They speak of evidence-based judgments, of facts, and, in frustration, of "one version of the truth," which means unquestionable truth claims. Such directives spoil genuine truth seeking. To see that, we need to spend some time listening to the post-truth siren songs. Stay close to your mast.

Kim Scott's *Radical Candor*, a best seller, stands for speaking one's mind freely and challenging directly without being a bully. Her work is about *compassionate* candor. She writes: "I chose 'candor' instead of 'honesty' because there's not much humility in believing that you know the truth. Implicit with candor is that you're simply offering your view of what's going on and that you expect people to offer theirs. If it turns out that, in fact, you're the one who got it wrong, you want to know."[2]

Really? Do we really want to listen to views that speakers do not regard as true? Indeed, if you are just offering views, you are not worried about truth; you are worried about having something plausible to say. And, yes, as an afterthought, you might want to know if what you said is wrong. However, if you are trying to say what is true, then you will *absolutely* want to know if you have it wrong. Getting it right is the point. Radical candor cannot have it both ways. If radical candor is about humbly offering and receiving views, then it is that way all the way down, including whether something is right or wrong. You are merely offering just another view. There is no switch that easily takes place between sharing views and seeking truth. The goal remains sharing compelling views and perhaps agreeing that one is most compelling. If, however, you are seeking and saying truth, then you are doing that top to bottom, and after hard thought and empirical work you and your colleague will agree that one claim is right and the others wrong. What will matter most will be the audacious—not humble—light of the new discovery that flashes out of the discussion along the way. Truth seeking has its own hard-fought rewards. Because finding truth is hard—not just a matter of offering views—and because we truth seekers are fallible, we must be humble. Truth tells us that in the end, even with all our carefully justified observations and reasoning and with the agreement of all, we may nevertheless still miss the truth. That is why truth is so important. But discovering a truth is seldom a humble moment. There is no reason to disguise it as such.

Brad Blanton is like Kim Scott. His book *Radical Honesty* is also a best seller. He says he cares about truth and detests the lying that he sees filling our lives. We could not agree more, especially about the self-deceit and other forms of deceit that fill the days of those who are not masterpiece creators. But truth is not so simple as Blanton would have it. It is not blurting out what comes to mind. Right at the beginning of his book, he writes: "If you get that distinction between being and mind you are at the very heart of learning about Radical Honesty. The being *notices*. The mind *thinks*. Radical

Honesty is simply reporting what the being notices."[3] In short, radical honesty is about blurting out what the "being" has noticed before the mind intervenes. Blanton's account is simply a bolder form of offering views. It is a far cry from seeking truth.

Creating a masterpiece requires the hard work of seeking and saying difficult truths.[4] Speaking your mind and expressing your being are important so far as they lead to the truth. Compassion is fine if it comes in ethical order after truth seeking and saying. Reporting what you notice does not face the difficulties of a truth-seeking discipline. Such reporting stops lying, and that is good, of course. But these popular books are still leading us, even if unintentionally, into a post-truth world, which is also a post-history, nihilistic world. It is a world of the eternal return of the same: one view after another. It is a world that does not include the bitter, hard work of finding oneself wrong and wrong again in pursuit of an understanding of what is going on. There are no masterpieces without that. That might sound strange to say, especially for followers of Nietzsche like us.

Nietzsche, one of the founding thinkers on masterpiece creation as the source of a good life, was among the first to write, despite this chapter's epigraph, of "*my* truths."[5] There is no question of that, nor is there much question over whether he inspired today's narcissistic, anything-goes relativism where one says, "What is true for me is based on my experience and might not be true for you."[6] Nietzsche did inspire, but he meant something quite different when he spoke of *his* truths. He was speaking of ways of being that he could not undo. He called those ways the "great stupidity." "My truths," for Nietzsche, are what we cannot think our way around or behind; they govern our experience rather than have their basis in our experience. Nietzsche was, in principle, a perspectivist but did not give up seeking truth in perspectives or adding perspectives together to obtain greater truth.[7] But he also thought that there could be infinite perspectives and that we could never add them all together.[8] He never gave up on seeking facts, an activity he saw that the Greeks and Romans gave birth to. Nietzsche rejoiced about "the *sense for* facts, the last-developed and most valuable of all the senses."[9] As this chapter's epigraph shows, Nietzsche honored truth seeking. He gave up seeking simply to be right to win an argument. He deplored that.

Scott and Blanton give us the seductive siren songs that lead to a post-truth-seeking world, but they only express with more vigor what goes on in much consultant advice giving. Consider the following. One top consulting firm persuades its clients that expressions such as "Her work is a mess" are not truth claims at all but expressions of an attitude. They say more about the speaker than about the messiness of the work. We have asked, "Why not acknowledge that a simple, old-fashioned proposition—'Her work is messy'—is in the first instance a claim that 'it is true that her work is messy,' just as the proposition 'The cat is sitting on the mat' is saying, 'It is true that the cat is sitting on the mat'?" If the claim is right, it is because the claim corresponds to some fact or state of affairs (even if we cannot explain how the correspondence works).[10] Or if saying that the claim *corresponds* to some state of affairs in the world is too realist, would not one want to say that it is true because it is useful over time to believe the proposition or that it coheres with other propositions taken as true?[11] All seem plausible accounts of truth. Yet the answer we received was: "Saying that the claim is true would make us into dogmatists. People who care about truth that much are dogmatic. They do not appreciate other people's different experiences."

Wow! That is the voice of the casual, friendly, post-truth world. Influenced by philosophers, as we are, we find such a statement mind-blowing for two reasons.

First, philosophers tend to think that if you do not know what it would take to make a statement true or false—what it would take for it to be true that the work is messy—you do not know even the *meaning* of the statement.[12] If you honestly have no idea of what could make work messy (or what it would take for it to be useful to believe so), then you have to ask, "What do you mean?"

Because, however, we use the word *messy*, let us assume that we do in fact have a shared meaning. You can already hear the post-truth relativist saying, "But 'messy' is subjective. Who decides what is messy?" Can we really have such subjective meanings? Famously, the philosopher Ludwig Wittgenstein argued against the possibility. He claimed that there is no such thing as a private language.[13] The argument not only is subtle and rewards study but also is intuitively appealing: if we do not have a community of people who coordinate their actions with the same words, then we cannot know whether we are using our words consistently. But we do have such a community. Therefore, we know that we are not using a word in the standard intersubjective way when someone tells us so. "That is not right. That is not what we mean by 'messy.' That is not even what you meant when you spoke last about messiness." Wittgenstein took such encounters as a fact of life.

How does truth seeking work? A truth seeker says "messy," which, like virtually all general terms we use, starts out unclear but not wholly confused. If the claim is intelligible at all, there must be enough consistency in its usage for adequate coordination. One observes that people in the same community understand each other when one says, "Please tidy up your room. It is a mess" or "This is a messy arrangement." We do not have to know the essence of the term *messy* to coordinate with appropriate actions and words. What matters is that we have learned to use the word in our community and on that basis can identify disagreements and then engage in further explorations and discussions to come to a more precise agreement about the meaning.[14]

Frequently, we do encourage engineers and scientists to contest their views as true or false, but we become cautious when the views concern people or community values. Truth, however, does not reside in science or engineering alone. It resides in any inquiry. We make a mistake if we believe that all truth must, like scientific truth, be universal. A community will have its truths, which might differ from another community's truths because each community institutes its own matrix of meanings. Each community copes with the world in its own way. Normally, truths would not contradict each other if we could translate them across communities; however, such contradictory truths might be possible under very narrow constraints.[15] Hence, a certain kind of highly constrained relativism might be coherent in principle. But we are unlikely to run into such cases in creating masterpiece organizations. The simple cases are clear: people in different communities mean different things by "love" or "patron," and the differences are open to explanation and then agreement. Once explained, we simply have the same word meaning different things.

So we think we can understand the sentence "Her work is messy" only if we can hear it as claiming a truth and understanding at least roughly what would make it so. Without that, it does become an expression of an attitude of disfavor.

Seeming subjectivity is only one reason for calling a truth seeker dogmatic. Another reason to treat the truth seeker as dogmatic is to suppose that person simply wants to be right. It is hard for philosophers to get a grip on this supposition. For philosophers, conversations involve making truth claims, supplying reasons, *and* almost always having truth claims contested. That is just part of the truth-seeking and truth-speaking business. Philosophers who care about truth also care about truth seeking, not just about being right. Contesting truth claims is part of common experience, and it is in working through the contest that new flashes of light and new truths happen. Dogmatists are the ones who have left the truth-seeking contest because in truth seeking, we regularly examine and contest truth claims. Sharing views solely in "candor" or in "honesty" enables dogmatists to state their claims without facing a contest. Truth seeking pulls the dogmatist from dogmatism.

Let us leave philosophers aside for a moment to get a breath of fresh air. We now turn to Albert Einstein, with whom we (the authors) grew up as a truth-seeking cultural luminary. Between 1907 and 1915, Einstein struggled to learn the geometry necessary for his general theory of relativity. The brilliant mathematician David Hilbert attended Einstein's lectures at the University of Göttingen in June 1915, got the point, loved the idea of general relativity, and started working through the mathematics of general relativity independently and quickly. Einstein set out to complete the theory in November 1915 and scheduled four Thursday lectures at the Prussian Academy in Berlin, where he wanted to showcase his completed theory. He failed on November 4. He failed again on November 11. (Interested in truth more than in winning, he sent his papers off to David Hilbert, who reciprocated, and indeed, he offered a session to go over his thinking with Einstein at his home on November 16. Einstein could not make it but received Hilbert's paper with his newest thinking on November 18, too late for him to use that day.) At the lecture on November 18, Einstein was able to produce the correct equations regarding Mercury's perihelion movement and the bending of light, but he had as yet no general theory of relativity. On November 20, Hilbert submitted his version of general relativity. Then Einstein gave his final lecture on November 25 and did succeed.[16] In speaking of his own paper, Hilbert acknowledged Einstein: "The differential equations of gravitation that result are, as it seems to me, in agreement with the magnificent theory of general relativity established by Einstein." Then in slightly backhanded summation (showing the state of psychological safety in this world), Hilbert states: "Every boy in the streets of Göttingen understands geometry in four dimensions better than Einstein. Yet, in spite of that, Einstein did the work and not the mathematicians."[17] Einstein's is a story of struggling to seek truth, of getting shot down in public again and again and again. He had to learn a form of geometry that did not come naturally. He had to go through the public humiliation of thinking he had it right only to discover he did not. That is what truth seeking and saying are like. Truths worth saying do not come easy. They never have.

We make a mistake when we think that a good case of truth seeking is like reading the temperature from a thermometer. We are merely coping with weather when we do the latter. We are determining whether to wear the overcoat. However, our technological convenience makes us think we really understand both thermometers and temperature. Unless we are certain kinds of scientists or engineers, we do not. We do not have a clear idea about what makes our utterance that "it is 70 degrees Fahrenheit" true. We would tend to say the utterance is true if it is, in fact, 70 degrees. But what configuration of molecules makes it 70 degrees? Unless we are experts, we do not know. We live in a community where there is, as the philosopher Hilary Putnam put it, a division of linguistic labor. When I say that the thermometer tells me the temperature is 70 degrees Fahrenheit, I mean by "temperature" whatever scientists in my community mean by "temperature."[18] Ordinarily, if a scientist or engineer were to tell us that we got something wrong in what we mean by a temperature or a thermometer, we would *without protest* amend what we said (just as Wittgenstein's private-language argument would have it). We would not claim that we have independent grounds for our claim that the scientist should consider. That is why our claims about the temperature are *not* exemplary truth claims. We are depending too much on community hearsay (Putnam's linguistic division of labor), which is necessary for coordination. But truth seeking happens when we are (1) *un*covering something unnoticed—Heidegger reminded us that the Greek word for *truth* is *aletheia*, "unforgetfulness"—and then (2) *verifying* through seeking both confirmation and disconfirmation that what we have found is real.[19]

Then, truth *saying* involves bringing to the attention of people in our community what we have uncovered and (when possible) verified.[20] We build masterpieces on hard truths that we come to through struggle, not through simple conventional actions such as reading a thermometer. Masterpiece builders, as we shall see, seek disharmonies in their own leadership styles and anomalies in their organizations' moral orders. They try to understand and then say what is true about the anomalies. We consider that process fundamentally important. Of course, the true statements we utter (and that depend on experts and their verifications) are important for coordination, and we abhor the frequent lying that takes place with truths that stay at the level of coordination and not discovery or verification. But the truth seeking and saying that matters involve truths one uncovers, verifies, speaks, and defends.[21]

Telling Truth to Power

We advise our clients and students to take pride in their truth seeking and saying. We run workshops on telling truth to power; those in power include customers, board members and shareholders, colleagues, key subordinates, and primary suppliers. Anyone who can damage your reputation counts as someone in power. The response to the workshop and exercises is shock and awe. Most people entering the workshop want to believe that leadership is primarily about execution. But masterpiece leadership requires more.

If you want to create a masterpiece, the first part of leadership is seeking truth. Leadership requires you actively to engage with your team in finding the hidden truths about your customers, shareholders, organization, and supply chain. Today, consultants have an agile way to avoid conceptual contests. Experiment and fail fast, and just do what works. Do not inquire much into the "why." If the small bag of cement does not work with the lower-income Mexican builders, try something else. Thus, innovation today frequently follows Chairman Mao Zedong's saying, "Let a hundred flowers blossom." We advise instead trying to get the whole picture in understanding your customers and others. Listen for difference. Then test the difference. Build your masterpiece on what you have discovered and verified.

The second part of leadership is telling the truth to others, even those who do not want to hear it. The question always arises: How do I get others to listen to me when I tell them an unexpected truth? The answer is never simply that you should supply data and make sure that your reasoning is based on evidence. The evidence for much of Einstein's theory of relativity has arrived only in the past few decades, not when he was working on it in the early twentieth century. The answer is also never to ask for a safe space free from interpersonal judgments. David Hilbert was breathing down Einstein's neck, and the Berlin lectures were heart-wrenching. Could Einstein avoid taking it personally when others undermined his reasoning? There are few safe spaces in the truth-seeking and truth-saying business.[22]

So, while acknowledging that speaking the truth is risky, how do you get others to listen? The first thing is to express the virtue of a truth seeker. Show that you are seeking truth. Talk about some of the things you tried that *failed*.[23] Accept wholeheartedly that you are wrong when you are wrong, as Einstein did. Truth seekers always know that they might be wrong. They know that they will never know it all. They are fallibilists. They do not lash out against those who disagree. On the contrary, they draw them into more advanced thinking through productive dialogue.[24] They intuitively appreciate what the philosopher Maurice Merleau-Ponty said about the value of dialogue: my interlocutor "draws from me thoughts which I had no idea I possessed."[25] Those are the virtues by which we recognize genuine truth seekers. We tell our clients that if they show those virtues, others will likely trust them and listen attentively to their words. This lesson comes from developing trust at first sight.

Beyond the most crucial point of exhibiting the truth-seeking virtue that will build trust in those who respect it, there are five other important, practical rhetorical considerations in saying truth to a particular person or group.

First, determine how important the truth is to the life of the person you are thinking of telling it to. If it is not important, there is no reason to risk the relationship. (Masterpiece creators have no time for unnecessary risks; there are more than enough necessary ones.) Also, ask if the person deserves to hear the truth. If the person will use it for ill to others or to themselves, you might have good reason to avoid telling the truth.[26] Likewise, if the effect of the truth will leave the person in a hopeless condition, you might have a good reason not to speak the truth. But do not let yourself off the hook easily. It should be a *King Lear* kind of case. In *King Lear*, Edgar at first lies to console his father, Gloucester. When later Edgar tells Gloucester the real events that have taken place, his father dies:

> his flaw'd heart
> . . . 'Twixt two extremes of passion, joy and grief,
> Burst smilingly.[27]

In other words, do not tell innocent people truths that will ruin their lives.

Second, evaluate your own reasons for telling the truth. Are they solid? Are they just barely compelling? Are they somewhere in between? Be willing to give this assessment clearly and honestly when introducing the truth claim. "Honestly" means honestly. Do not out of misconceived politeness claim that your truth is less well verified than it is.

Third, make sure you have cultivated an identity that will make the other want to hear you. Beyond cultivating the identity and virtue of truth saying, show that you care for the other as well. We tend to listen to people whom we credit as wise *and* as caring about us.

Fourth, figure out what the other might think and work through the other's thinking. What reasons would the other have to doubt your claim? What else is the other being told and why? See how you could answer those thoughts or objections in a compelling way by reconfiguring your initial argument. Remember that truth seekers are willing to learn about how to express their truths so that others can hear them. Sometimes that means discarding some personally strong reasons to persuade the other.

Fifth, compose what you are going to say so that the other can easily understand it. Truth seekers and sayers do not clutter their speaking by listing all who agree or by overloading their speech with evidence. Nor do truth seekers and sayers just blurt out truths unless, like the ancient Cynics, they have carefully developed an identity of blurting things out. So, unless you are going to live in a barrel like Diogenes, compose what you are going to say carefully for the easiest understanding possible.[28] Table 5.1 summarizes the rhetorical issues of speaking truth to power.

Yes, There Will Be Strife, but Hold On to Truth Seeking and Saying

Our advice so far runs smack against today's grain. Francis X. Frei and Anne Morriss say in the *Harvard Business Review* that people trust those who are authentic (true to their real selves), empathetic (listen to others attentively), and logical (which means exercising sound reasoning but not necessarily being in possession of the truth).[29] When you see articles like this, we advise asking of each main claim: Is it true? That is really the only way of holding on to the truth-seeking and saying course. So, regarding claims like those in the article, ask yourself: Do you have a real self? Twenty-first-century philosophers and psychoanalysts have argued that we are deep down changeable and that the notion of a real self is a Romantic-modernist myth. In other words, you have a flexible self that you, like an artist of life, are adjusting.

Table 5.1
Rhetorical Considerations of Telling Truth to Power

What is at stake?	• How important is the truth to your auditor? • If it is not important, do not risk the relationship.
What are your reasons?	• Are your reasons solid or barely compelling? • Be up front and clear about this evaluation.
Do you have a truth-telling *and* caring identity?	• Does your auditor know you care about truth? • Does your auditor know you care about him or her?
What will your audience's response be?	• Think about how the auditor will respond to your claim. Why would the auditor disbelieve the claim? • Are others making contrary claims? What are those claims? • Explore how you might respond to such claims. • Supply reasons compelling to the audience.
Are you being considerate?	• Compose what you are going to say so it can be listened to. • Blurt out thoughts only if you have managed the context.

As discussed earlier in this book, for Heidegger and Sartre being authentic meant being true to the changeable nature of human being.

Do you trust people who listen to you attentively and with empathy? Truth seekers and sayers will find that they trust people who listen carefully and attentively *and* who probe and ask about how we came to our conclusions. They might ask about personal motivations to get a clearer picture. But they are listening to what the person says or is trying to say. It is the content that counts. Caring is nice. Empathy is nice. But also remember that con artists show care and have empathy. We demand more than that. We trust those who seek truth and therefore question and probe us about what we say.

Masterpiece creators frequently ask here whether they should act authentically and empathetically to people who are not truth seekers and sayers. We advise erring on the side of treating them as if they are. Most people, even if they are not consciously truth seekers, will find it flattering and absorbing if you treat them as such. They will speak more freely and will say that the conversation with you was like having a good meeting with a therapist.

And what about data-driven reasoning? When consultants advise that credibility arises from strictly well-constructed, data-driven reasoning, they are putting the cart before the horse. They are advising you to deliver the truth of verification (the cart). But without the truth of discovery (the horse) preceding the verification, the data-driven bits of reasoning look like special pleading. We judge claims to be true—the truth of discovery—when they reveal the world to us in a new way that is different from what we thought before and that is better because it resolves confusions. In developing the theory of general relativity, Einstein bore witness to the truth of discovery by working so valiantly to develop the theory, and then people saw it as true because it resolved numerous confusions between electromagnetic theory and gravity. Such interpretive truth is the truth of discovery, which later seeks the truth of verification. Our data-obsessed culture makes it easy for us to appreciate the latter and ignore the former. But we should pay attention to both. We want to resolve confusions and solve puzzles, and that means we want to discover and verify.

Why Do Feelings Seem So Important?

What is going on with us at this moment in history that we should focus on feelings and on empathy and authenticity so much? Why are we told to be true to our feelings to be authentic? Why does empathy matter more than argument? Why do we avoid contestation of ideas to make sure no one feels we are dogmatic? The philosopher and historian Michel Foucault gives the most illuminating answer.

Foucault says that changes in our core codes of ethics (rules and guidelines for how we treat others, including how we lead) over the past 2,500 years (from endorsing slavery to outlawing it) have not been *as radical or as deep reaching* as changes in what we apply our codes to. That is a huge claim. However, his historical claims are compelling. The ancient Greeks applied ethical standards to pleasure (and mastering pleasure). The king stayed faithful to his wife to show his mastery over himself. As part of showing mastery, he must desire other women and then master the desire. The Christians applied the rules of ethics straightaway to desires. There were permissible and impermissible ones. Hence, Christians developed institutions for confessing inner desires and dealing with them through penance. During the Enlightenment from 1770 to 1900, ethical principles were applied to intentions and judgments. One intended to do one's duty. If things did not go well, the intention was paramount. If the intention was wrong, and things nevertheless went well, one had still failed ethically.

Foucault claims that today we apply our ethics to our feelings. He encapsulates the claim when he says that if you have a good feeling about your spouse, your affair with another does not matter.[30] Thus, when we try to understand or describe leadership, we look to the leaders' feelings and how they express and manage them. Does the leader show authenticity and vulnerability? Is the leader empathetic and compassionate? Does the leader respect and empower the feelings of others? And so forth. Leaders who fail to exhibit the right feelings receive harsh treatment. Consider the former head of the Metropolitan Police in the United Kingdom, Cressida Dick, who early on received praise for her "warm gestures" to the rank and file. She was forced to resign over not listening to advice.[31] Leaders who can project empathy and compassion seem to win the game of public opinion. But is that enough?

Foucault did not know it, but top management consultants bring the ethics of feelings down to the micro level. A 2020 McKinsey article advises that a leader should show compassion during difficult times. According to the writers, compassion involves tuning into one's own feelings, expressing gratitude, listening to others, showing vulnerability, and, finally, fostering inclusion. This advice is all about giving high regard to feelings, not to figuring out what to do to get out of the difficulty. It *feels* as though McKinsey is opening a therapeutic space. For facing stress, the article has the following advice: "A simple practice during these times is to engage in deep and intentional breathing. Deep breathing slows the heart rate and restores the body to a calmer and composed state."[32] It does not advise asking what is true about the situation and what is unknown.

Did or do Jeff Bezos, Elon Musk, Reed Hastings, Madam C. J. Walker, Anita Roddick, Steve Jobs, Ray Dalio, and Phil Knight build trust as therapists? Did or do they lead with compassion first? Deep-breathing exercises are fine but insufficient for leaders. Do not internalize the voice of the therapist. When stress comes, as it will daily, stick primarily with seeking truth to weather the storm. When people around you are panicking, you need to be cool and ask, "What things do I know to be true about this situation?" Knowledge is not what you have heard. It is not a matter of accepting and passing the word around. What do you know that you or you and your team have discovered? What do you know after working hard on the problem? Use that knowledge as your foundation. This process calms and focuses. Then ask, "What are the fearsome speculations that others and I share? Which parts of them should I ignore? Which should I investigate personally? Which can I trust a team to investigate?" Leaders who create masterpieces find out what is true and act on it. They do not worry about charges of micromanagement.

The Ancients Knew Better

In response to today's regard for feelings, we, the authors, say that people should reenlist in the 1,000-year tradition (400 BCE to 600 CE) of telling truth to power that the ancients called *parrhesia*. Foucault lectured on this tradition in the last years of his life.[33] The ancients had a better understanding of leadership than we have. Read Sophocles and you gain far deeper insights into the complexity of leadership than you would get in most popular management books. The leaders we listed earlier show three key aspects of ancient leadership. They seek and unconceal (discover) a truth that others do not see about their world; they take a public stand based on that truth; and they take moral risks for the sake of the truth.

Consider Jeff Bezos. In 1993, with web usage growing like wildfire, he saw the truth that only a few others—eBay's Pierre Omidyar, Yahoo's Jerry Yang and David Filo, and Google's Larry Page and Sergey Brin—saw: that the internet in all its wildness could take over our lives and drive us to distraction. Bezos saw that it could undo all the stabilities of retail. It could create a bazaar with no fixed prices and no fixed products. Everyone loved all the miscellaneous boards and groups. But Bezos saw the wild growth of the web as a moral anomaly that he would understand and face. His second truth was his vision that an "everything store"—Amazon—could tame the web. These are truths of discovery. Only the success of Amazon and a tamed internet could verify these truths. Based on these truths, Bezos took a stand and as part of that developed a strategy to start an everything store that sold books. To ensure Amazon's success, he believed he had to surround himself with only the best and the brightest. So, over the years, he has had to take the moral risk of forcefully retiring many of those who were closest to him.[34] What kind of leader is Bezos? Judge him by feelings—his empathy, compassion, vulnerability, authenticity, coaching skill, capacity to build consensus and diversity—then he is a nasty and obsessive leader. Judge him by the seeking and saying of truth and the commitment to act on it (which we consider part of truthfulness) even with moral risk-taking, then he is a great leader.

Have we been too hard on compassion, authenticity, empathy, vulnerability, empowerment, consensus seeking, and the acknowledgment and cultivation of diversity? Many will think so. Can these virtues be parts of a masterpiece? Of course they can. But first and foremost, build your masterpiece on truth seeking and saying. Feelings such as compassion, authenticity, empathy, vulnerability, and others like them can create admiration directed toward a masterpiece only *in the service of truth*. Without that, they lack purpose—they stifle growth and create narcissistic obsession. That is not our wish for masterpiece creators. "May you always know the truth / And see the lights surrounding you."

6   Safety, Moral Risk-Taking, and Developing the Warrior Spirit to Change Moral Orders

For believe me: the secret for harvesting from existence the greatest fruitfulness and the greatest enjoyment is—to *live dangerously*! Build your cities on the slopes of Vesuvius! Send your ships into uncharted seas! Live at war with your peers and yourselves.

—Friedrich Nietzsche, *The Gay Science*

And my car's out back if you're ready to take that long walk
From your front porch to my front seat
The door's open but the ride ain't free

—Bruce Springsteen, "Thunder Road"

The Moral Elevation of Safety

The moral valuation of safety is on the rise.[1] There is a good chance that we have already witnessed its transformation in North Atlantic or Western culture from a prudential value that offers a guide for optimizing outcomes to a moral evaluation that sets requirements on us independent of our particular circumstances. In short, ensuring safety in all circumstances is coming to be like preserving innocent human life, honoring agreements, and respecting property.

Safety previously mattered not as a moral guide for what is good in life but as a matter of prudence. Consider the United States in the 1960s: though the Census Bureau had declared the frontier closed in 1890, many people in the country still admired and sought to have a do-it-yourself, independent, risk-taking, pioneer spirit. President Kennedy famously reinvigorated that spirit with his moon mission. Of course, pioneers, astronauts, and their support teams had an intense focus on safety because their missions were distinctly risky. They had a prudential sense of safety. For people who work on high-voltage lines, who fly planes, who run nuclear reactors, and so forth, safety is a major preoccupation. In organizations that require high reliability, safety is an outcome that comes about through people retaining their vigilance, resourcefulness, and determination, not though simply avoiding taking risks.[2] But until recently safety did not have the status of a moral evaluation. Consider the sense of safety practiced in university and school classrooms across the United States, where the moral valuation of safety requires that students not hear views strongly countering their own heartfelt views. It is not a matter of politics (we see this at both ends of the political spectrum) but a generalized attitude toward views that cause discomfort. As a moral matter today, people should not suffer forcible verbal challenges because such challenges make them feel unsafe. Psychological safety comes before speaking truth. Would we have ventured to the moon if safety had a high *moral* evaluation?

What is this moral psychological safety? According to leading management thinker Amy Edmondson, "Psychological safety is broadly defined as a climate in which people are comfortable expressing and being themselves. More specifically, when people have psychological safety at work, they feel comfortable sharing concerns and mistakes without fear of embarrassment or retribution. They are confident that they can speak up and won't be humiliated, ignored, or blamed."[3] Likewise, feeling safe, says a Google study of effective teams, means that team members can take "risks" without worries about insecurity or embarrassment.[4] McKinsey declares that "the benefits of psychological safety are well established."[5] Edmondson and Mark Mortensen repeat the mantra in the *Harvard Business Review*.[6] Psychological safety above all else, the chorus chants!

But what if the mistakes and concerns people share are blameworthy? Why would anyone think there is such a thing as *safe risk*? If an action is risky, it is not safe. What risk is there if there are no worries about embarrassment? If one makes a boneheaded mistake that causes a project or business to fail, acknowledging what one did would involve embarrassment. What kind of person would not feel embarrassed in such a case? Rowan Williams, former archbishop of Canterbury, invites us to think not only about the benefits of safety but about its costs too: "The search for the reasonable and safe course of action will always bring disaster sooner or later to the extent that it presses us to ignore the unavoidable costs of safety."[7]

To begin to understand the motivation for so vexed a distinction as *safe risk*, we need to see the foundation of Edmondson's thinking. Taking her cues from interactional sociology, she says, "We are constantly attempting to influence others' perceptions of us." She continues, "Whether explicitly or implicitly, when you're at work, you're being evaluated. In a formal sense, someone higher up in the hierarchy is probably tasked with assessing your performance. But informally, peers and subordinates are sizing you up all the time. Our image is perpetually at risk. At any moment, we might come across as ignorant, incompetent, or intrusive, if we do such things as ask questions, admit mistakes, offer ideas, or criticize a plan." Thus, people do not speak up at work because they are trying to look good, and silence is less risky than speaking in the looking-good business.[8] (It is worth noting what Brené Brown makes of a similar starting point.[9])

There is some truth in these claims, but Edmondson downplays the difficulties involved in seeking and saying truth. Specifically, she ignores how hard it is to formulate your thoughts in a way that will draw others to listen to them, neglects the cultivation of courage necessary to think beyond what is normal, and stands against people feeling ethically responsible for having to say what they believe to be true. There is no "if you see it, say it." Indeed, her exemplary case of someone failing to speak up, to which she recurs in her book, is of a nurse who had recently been in a training program that advocated administering a certain medicine to babies born prematurely. She saw that the doctor she was working with did not order the medicine for premature twins, and she did not speak up because she had seen the doctor berate another nurse earlier. Edmondson sympathizes with the nurse and sees her not speaking up as the problem of the unsafe climate.[10]

Taking the example as Edmondson lays it out, notice that the nurse does not feel responsible for figuring out how she could compose her remark to the doctor so that the doctor would listen. For instance, "Doctor Drake, I went to a training program on medicine X, and the speaker suggested that we should normally administer medicine X to premature born babies. I know that we don't do that as a matter of course. What do you think?" According to Edmondson, the nurse does not have that responsibility. The onus is strictly on the doctor for not being appreciative enough to other nurses in the past and thus for creating an unsafe climate. Assuming the twins did not die, we follow Edmondson in giving the nurse a pass. Had the twins died for lack of the medicine and the parents found out that the nurse did not speak up out of concern for her image, the parents would think her action one of petty-minded, self-regarding cowardice, and they would have a point. Edmondson is clear that she does not consider speaking up an ethical requirement.[11] It might not now be a general ethical requirement, but few masterpieces could happen without it.

If we ignore the virtues of truth seeking and saying, of courage, of the responsibility to compose statements carefully so that people will listen to them, and finally of the ethical responsibility to speak out against wrongs, then the reasoning behind psychological safety becomes plausible. Of course, we concede that if a business or institution reduces the fear of negative assessment from colleagues and bosses, people will speak up more. But will they be doing so in a useful way? Will they say things others might find challenging or unorthodox? That is not clear. Of course, reducing social fear might be the right course for children learning but when applied to responsible adults, psychological safety advocates wed themselves to three incoherent claims that inhibit masterpiece creation.

First, we have in psychological safety the idea of safe risks, which are risks taken without worry that your immediate boss or members of your team will humiliate you if you speak out. Second, in the climate of psychological safety, if you speak out in a way that harms the business, consequences must follow, but the assessment of consequences should be somehow impersonal rather than "interpersonal."[12] Perhaps, Edmondson has in mind a market failure. However, without an oracle at Delphi, it is hard to tell what such an "impersonal" assessment would be like. Edmondson's case of Google's firing of James Damore in 2017 as impersonal remains unconvincing. Surely, Damore did not take the assessment as having Delphic impersonality. Third, another way to explain the oxymoron of safe risks is that they are the risks that come in a climate where one is free to fail. But even at Google, where managers have endorsed and absorbed psychological safety, it turns out that people are not exactly free to fail. CEO Astro Teller at Alphabet's X speaks for rewarding tough judgments to close a project *before* it fails at the same time as he speaks for psychological safety.[13]

Edmondson believes that not speaking up comes from fear of others' judgments, *not* from the inherent difficulty of mustering the courage to seek and say truth and *not* from the inherent compositional difficulties of finding a way to say the truth so that the listener will listen. Thus, it looks to Edmondson as though every organization where people speak up is one that has psychological safety. She even puts Ray Dalio's Bridgewater in her camp. Bridgewater is, in fact, an exemplary case of an organization where people speak up *despite* fear, not because Dalio has reduced fear. People there have developed virtues that are more than a match for the fears around looking good. They stand for the ethical requirement of courageous truth seeking and saying. Dalio considers it an ethical responsibility to speak out; candor is useful only as a part of and in the service of truth seeking and saying. At Bridgewater, employees must earn their right to have an opinion.[14] If a worker sees interpersonal fear as the main blocker to speaking out, then that worker will not see that the virtues Dalio hires for and instills in his team enable them to face fear and speak up.

What does the world look like when people are courageous, feel responsible for taking stands to do the right thing, and seek and speak truth? Do people really speak freely, listen to others, and thrive in such an environment? Let us turn to Ray Dalio and Bridgewater.

Ray Dalio's Masterpiece Creation of a New Moral Order: An Idea Meritocracy at Bridgewater

> And since your journey . . . will certainly be a struggle, I hope that these principles will help you struggle and evolve well.
> —Ray Dalio, *Principles*

Bridgewater is the world's largest hedge fund and has made more money for clients than any other hedge fund.[15] According to Matt Wirz of the *Wall Street Journal*, between 1991 and 2016 Dalio's flagship fund earned 12 percent per year on average.[16] However, we focus on Dalio's innovative management practices, which he sees as destined to change the way organizations work in the twenty-first century.

Understanding and Committing to Resolve a Moral Anomaly
Dalio noticed that with modern communication technology, social media, and so forth, we will lose any robust sense of privacy. He saw that as damaging primarily our ability to think and reflect. Anything we write down or

say could go out into the web.[17] We would tend to respond with a curated self-staging that involves sending cleverly crafted attitudes into cyberspace; consider X or Instagram, for instance. Dalio did not consider such behavior fully ethical and became committed to preventing it from taking over. He committed himself to saving truth seeking over sharing attractive views.

Figuring Out and Advocating for a Solution to the Anomaly

Dalio had a guiding intuition he could transform the radical transparency that information technology brings into motivation for people to speak to each other with greater frankness and in a community of truth seeking. He writes: "I wanted to surround myself with people who needed what I needed, which was to make sense of things for myself. I spoke frankly, and I expected those around me to speak, frankly. I fought for what I thought was best, and I wanted them to do so as well. When I thought someone did something stupid, I said so and I expected them to tell me when I did something stupid. . . . Operating any other way would be unproductive and unethical."[18]

Dalio started shaping digital practices to turn radical transparency into a call for frank speaking and by that means to turn Bridgewater into an idea meritocracy. He explains what the "idea meritocracy" came to mean to him some years after he started creating it:

> A community in which you always have the right and obligation to make sense of things and a process for working yourselves though disagreements—i.e., a real, functioning idea meritocracy. I want you to think, not follow—while recognizing that you can be wrong and that you have weaknesses—and I want to help you get the most likely best answers, even if you personally don't believe that they're the best answers. I want to give you radical open-mindedness and an idea meritocracy that will take you from being trapped in your own heads to having access to the best minds in the world to help you make the best decisions for you and for our community. I want to help you all struggle well.[19]

What was the key to creating this community? Dalio established a culture where everyone is constantly making assessments of everyone else's performance in meetings. He developed automated, digital devices to enable constantly making and publishing assessments so that people can see how their colleagues are judging their performance as they speak in meetings. He wanted performance evaluated in real time.[20] He did this without much regard for people's feelings. He accepted fully that life is a struggle.

It demands the cultivation of courage far more than it does the reduction of fear. Today, WhatsApp and Zoom enable such real-time interaction, but, in contrast, Bridgewater stands out for frankness without *sniping*. Dalio brags about a young associate who publicly gave him low marks for his failure to balance open-mindedness with assertiveness.[21] As part of his commitment to making things extremely clear, Dalio has gone so far as to convert management and investing principles for making decisions into algorithms.[22]

During the time Dalio was creating this culture, the press accused him of being a cult leader and Bridgewater of being a cult.[23] But rather than being cultish, Dalio developed a culture that resolves disagreements with practices like those of the adversarial common law: disputants argue for their claims, and, like lawyers in the common law, Bridgewater disputants love the practice and the tradition.[24] Researchers Adam Grant as well as Robert Kegan and Lisa Laskow Lahey claim the community works.[25] (Journalists now write about radical transparency at Netflix as though it is part of the ordinary business lexicon.[26])

Moral Risks Necessary to Create the Moral Imperative of an Idea Meritocracy

In 1981, Dalio's models showed an impending bank-debt crisis because of money lent to emerging markets. He became a media star for issuing warnings and then was proven wrong when the Fed brilliantly handled the problem. Bridgewater lost everything. Dalio had to let everyone go except his thinking partner, Paul Colman. He had induced Colman to leave Oklahoma, bring his family to Connecticut, and join Bridgewater. Colman's and Dalio's families had become inseparable. Yet when the choice arrived between giving up Bridgewater and going back to Wall Street or letting Colman go and keeping a vestigial Bridgewater, Dalio let Colman go. He describes the families' tears when the Colmans departed, never to return.[27] This decision signaled that Bridgewater would remain in the image of Ray Dalio. Dalio took a moral risk. He could not know then whether an alternative—for instance, both Dalio and Colman getting their finances in order by returning to Wall Street—would have been better. The only way he could justify the stinging termination would be to keep Bridgewater in his image and make it extraordinary. Otherwise, we would say that he treated his friend ruthlessly. The Colmans and the Dalios surely realized that.

Dalio's other documented morally risky action came in removing Greg Jensen from the co-CEO position at Bridgewater. Though Dalio had treated Jensen as a son for 20 years and expected Jensen to run Bridgewater, Dalio realized that Jensen was failing. Dalio reports this sacrifice of Greg's identity as one of his most painful actions.[28] It surely showed everyone at Bridgewater that Dalio would stop at nobody to make Bridgewater's idea meritocracy sustainable. He would even sacrifice a son. The adversarial debates became a grounding norm, making frank assessments frequently became the clarifying moral norm, and maintaining an idea meritocracy became the organizing moral norm of Bridgewater.

With the example of Dalio, we can better see the contrast between a masterpiece-creating team and a psychologically safe team, as shown in table 6.1.

Table 6.1
Masterpiece Teams and Psychologically Safe Teams

	Masterpiece-Creating Teams	Psychologically Safe Teams
Mission and Status	I have committed to a hard mission with *pride* because I believe in it and hope to have the *courage* to make it succeed.	I have committed to a motivating mission with the knowledge that I do not know how to accomplish it and must be a *humble learner* who, equally with everyone else, *messes up* and is *vulnerable*.
Asking Open Questions	I ask open, serious questions because I want to find out what is true.	I ask open questions because I need to learn and do not want to trigger natural defensive silence.
Speaking Up	I owe it to the community to speak up and do so *even if others will judge my thoughts stupid*. I sacrifice my vanity for the community.	I speak up because *others do not blame or humiliate anyone here.*
Responding to Speakers	I engage fully with the content of any speaker's claims; *I am obliged to determine their value and their truth.*	To anyone who speaks out, I respond with *thanks to make the person feel safe* and then turn to the content.
Failure	I experience failure regularly; it shows that I am doing my part. If I had no bruises to show, I would not be in the fight.	I feel free to fail because my team consoles me, does not pass harsh judgments, and offers a bonus if the failure happens early.

The masterpiece organization has teams work by cultivating as a second nature the virtues of taking on difficult odds, courage, self-sacrifice, truth seeking and saying, and a commitment to face hardship. The psychologically safe team avoids the triggers of interpersonal fear that comes from wanting to look good. It requires virtues of empathy, kindness, and keeping safe. Openness and truthfulness remain subordinate.

Courage, Self-Sacrifice, and Truth Seeking and Saying

Do not fall for the claim that the only way to get people to speak up is to create a psychologically safe workplace. Dalio's Bridgewater shows it is not so, as does Reed Hasting's Netflix. The cultivation of masterpiece virtues lives on in our traditions and still maintains a subterranean life, which we would like to raise to the surface. Writing in the *Harvard Business Review*, Laura Delizonna describes places that do not have psychological safety as places where the leader metaphorically "cuts off heads."[29] For Delizonna, such a culture is obviously stifling and will not be innovative. We want to look instead at what courage, self-sacrifice, and truth seeking and saying can do.

What about a culture where heads are not metaphorically but really cut off? What does history show about cutting heads off and creativity? Let us look at one of our favorite creatives: William Shakespeare. As he rode into London, he saw on London Bridge the heads of Catholics on pikes. His father was likely a recusant Catholic. Two of the heads on pikes were his kin.[30] Nevertheless, many of Shakespeare's top, creative, market breakthroughs, including *A Midsummer Night's Dream* and *Hamlet*, show distinct Catholic sympathies. There was no psychological safety there. We have already written about the thousand-year, risk-filled tradition of speaking truth to power. For their truth telling, Socrates accepted judicial execution, and Plato was sold into slavery; closer to Shakespeare, two of England's greatest and most creative political leaders, Sir Thomas More and Sir Thomas Cromwell, had their heads chopped off. We discussed Einstein in chapter 5. Much more recently, senior physicists drummed the signally brilliant quantum physicists David Bohm and Hugh Everett out of the physics community for telling truth to power; nevertheless, they did not shirk from creating their theoretical masterpieces.[31]

But surely we are being unfair. Delizonna is not speaking about such freaks of nature as Shakespeare, Socrates, Plato, and Einstein. She is writing about, as she says, "moderate risk-taking." We do not know how she would classify Bohm and Everett. But let us look at the academic literature on *successful* management of average creatives and risk-takers. We found that, generally, most organizations that employ creatives—theaters, restaurants, recording companies, video game makers—*successfully* manage creatives by keeping the situation anything but safe.[32] Realizing that creatives *need* to be creative and cannot negotiate around that need, these organizations offer them a bare platform for the expression of their creativity. Creatives will acquiesce to other demands, in particular lower job security: they frequently go to work each day fearing their termination.[33] Your average or even near-great actor, chef, game coder, or recording artist works in an environment with no psychological safety.[34]

Leaving Google aside, many creatives in other industries work with significant insecurity and little psychological safety. Read about how Nike founder Phil Knight treated Jeff Johnson. He gave him a platform to serve runners but virtually no support and only a few shares.[35] Down deep, we know this fact about managing creatives and truth sayers: those who absolutely *need* a platform to exercise their creativity or truth saying have poor negotiating positions. Creativity and truth saying are not for them an option that they can trade away but rather a way of life.

Creatives and truth seekers and sayers break norms and therefore take risks. They are passionate about innovation and working and thinking hard and therefore have developed courage. Why courage? Truth seeking and saying are moral commitments. Very frequently, those enacting them need moral luck to succeed. Taking those sorts of risks is at the heart of masterpiece creation. So we turn now to moral luck and its implications for leaders seeking to create masterpieces.

Moral Luck

> I cannot praise a fugitive and cloistered virtue, unexercised and unbreathed, that never sallies out and sees her adversary, but slinks out of the race where that immortal garland is to be run for, not without dust and heat.
> —John Milton, *Areopagitica*

The Google wish for safe risk-taking, like the wish for trust and love without betrayal, is the wish for a rose without thorns. The examples of

Shakespeare, Socrates, Plato, Einstein, Bohm, Everett, and even today's average actors, chefs, musicians, game coders, and running-shoe designers (not to mention small-business owners) show that they create and tell truth to power in defiance of safety. Is that something essential to being human or at least to creating masterpieces? Outside of the Google thornless rose garden (if it is really such), life is not set up so that we can take risks with safety, have trust without the worry of betrayal, or enjoy roses without thorns. To think otherwise is not just to be naive but also to miss an important—and, we would add, beautiful—feature of moral life: the possibility of moral luck, which the late, great philosopher Bernard Williams brought out clearly for us.[36] Results matter economically, prudentially, and surprisingly *morally*.

For most people, luck is repugnant to morality. When we say that someone is a good person, we are speaking as much as possible about that person's core, and we are not saying that the person is lucky. To think otherwise seems precisely to give up any sense of morality. In contrast, Bernard Williams tells us that when we think that way, we are blind to how we make genuinely moral judgments, and we are missing something profound about our involvement with each other. He shows that though people normally avoid moral risks, at certain points in their lives, they nevertheless take them. They take an action whose outcome they cannot anticipate and for which they know they themselves and others in their community will judge them morally. As a simplest instance, I decide to put off fixing my brakes today though I know they are in bad shape. We can agree that this is a bad act, but it could become really bad. Let us turn to the examples.

Suppose both person A and person B are negligent about repairing their cars' brakes. They spend the money, let us say, on something good like gifts for their suffering grandmothers. As A drives through an intersection, the light changes, and her brakes fail. However, she sails through free as a bird. Person B is not so lucky. In the same circumstance, his brakes fail, and he runs over a pedestrian. Many—but not everyone—feel that person B is morally culpable far more than person A. Both are culpable for negligence. However, others and B himself see B as guilty for taking a life. Therefore, B should suffer both economic *and* moral consequences. Why? For Williams, our lives are that involved (intertwined): when we hurt someone even unintentionally, our connection is such that we have a moral guilt and obligation to do something about it.[37]

To get a clearer sense of what moral luck means for masterpiece creators, we turn to Williams on good moral luck as he describes it with the example of a slightly fanciful Paul Gauguin. Williams's Gauguin had a wife, five children, and a failing career as an artist. He sensed he needed a new, nonbourgeois inspiration and decided on abandoning his family to move to Tahiti. This inspiration was his moral anomaly. Obviously, his bourgeois moral norms said that he should treat the call as a merely whimsical impulse. Acting on it would be immoral. Yet not acting on it would leave him practically a failure, which was also unacceptable in a bourgeois milieu. He took the moral risk of treating the impulse as a moral calling. He abandoned his family, ran off to Tahiti, and produced the great art that the real Gauguin created. Assume that you appreciate the art of Gauguin. Did the romanticized Gauguin do the right thing? Or should he have stayed with his family and produced poor art? *Assume those are the only choices.* The only way you get the great art is to have the roguishness of Gauguin. (Likewise for Apple and Steve Jobs.) Which seems more right to you: to have the great art and a nasty rogue who injured his family or to lose the great art and have a man who preserved an unhappy, conventional, bourgeois marriage? The choice is not meant to be obvious, and people do find an easy way to let themselves off the hook. They want to enjoy and learn from the great art and punish the moral monster. In short, they want to punish egg breakers and enjoy omelets—condemn Steve Jobs as a monster as we write on our Apple computers and listen to music on our iPhones. Yes, we can do that, but that is surely not a *moral* position. Our enjoyment of omelets at the very least encourages egg breakers.

Those who, like us, say that Gauguin did the right thing say it in gratitude for the greatness of the art—its primitive, erotic beauty—which also and importantly changed our evaluation of bourgeois norms. These moral consequences show to us that Gauguin was right in his intuition that his anomaly was a moral one. There was no right way to act. Abandoning his family would be bad. Staying with them and creating poor art would be bad. Both would be bad in bourgeoise terms. However, part of what Gauguin did with his art was to change our moral evaluation of a bourgeois life. That makes it easier to endorse his actions. We regret the injury to his family, but Gauguin, like a leader who must sacrifice a few to save many, did the right thing. If we must suffer rogues for such beauty and shifting moral evaluations, so be it, at least to the extent the rogue was a rogue in the thought experiment. Of course, had Gauguin failed to produce his great art, then he would have done the wrong thing. It all depends on a twist of moral luck.

To take a less romanticized version of moral luck, we recall the Churchill story from chapter 1; Churchill sacrificed all the soldiers in Calais to try to save the British army at Dunkirk.[38] It was a desperate move, with only a slight likelihood of success. Failure would have been disastrous, the loss of both the army at Dunkirk and the troops in Calais.[39] Churchill had, in fact, taken a similar moral risk earlier at Gallipoli and lost. Many reviled him as an immoral, murderous wrongdoer who loved war more than his soldiers' lives. Churchill himself later acknowledged he had acted immorally at Gallipoli; he was "too ready to undertake tasks that were hazardous or even forlorn."[40]

However, Churchill faced a moral anomaly in Hitler. During Churchill's decade out of power, he said that Hitler was after ferocious conquest, but in the high-minded, buoyant moral order of Britain that claim made no sense. In facing Hitler, Churchill knew he had to do shocking things that would change the moral order. It was only the threat of Hitler that persuaded the English to accept him as prime minister, and he had to take the risks to show it was the right call.

Regarding the troops at Calais, we say that Churchill did the right thing, perhaps changed the course of the war, even though he regretted the loss of the troops. We evaluate his action as good, as morally right. Yet the terms of its rightness did not become clear immediately. Only when he committed the morally shocking act of destroying the Allied French fleet at Oran did he change the moral order of Britain. With these moral risks, the British came to see that to defeat Hitler they had to look at the world with brutal realism and organize themselves with ruthlessness. So, like Gauguin and other artists and leaders who have moral luck, Churchill changed moral norms. Had he failed and England suffered the consequences—invasion—he would be seen as evil, too focused on his personal glory and too careless of the lives of his troops. That is how life and history work: we take our moral risks and enjoy or fail to enjoy moral luck.

Together with Bernard Williams, we are not *simply* saying that ends justify the means. Normally, when we say that the ends justify the means, we mean to say that the *anticipated* ends justify the means. That is the reasoning behind the COVID-19 lockdowns, which abrogated rights of free assembly. The ends of the lockdown—the saving of lives and hospital space—are clear at the outset and justify the temporary abrogation of rights. In the moral-risk cases, however, neither person B nor Gauguin nor Churchill had anything like clarity around anticipated ends. B, Gauguin, and Churchill could only hope for a good outcome in some shape (and not one that resembled the old order). They all took a genuine *moral risk*, and person B suffered bad moral luck, while Gauguin and Churchill experienced good moral luck.

Who disagrees with advocates of moral luck? Rational moralists such as Kantians believe that there are rational principles such as the golden rule that we should always follow. Similarly, utilitarians believe that you do the right thing if you make a responsible calculation in advance of the greatest good for the greatest number and then act on it.[41] Many nonphilosophers just recoil against the unfairness of moral luck. They claim that person A and person B should receive the same moral penalty and suffer the same moral guilt for negligence in taking care of their brakes. Whether person B or person B's insurance ponies up some money is a nonmoral issue, a public-order issue. Likewise, moral-luck rejectors will claim that Gauguin should not have fled even if it meant giving up the great art that has changed our moral evaluations for the better. The moral elevation of safety certainly feeds into these moral intuitions. Valuing safety means avoiding moral risk-taking and hence giving little credit to moral luck.

Let us examine what the high evaluation of safety threatens to do for creatives, truth sayers, and leaders who are making market breakthroughs. Do their breakthroughs require moral risk-taking, moral luck, and hence the possibility of interpersonal moral condemnation? In almost all cases, creative achievements or telling truth to power requires breaking a *moral* norm, not a mere convention or a prudential norm. But what does it look like when in the name of psychological safety management tries to remove the negative judgment from unsuccessful moral risk-taking? Both person A and person B take a moral risk with a marketing campaign that breaks a privacy norm. Person A's campaign succeeds gloriously with huge financial rewards and happy customers. Person B's campaign fails with huge financial losses, betrayed customers, and a nasty lawsuit. In a world that esteems psychological safety, both A and B deserve the *same interpersonal moral reward* for their bold creativity, whereas the market doles out reward or penalty with Delphic *impersonality*. But are we to imagine that the team praises A and B alike for the risk-taking, consoles B for the market's response, and gives a bonus to neither or to both? Google might have enough money to pay meaningful bonuses on such a psychologically safe bonus scheme, but we are doubtful that Google really does that.[42] If it does, then we would follow the poet John Milton in calling Google a cloister that cuts people off from genuine involvement with others. When B fails, the company suffers, and we in the company suffer. We are involved with each other and the markets.

Why say Google is a "cloister" (while doubting that it really is)? Milton coined the term *cloistered virtues* for virtues that people could successfully cultivate and maintain only within a cloister.[43] For most of us, breaking a moral norm and thereby causing a huge financial loss might well bankrupt our companies. Moreover, we would expect *and want to* feel the moral emotions of guilt, shame, and embarrassment if we did that. Would we not be moral monsters—indeed, sociopaths—if we felt none of those moral feelings? And would we not expect our colleagues to act on moral evaluations like our own? Likewise, when we dare to break a moral convention and that break leads, as it does sometimes, to better lives for most and huge financial gains for our organizations, we would feel morally justified in believing we had done the right thing. We changed the world even if it took luck to get there.

For people living in the real, historical world, moral risk-taking and luck play a key role in their moral evaluations. Creatives, truth sayers, and leaders take moral risks and receive their appropriate moral awards. Trying to avoid this logic leaves us as either sociopaths or cloister dwellers, which poses an important question for masterpiece creators, particularly today when safety is a moral evaluation. How do we prepare ourselves to be moral risk-takers in such a time?

Reviving Our Warrior Spirits

> Our highest insights must—and should—sound like follies and sometimes like crimes.
> —Friedrich Nietzsche, *Beyond Good and Evil*

As we said, giving safety a high moral evaluation takes people out of the moral-risk-taking business and puts them into the cloister, where a refined morality judges only their desires, intentions, and feelings and not their actual acts in the world. Evaluating safety highly therefore reveals a deep conceptual, moral confusion about what really matters morally. It leaves everyone tending toward the sociopathic avoidance of guilt.

Yet that conceptual confusion is *not* what troubles us most. We are most disturbed by the many people who are trying to turn their businesses into cloisters, succeeding at it, and then thinking they have created genuine masterpieces. (As we explained at the end of chapter 2, we believe psychologically safe Google is, in fact, a genuine masterpiece that succeeds, but only through moral acrobatics. Try those moves at your own risk.)

Instead of focusing on Google, here we ask: What happens in most of these so-called masterpieces where safety is king? Remember, if you do not feel safe, you do not have to speak up or act. Cloister builders find themselves constantly having to ratchet up levels of safety as people become insecure over what, in the past, they would have considered just normal levels of risk. As business advisers, we travel from company to company and hear the new litany: "I can't do that because there are a bunch of people who will oppose it." More fashionably, "I can't do that without my team's support."[44] "I can't say that because most people will disagree." "I can't act that way because no one has my back." "I can't make this vital change because I do not have a consensus." "To succeed, we absolutely need to change the process here, but we are stalled since we don't have Finance behind us." Our favorite, because it is so devious and even seems to support moral risk-taking, is: "I'd rather ask for forgiveness than permission." Do you hear the wobble in the last banality? A person who takes moral risks and fails always knows she has committed a bad act. In the world where actions matter, she can ask for leniency, but she would not want to ask for forgiveness. She wants to face a lenient version of just deserts. It is in the cloister of safety where one asks for forgiveness and receives it. Just to be extra clear, when people start speaking in the ways just rehearsed, they are not speaking merely prudently. They are *not* saying, "At this moment, it is not prudent to take the risk. It is, however, a risk worth taking, and I will find the moment." They are saying that it is wrong to take the risk. We know this because clients frequently tell us, "We are working hard to build a psychologically safe environment here. Haven't you read Amy Edmondson or the Google article?"

When we hear these expressions, we urge our clients to speak to someone used to taking on difficult odds. We say that this practice shows a warrior spirit. People with warrior spirits will say: "It's worth doing in part because most people oppose it." "It's worth my while saying this precisely because people will disagree." "Since no one will have my back, I'll stand for what I believe in and take on the whole group alone." "Because we can't reach consensus, I will decide and act." "Because this action is necessary, we should take it now and bring Finance along later." And last, "I'll ask for high honors if I succeed and no more than justice if I fail."

Leaders today and in the recent past have like warriors taken on moral risks. These leaders include Jeff Bezos, Reed Hastings, Elon Musk, Ray Dalio, Phil Knight, Julia Robertson, Oprah Winfrey, and, further back, Anita Roddick, Steve Jobs, Madam C. J. Walker, and Winston Churchill. By our rough calculations based on our reading of biographies, such leaders take on average one significant moral risk each year.

What is it like to live like this? Churchill's memoirs come closest to giving a solid answer.[45] Most memoirs and biographies do not, in part because of the confusion about moral risk-taking. Even Winston Churchill is not fully clear. We suppose that the pain of Gallipoli and 10 years of exile from ministerial office scarred him too deeply for greater moral clarity. However, we have a savior who can give us a far richer sense of what the heart of a moral risk-taker is like. William Shakespeare, the creative who could face real beheading or other judicial execution, takes us directly into the heart of moral risk-taking by bringing us into the heart of a warrior spirit. We have already discussed the moral risks Shakespeare took in his writing. No doubt he took them in his business as well. He was a preeminent business leader in early-modern England. He expresses this moral-risk-taking spirit clearly in his second Henriad: *Richard II, Henry IV, Part 1, Henry IV, Part 2*, and *Henry V*.

Bolingbrook in *Richard II* dethrones Richard II and takes the throne as Henry IV. It is a story about moral risk-taking through and through, which Shakespeare signals by Bolingbrook's return from exile before he has a legal excuse to do so. But for speeches that tell us what it is like to take moral risks and inspire others in doing so, *Henry V* stands above the others. Let us look at a short excerpt from this historical play. Here King Henry gives his famous speech to the English troops as they face five-to-one odds before the Battle of Agincourt. Think of all the "we cannot do this because" excuses mentioned earlier as you read it.

Westmerland: Of fighting men they have full threescore thousand.

Exeter: There's five to one; besides they all are fresh.

Salisbury: God's arm strike with us! 'tis a fearful odds.

•   •   •   •   •   •

Westmerland: O that we now had here

But one ten thousand of those men in England

That do no work to-day!

King Henry: What's he who wishes so?

My cousin Westmerland? No, my fair cousin.

If we are mark'd to die, we are enow

To do our country loss; and if to live,

The fewer men, the greater share of honor.

God's will, I pray thee wish not a man more.

•   •   •   •   •   •

Rather proclaim it. Westmerland, through my host,

That he which hath no stomach to this fight,

Let him depart, his passport shall be made,

And crowns for convoy put into his purse.

We would not die in that man's company

That fears his fellowship to die with us.[46]

Watch the whole speech as Kenneth Branagh delivers it.[47] Many feel its power.[48] But others respond to the speech with seemingly smart skepticism: heroes are foolish instruments of another's power; there is no glory in risking life, fortune, or reputation; if you are smart and wily, others will make sacrifices for you. Yet what is the point of a life that breeds such cynical wisdom? Achieving health, fortune, and high repute by manipulating others into taking risks? That is most likely a fantasy bred in a cloister. And if not, if it is the genuine manipulativeness of a Phil Knight or the brilliant storytelling of Oprah Winfrey, then it, too, is moral risk-taking through and through. Thus, it turns out that even post-heroic leaders who manage by brilliantly bending and breaking rules and manipulating people into consensus or making them feel deeply understood do take moral risks—usually in telling lies—and in doing so create their masterpieces.

Heroic and post-heroic leaders and people who take moral risks have the courage of warriors. If we break conventions, we risk our careers (Bohm and Everett) and reputations. Think of cancel culture. Masterpiece creators do not shirk when others will not agree, understand, or have their backs. They do not wait for Finance to come on board. They do not wait to do what they know they ought to do. They do what is essential. And when they do claim to *know*, it is because they are truth seekers. Of course, they speak their truths with careful attention and composition and take their actions after looking as many moves ahead as they can.

We have described mostly grand moral risks that signal masterpieces. But moral risks come in varied sizes, and all can be in the service of creating a masterpiece. As Shakespeare shows at the end of *Henry V*, all moral risk-taking requires courage, but sometimes the risks can be modest. At the end of the play, Henry V persuades Kate (the French princess) that together they will take the weak moral risk of changing mild social moralisms. In this case, Henry wants Kate to kiss him in public before their marriage. He says: "Dear Kate, you and I cannot be confined within the weak list of a country's fashion."[49] She agrees. Moral risk-taking can have the virtues of compassion, empathy, vulnerability, and the rest, but it cannot have safety without moral acrobatics. We advise against seeking such safety.

From Concept to Practice

The most important focus of this chapter has been on the need for moral risk-taking in breaking moral norms to create a masterpiece. The transformation of safety into a high moral evaluation threatens any moral risk-taking. The proposition that you can have risk-free innovation is a fantasy that lives only in cloisters. The following chapters offer practical suggestions and detailed examples on how to create an actual masterpiece. For now: Do not let your business become a cloister. Adopt a warrior's response to the feeling that the odds are against you. Listen to or read the Henry V speech when you begin to panic or when you think you cannot win. Given the conceptual nature of this chapter, the most practical suggestion might be simply to remember the examples. Remember Williams's Gauguin. Remember Shakespeare traveling into London, seeing the impaled heads, but nevertheless writing breakthroughs sympathetic to Catholicism. Remember Churchill: already scorned as a callous warmonger, he made the difficult decision to have the troops at Calais fight to their deaths and then engaged in another piece of morally shocking behavior to change the moral order of his country and thereby defeat Hitler. Remember that we do not live in a world of roses without thorns. Let us stop building cloistered businesses out of a desire for safety and easy trust. Give safety no more than its due in the rough-and-tumble world where we make change happen. Elevate safety when learning a new skill or conducting a momentous truth-and-reconciliation process; otherwise, keep it inside routines. Seek nobility. Cultivate courageous organizations. Listen to Ray Dalio's voice. Let us build our masterpieces with a warrior spirit. No other spirit builds masterpieces.

7   Designing an Organizational Culture Masterpiece

with Christopher Davis

It was her voice that made
The sky acutest at its vanishing.
She measured to the hour its solitude.
She was the single artificer of the world
In which she sang. And when she sang, the sea,
Whatever self it had, became the self
That was her song, for she was the maker. Then we,
As we beheld her striding there alone,
Knew that there never was a world for her
Except the one she sang and, singing, made.
—Wallace Stevens, "The Idea of Order at Key West"

Leaders play a decisive role in making their organizational culture admirable. They craft the *norms* and *practices* according to which people in the organization will live and work. Though seldom recognized as such, it is a work of huge moral artistry, like the devising of constitutions of ancient city-states or of modern countries following a regime change. In shaping a culture, leaders establish ways they think people should work and live and invent practices for getting them to work and live that way. They do that by adjusting and updating practices people already have. The American Declaration of Independence, for example, articulates a moral vision of egalitarian freedom (still in progress) for the country and does so based on such English common-law practices as juries, town councils, and so forth. The same for South Africa's Constitution, which developed following the overthrow of apartheid and, while keeping representative structures, clearly echoed Mandela's voice in saying that South Africa is to "heal the divisions of the past and establish a society based on democratic values, social justice, and fundamental human rights."

In this chapter, we recall the emphasis on artistic skill we brought out in the introduction and focus on the artistic basics for developing a masterpiece organizational culture. We give examples and advice on using those basics. We are quite serious about considering masterpiece-creating leaders as artists who strengthen or change their cultures. Most leaders grow divided, thin cultures.[1] In contrast, Jeff Bezos, Oprah Winfrey, Ray Dalio, Reed Hastings, John Mackey, Larry Page and Sergey Brin, Ed Catmull, Anita Roddick, Madam C. J. Walker, those following their examples, and some others have been quite mindful about the cultures they created. However, these leaders learned mostly through trial and error. In our practice, we see that culture creation can be an art, and the masterpiece leaders we are hoping to develop are like screenwriters who hone their craft by learning how to use the conventional artistic tools.

We start here with the basic elements of a culture, which are its shared skillful practices for dealing with things, others, and selves. For the culture creator's initial purpose, the diverse practices are not so important as two unifying aspects of the practices: the practices' *mood* and their *style*. We will define mood and style more clearly later. But notice that there are cultures as different as Apple's, Google's, Amazon's, and W. L. Gore and Associates' (with its small interdepartmental teams). They have different pervasive moods—Apple's hope (to change the world), Google's admiration (for all employees), Amazon's zeal (to execute a hyperintense form of customer care), and Gore's joy (in helping everyone so that the teams succeed astonishingly well)—and different styles, which we will set out later. In addition to mood and style, strong cultures have certain widely used, economic-value-creating practices that manifest the mood and style. In a working culture, we call those practices its *signature practices*. In shifting a culture, the leader who wants to bring a new mood or style (or simply sharpen one) works with basic, stripped-down versions of the signature practices, which we call *conveying practices*. These basic building blocks are like the constitutive elements of a screenplay: the main characters, story or plot, mood, patterns, and pacing.

Once we are clear about these building blocks—mood, style, signature practices, and conveying practices—we will describe the typical kinds of culture that different combinations of mood and style produce. If we were writing a screenplay, we would be going through the various common genres of screenplays: mystery, action adventure, romance, science fiction, horror, historical fiction, sitcom, and serious drama. A leader's starting culture is likely to be a thin, rough-hewn version of one of the typical organizational cultures or a mixture of them.

A cultural artist begins well by using our accounts of the various moods and styles to identify his or her present organization's dominant culture. Once such leaders identify the culture they want—much like the screenwriter determining the genre—they will start considering the conveying practices that will strengthen or change that culture. Masterpiece-creating leaders want a culture most suited to their skills and the way the business produces distinctive value, just as screenwriters seek a genre most suited to the skills they start with and the audience they understand.

Then the culture artist in her or his study designs the key practices that will convey the sought-after culture. As we said, these conveying practices will be ones that are widely used by people in the organization, produce economic value, and are dramatic in their application. We find four common categories of practices: *formal and informal performance-evaluation practices, coming-to-resolution practices* (where a decision is made in such a way that people happily enact it), *handoff practices* (where one person expects another to complete the next step), and *achievement-celebration practices*. We list these four because most companies have them, track them, have most employees engage in or witness them, and find that these practices have a dramatic, memorable character. Last, when done well these practices create significant economic value. These practices are like the screenwriter's scene setting, character introductions, opening of the plot's main problem, plot twist, and resolution. And just as there can be other important moments in screenplays, many other organizational practices could serve for conveying the culture; consider, for instance, design freezes in design-heavy companies, risk-and-opportunity meetings in project-oriented companies, and so on.

Working in their studies, leaders will usually design or refine a practice by setting out the objective, participants, and overall flow of steps, including those for rolling out the practice. Then these leaders will try out this practice with the senior team. The leader and team refine it over the course of a few months and, when successful, have the new practice percolate down the organization.

In this chapter, we focus on how different variations of a coming-to-resolution practice (making a decision that people will happily follow) convey different cultural types. We consider Pixar's highly inventive variation on coming to resolution and end the chapter with advice on how to roll out conveying practices. We promise that by the end of this chapter you will have a sense of the kind of culture your organization currently possesses, how to determine which one you would like, and some standard conveying practices that you might adapt to bring about the culture you want. You will be ready to design your conveying practices first in your study and then in action, typically first with your senior team and then with their reports. You, of course, will learn much more as you see how people react to your new practice. But unlike most organizational leaders who have come before you, you will be practicing your art in mostly charted territory, as most artists do. We turn now to the basic elements of a culture and how they work to give a culture its character.

How Do Organizational Cultures Work?

Ordinarily, we do not notice our culture in our everyday ways of going about business. The norms we follow fade into the background, as do the rules of grammar when we speak. Paradoxically, the more familiar we are with a culture, the less we can describe it. Tacit know-how or practices for making sense of things and getting things done constitute the bulk of any culture. Our explicit beliefs are far more limited. We can identify and talk about rituals and celebrations. We know about the founding documents and stories of the founding leaders. We hear a bit about the founders who set up the first operations. But we have no overall picture. We notice pieces. We have some memories of what we thought was odd when we first started. We have some comparisons with other cultures, and know of some breakdowns—confusing accidents—that reveal the little-noticed understandings that made the accident possible.

When we join a new company, we first experience it as alien, wonder about it, and notice its key features. But unless the culture is extremely different from what we have experienced previously, we will find that within a few days we are already seeing many things from the organizational culture's point of view, and the culture will have lost its strangeness, even if certain events and situations still do not make sense; in short, its normativity quickly becomes absorbed and taken for granted. It is like adjusting to the mood of a party. We do it quickly. We learn new cultural practices far more quickly than we learn a new language.

When film writers and directors create powerful movies, they have the moral imagination to bring out the main elements of the cultures of their imagined worlds. They can do so because, for them, inventing behaviors that exhibit a distinctive culture is an essential part of their artistic discipline. Consider how quickly viewers tune into *Star Wars*. It takes place in a shared mood of hope. Ambitions matter if they are valuable and require going up against extraordinary odds—"Never tell me the odds"—but do not matter if they are normal and low risk. In *Star Wars*, the prevailing cultural style of how people do things and what counts as good is opportunism: find opportunities and act on them even if they pull you away from your community— for instance, by having to go to another planet to become a Jedi warrior.

In contrast, we may be a little slower to tune into *The Hunger Games*, but once we do, we get what Katniss is up against and how she and Peeta come to have feelings for each other. Now, try to imagine Princess Leia connecting with Katniss. Why is it so hard to imagine? It is not that their roles are so different. Both are rebels up against an evil state. It is not their personalities: they sense that they are special, draw admiration from people easily, have a deep-seated sense of doing what is right, are courageous and noble. The dividing wall is their distinct cultures. *The Hunger Games* has a shared mood of resentment. In fact, the Hunger Games themselves are the signature practice of resentment: a lottery selects individuals from the losing side of a war to hunt and kill each other. In this mood of resentment, things matter insofar as they are causes for anger but do not matter if they are not. *The Hunger Games* is a little more difficult to tune into because the style of the rulers is trendiness—hence the fashions—while Katniss has a style of seeking justice, hence her slowness to kill.

Hope and resentment are famous opposites. Likewise, styles of opportunism, justice, and trendiness stand against each other. Opportunism looks unjust to people whose style is justice. Justice looks dull to the trendy. Leia to Katniss: "Should I marry Han and remain close to my brother, Luke?" Katniss to Leia, if she could even understand such a question: "No, I can't guess what you are thinking. Do you not see that they are unbearable opportunists?" In organizations where there are multiple cultures, communication fails, as between Leia and Katniss. When a company does not understand how its culture is different from various customer segments' cultures, its communications in important matters likewise fail. To prevent that, leaders must build bridges not safety zones. When the culture has a positive mood and clear style, diverse spirits soar. Hearts are clear. Thinking is on fire. People understand each other, really understand each other, automatically.

Building Blocks

Why do we say that the keys to culture are (1) a shared mood (how things matter), (2) a shared style (which determines what is most appropriate to do), and (3) signature practices (established emblematic practices that started out as conveying practices) that manifest the mood and style? We follow the philosopher Martin Heidegger, who claims that *practices*—skillful ways of living—are basic to our making sense of the world. That claim was revolutionary in 1927, when Heidegger made it.[2] For centuries, we thought that fundamentally we are *thinking* beings. Remember Descartes's famous aphorism "I think; therefore I exist." Heidegger turned it on its head: I exist (get on) with others and things, and therefore I think. He convincingly showed us that our basic way of being is to cope with others and the world using the habitual, intertwined social practices we dwell in. They are the source of our concepts. For example, we understand the hammer by *hammering* just as we understand what a step is by *walking* or what virtual communication is by *interacting* on Zoom. The critical point is that *activity comes first*.[3] We know something not by being aware of it abstractly but by using it or doing it. However, note that hammering does not occur without something to hammer (say, a nail), without a purpose for which to use the hammer (to make a piece of furniture), and some rules to follow when hammering. In short, any activity requires context.

We might go along so far and say, yes, we have practices organized by the outcomes they produce. Heidegger tells us to go one step further, though. How do we come to believe that one outcome or another is worth producing? If you think that we are primarily animals, then you might say that the need to survive rules. And we certainly have an animal-first nature. But our second nature has come a long way. Just consider all the human beings who have died for reasons other than mere survival. Our purposes derive mostly from our second nature. In part, our practices cohere and give us a sense of a unified world and self because the practices mostly share a way things *matter* to us. That shared sense of mattering is what Heidegger calls our shared *mood*.[4] In a shared mood of fear, for example, things matter according to how threatening they are. Activities matter so far as they can lower or raise the threat. The same case holds for other moods. However, what is worth doing does not derive from mood alone. If you have a mood of fear, that mood will drive you, classically, to hide out, flee, point the threat at another, or fight. How does one of these solutions take precedence? It is not a matter of first nature.

For the choice of action in reaction to a threat, we need to understand how our practices cohere according to a style that determines what is most valuable. Heidegger claims that on the level of practices—in the way we walk, the way we drive, the way we build things, the way we manifest one gender or another—there is a *style* that shows what is appropriate and valuable and what is not appropriate or valuable.[5] In business, the style manifests itself in the way we come to agreement, hand off work, evaluate performance, and celebrate. For many, the easiest way to see style-oriented evaluation of actions is in driving practices. For instance, the style of driving in New York City is aggressive. If you do not move quickly and decisively to get the spot you want in traffic, you lose it. In New York, it seems good to dash through a changing light, and many slip through red lights. In the small towns of the US Midwest, drivers drive courteously. They try to make other drivers feel comfortable. They would feel guilty about dashing through a changing light. Embodying a style involves making thousands of distinctions in our demeanor, in the choices we make, in the thoughts we entertain. Styles give us our objectives. Styles are not as surreptitious as moods in taking us over, but nearly so. They are just as contagious. It is certainly possible for a New Yorker to find herself in the Midwest and pausing to let some hesitating drivers go and then wondering, "What has become of me? Am I becoming midwestern?"

A style is part of our second nature and is composed of a disposition to notice certain things and hold high or low evaluations of those things. When we have a perfectionist style, we just see ideals and flaws, the perfect product design as opposed to what we have. That is just how we have developed our second nature. Similarly, an opportunistic style sees subtle disharmonies that might be opportunities. While others see the hot new tech company and invest in it along with the herd, the opportunistic investor instinctively attends to the company from which the investment money is flowing away.[6] For the perfectionist, coming as close as possible to the ideal is good. For the opportunist, it is good to find an opportunity that others are ignoring. To speak like philosophers, we can say that the style gives us an epistemic order (what we see) and a normative order (how we value what we see morally or practically or otherwise). In changing a style, you change both the epistemic and the normative orders. Here we focus on changing mood and style and therefore changing both orders. In the next, we focus on changing moral orders though, in the second case, we also show an epistemic change from a developmental to a pragmatic style.

Different regional cultures have different styles; different organizations have different organizational styles; and different styles interact differently with moods. Suppose Jack Welch's playing-to-win GE gets into a mood of fear; it will find the most *aggressive* reaction to threats that it can. If customer-loving John Lewis or Starbucks were to get into a mood of fear, each would either find or invent a *friendly* form of backing down. In an opportunistic culture, a schemer is the most intelligent player, and in fear and opportunism a schemer points the threat at another. In a culture that prides itself on justice, an impartial judge is the most intelligent, and in fear, the judge's impartiality comes out in reaching a compromise that least upsets both sides.

A culture's style and mood manifest themselves most emphatically in signature practices.[7] For instance, Nordstrom and Starbucks are famous for peers celebrating and evaluating each other. In its heyday, GE was famous for its exacting performance evaluations, by means of which GE managers cut the bottom 5 or 10 percent of workers each year.

With this philosophically oriented approach, we are opposing mainstream—cognitivist—views that see culture coded in our implicit beliefs about (or values concerning) important things, such as intimacy or safety.[8] It follows from the cognitivist view that people can bring their implicit beliefs to the surface and then change some in light of others, which, at another time, could also be brought to the surface. Thus, on the cognitivist view, a leader can change the culture by surfacing implicit values and changing them. That is why much of the popular culture-change literature focuses on values. The literature has the same reasoning as New Year's resolutions, which sometimes do succeed. But lasting change really happens at the level of habit-forming, skillful practices. Unless we build new habits—new ways of doing things—cognitive change alone will not last. To will to change something is one thing; to change it successfully for the long term is another. Human beings are much more than cognitive machines; we have bodies trained in certain behaviors and embedded in communities of practice. As Aristotle and John Dewey all too well knew, unless we develop new habits, we cannot complete a change. In short, to change important cultural evaluations, you must work on some of those deeply embedded ways of doing things that people absorb as a whole.

So, in organizations, we change cultures by designing and imposing new conveying practices, such as the practices for coming to resolution (making a decision that people will follow), evaluating performance, handing off (usually with promises), and celebrating. We focus on these practices because most people in a company engage in them, because they clearly affect financial and other forms of success, and because, when done well or poorly, they tend to be dramatic and memorable. Thus, changing these practices resonates throughout the culture. For instance, in a culture of fear, taking a strong stand on an issue to bring about a resolution feels dangerous. However, if we put some people in the formal role of change proposer and others in the formal role of advisers, then people in fearful cultures start taking stands as part of acting those roles. Of course, they initially do it because they find it more threatening to reject the game than to play it. They do it out of fear. But (recalling William James from chapter 3) the theatrical quality of playing the role gradually wears away. People find that as they habituate themselves to taking stands, they are moving from a mood of fear to a mood of zeal or hope. Since they are taking stands, they are likely to start adopting a style of perfectionism (getting things right) or of opportunism (seizing an opportunity). As they make this movement, other practices gather to support stand taking.[9] Thus, the conveying practice becomes a signature practice of a culture with a new mood and style. That is the short version of how to change your culture.

Going forward, we will describe using conveying practices to bring a new mood and style or to intensify a mood and style in an organization whose signature practices have fallen into desuetude. In the first case, when bringing a new style's moral order to a culture with an already strong style, the masterpiece-creating leader will have to take moral risks. Succeeding in taking such risks will create a masterpiece with a significant competitive advantage. In the second case, the strengthening of decayed practices, the leader need not face significant moral risk-taking. In the next chapter, we describe in more detail the way a masterpiece-creating leader takes moral risks to change a culture and gain a competitive advantage. Here we point out what is common in both cases, organizational culture change and organizational culture sharpening, after we go through the typical organizational moods and styles.

Typical Moods of Organizational Cultures

In our work, we typically find four negative and four positive shared moods in organizations. The negative moods are resentment, fear, resignation, and arrogance. The positive ones are hope, admiration, zeal, and joy. As we have said, moods determine how things matter. With *Star Wars*, we see that in hope what matters is a world-changing breakthrough. With *The Hunger Games*, we see that in resentment what matters is defeating or punishing the opposition. In resignation, things matter so far as they keep us on a steady keel. In arrogance, things matter so far as they lend themselves to us ruling the roost. In admiration, things matter so far as they increase affection for others, usually colleagues and customers. In zeal, things matter so far as they further the mission in a disciplined way (not just by good fortune). In joy, things matter so far as they enable us to help another colleague create a great, shared performance.[10] It takes artistry and a little calculative ability both to determine which mood is best for the organization and then to deploy it. Figure 7.1 shows the common moods.

Mood

An organizational mood shows how things matter and is usually attached to a feeling. For example, in a mood of fear, things matter according to how threatening they are, and, since people are looking for threats, most will find them. In contrast, in a mood of zeal things matter so far as they are part of a mission. The figure on the right shows each mood, its twin, and its most noteworthy behavior.

Blame	Trust
Resentment	Hope
Hide	Celebrate
Fear	Admiration
Appease	Seek Discipline
Resignation	Zeal
Deceive	Improvise
Arrogance	Joy

Figure 7.1
Organizational moods.

Typical Styles of Organization Cultures

We also typically run into nine cultural styles today. (Typical styles change regularly over time. For instance, loyalty used to be a common organizational style.) The mood-and-style configuration determines whether the culture is positive or negative. An opportunistic style joined with hope is *Star Wars* positive but joined with arrogance is Enron negative. The main styles are perfectionist, pragmatic, developmental (developing people), opportunistic, trendsetting, just, playing to win (competitive), getting stuff done (productive), and collegial. See figure 7.2.

A *perfectionist* style with a mood of hope gives you Steve Jobs's Apple, which focuses its perfectionism on design. A perfectionist style with fear or resignation becomes obsessive covering of one's tracks. A company with a positive mood and a *pragmatic* style has managers who are skilled at *and take pride in* making tough trade-offs quickly. With a negative mood, however, such companies accept trade-offs that lead to shoddy work. Microsoft and Dell would stand out as companies with a mood of zeal and a pragmatic style. Pragmatism with fear leads to avoiding stands and to overemphasizing glossy PowerPoint presentations with anodyne recommendations and long appendixes that merely list myriad facts and stymie analysis. A *developmental* company tries to develop the capabilities of employees, customers,

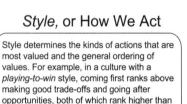

Style, or How We Act

Style determines the kinds of actions that are most valued and the general ordering of values. For example, in a culture with a *playing-to-win* style, coming first ranks above making good trade-offs and going after opportunities, both of which rank higher than being just.

Perfectionist	Strive for absolutes. Never settle for what is good enough.
Pragmatic	Deliver what is good enough by making brilliant trade-offs.
Developmental	Develop capabilities of individuals, teams, customers, and shareholders.
Opportunistic	Seek and exploit advantages.
Trendsetting	Lead others by having compelling opinions, designs, or actions.
Just	Do for others what is their due.
Playing to Win	Seek first place always.
Getting Stuff Done	Improve productivity. Always be in action.
Collegial	Maintain harmony above all else.

Figure 7.2
Organizational styles.

suppliers, and shareholders. When in a positive mood, such companies are enormously productive. Consider Bridgewater, Google, Starbucks, and John Lewis.[11] In a negative mood, as is the case commonly with utilities, the developmental style leads to low productivity because everyone develops the style of nurturing friendly relations and avoiding challenges. Successful hedge funds and venture capitalists have a mood of zeal and an *opportunistic* style. They go after the next new thing in a highly disciplined manner. Consider Leon Black and Marc Rowan's private-equity company Apollo. In contrast, a mood of arrogance and style of opportunism give you Enron. (We pick up the downfall of Enron in the next chapter when we describe what led to Andrew Fastow's bad moral luck.) We love companies that maintain a mood of joy and a style of perfectionism or even pragmatism. In these companies, people enjoy picking up the ball when someone drops it and hence have high ambitions. W. L. Gore and Associates (hereafter Gore), the maker of Gore-Tex and other advanced materials, has a mood of joy and style of opportunism. Morning Star, the tomato-processing and packing company, has a mood of joy and a style of pragmatism. The Caribbean mobile telephone company Digicel had in its high-growth days a mood of joy and a style of *trendsetting*. It set trends in determining which first-world product to bring out next.

We round out our account with examples of companies with just, playing-to-win, getting-stuff-done, and collegial styles. Ben and Jerry's operates with a *just* style. It has a mood of hope and, with its resonating positive messages tied to its mission, has many fans. When the just style comes with resentment, people in the organization fashion themselves as victims. Under Welch, GE had a *playing-to-win* (competitive) style and experienced enormous growth. However, when playing to win joins with arrogance or resentment, internal competition rules and organizations stall or decline. A *getting-stuff-done* (productive) style makes a zealous company enormously productive. Most of what gets done is on mission. In a company in the mood of resignation, getting stuff done drives a focus on compliance and governance. When a *collegial* style—getting along with each other as each pursues her or his agenda—joins with a mood of hope as in a research company, innovations arise. When a collegial style joins with fear or resentment, people act with studied niceness as they harm others. (We call those assassination cultures.)

Which cultural configuration (mood and style) does your company have? Take the practices that seem most dramatic and pervasive or take the four basic ones of coming to resolution, evaluating performance, handing off, and celebrating. How do things matter when you and your team are engaged in those practices? For instance, do you make decisions more often to reduce threat or to keep things on an even keel or to follow a huge, risky opportunity or to create an industry-changing product? What style determines what counts as a preferred response to something that matters highly? Do you more often praise making trade-offs or developing people or something else?

Common Pairings of Business Focus and Culture

How do you determine whether you should strengthen your current culture or change it? Ask yourself: Are your signature practices producing the economic value you want? Are they bringing out the capabilities you want your employees to have? Do your customers admire your culture? These are the critical questions. However, certain cultures go with certain business focuses.[12] A mood of hope and style of perfectionism goes well with competing on product leadership. A mood of admiration and developmental style will give you the edge in competing on customer intimacy. Zeal with pragmatism will enable brilliant execution that gives you an edge with operational excellence. Admiration with trendsetting will be well suited to building network effects. Joy with a style of trendsetting goes well with growing in a niche, where you are continuously an innovator. Digicel grew a trendsetting mobile phone empire in island countries in the Caribbean and South Pacific. The company had a knack for bringing just the right first-world innovation to the island and a famous variant of a coming-to-resolution practice: a weekly meeting where participants had to answer the question, "Why should our customers marry us this week?" Table 7.1 lays out a more complete alignment of business focus and cultural configurations.

Using Conveying Practices to Create Your Masterpiece
Organizational Culture

Designing your conveying practices is the heart of a masterpiece-culture creator's art. We advise leaders seeking to create a cultural masterpiece to

Table 7.1
Aligning Business Focus with Cultural Configurations

Focus of Business	Aligned Moods	Aligned Styles
Product Leadership	Hope or Joy	Perfectionist Opportunist Trendsetting
Customer Intimacy	Admiration or Joy	Developmental Getting Stuff Done (Productive) Collegial Trendsetting Just
Operational Excellence	Zeal	Pragmatic Getting Stuff Done (Productive) Playing to Win (Competitive) Perfectionist
Network Effects	Admiration or Zeal	Trendsetting Opportunistic
Niche	Joy or Admiration	Perfectionist Trendsetting Opportunistic Pragmatic

practice designing different conveying practices for different kinds of culture, the way a screenwriter experiments with creating scenes for different genres: introducing the main characters, the main challenge, the complications, and so forth. That regimen sharpens the screenwriter's sense of what will work and what will not, even if the screenwriter writes strictly within one genre. A similar regimen is just as important for a cultural artist. Creative insights come from comparing and contrasting.

To get you started, we take one typical conveying practice, the *coming-to-resolution* practice, and show how variations on it make it suitable for important, conventional culture types. In its abstract, bare-bones form, the coming-to-resolution practice typically works by having a leader identify champions of the principal options and then getting everyone else on the relevant team to take on the leader's perspective and advise the leader on which option to adopt. The leader then summarizes the champions' positions and the advice received and declares a decision. Let us now look at the variations that make this practice convey different cultures.

Moving from the bare-bones version, we look at cultures of hope with styles of perfectionism or opportunism. Such cultures are suited to innovating on product or service. Successful high-tech, life science, venture capitalist, and some hedge fund and private-equity companies have this type of culture. Second, we look at cultures founded in admiration with a developmental or collegial stye. Such cultures are suited to creating companies that customers and employees love. Organizations with such cultures tend to compete on customer experience. Third, we look at the coming-to-resolution practice for zeal with a perfectionist style and a slight variation for zeal with a pragmatic style. Such a culture goes well with operational excellence and lends itself to driving up margins. Because there is much confusion over zeal cultures, we provide more detail for them than for cultures of hope or admiration. Fourth, we look at a mood of joy with a pragmatic style. This cultural configuration works extremely well for companies who want to own niches where they can combine innovation, care, and operational excellence. Again, because the study of joy cultures is fairly new, we give some additional details on them. Table 7.2 summarizes the variations on the coming-to-resolution practice conveyed in different cultures.

Cultures of Hope with Perfectionism or Opportunism

Hopeful perfectionist or opportunistic organizations elicit many debates over which objective to pursue. People are not afraid to think out loud in front of each other. There is no concern about airing dirty linen. Once people have spoken their views, and it is time for resolution, the leader selects the champions for opposing views and has them make the best case for both their own and *the other's argument*.[13] Conversions frequently occur in that process. Such debates always narrow differences, which enables the leader to settle on a compromise position or select one with the goodwill of all. The magic happens when everyone sees things through the other's eyes, speaks honestly in giving advice to the leader, and hears how the leader has taken the advice into account even if rejecting it.

To get to the point where such meetings work, the leader probes people to find out who has the best grip on each of the views. Those people become the champions, who must then understand the opposing view well enough to argue for it, which requires getting behind another's position and thinking it through. What are the odds against doing this well? They are high. It takes devotion to getting things right or eagerness to exploit an

Table 7.2
Summary of the Variations in the Coming-to-Resolution Practice

Main Elements of Coming to Resolution	Variations for Conveying Mood and Style			
Standard Form	Hope with Perfectionist or Opportunistic Styles	Admiration with Developmental or Collegial Styles	Zeal with Perfectionist or Pragmatic Styles	Joy with a Pragmatic Style
Pre-meeting work.	Leaders identify champions who understand both sides. *Leader tells them to focus on getting things just right or on the size of the opportunity.*	Leaders seed new practices or find successes in going the extra mile or in taking care of others.	The leader creates a mood of zeal: the leader writes crisp mission statements. *Perfectionism: getting the details right.* *Pragmatism: looking for trade-offs.* Leader sets an arbitrary rule for making the decision.	Leader finds team promises whose fulfillment might be missed or enhanced.
Champions speak.	Champions argue both sides.	Manager of person who went extra mile or who took care leads celebration.	Champions argue for their positions.	Team member whose promise could be missed or enhanced speaks for the problem or opportunity.
Participants adopt the leader's perspective and advise on which course to take.	Advisers advise but note any personal conversion.	Advisers refine to remove bad consequences and develop rollout. *Trainers trained for developmental; handholding training planned for collegiality.*	Participants adopt the leader's perspective and advise on which course to take.	All participants look to contribute their part to a solution in a "yes-and" mindset. *Leader facilitates for a pragmatic—good enough—or another kind of solution.*
Leader summarizes and decides.	Standard: Leader summarizes and decides.	Leader accepts rollout plan and appoints team.	Standard: Leader summarizes and decides.	Team votes on the solution to adopt.

opportunity to come to agreement. *Getting things right conveys a perfectionist style. Exploiting the opportunity conveys opportunistic style. Going against high odds conveys hope.* In giving instructions, the leader sets the stylistic focus on getting things just right or on seeking the cool opportunity. In the end, if one champion converts the other, that is even more a matter of hope fulfilling itself. The shared experience of the meeting makes the decision one that participants happily follow.

Cultures of Admiration with Developmental or Collegial Styles

Admiring developmental or admiring collegial organizations reach resolution when members of the senior team see a desirable behavior achieving a great outcome and resolve to adopt it across the organization. The coming-to-resolution meeting is then a matter of (1) celebrating a success, (2) vetting the practice for hidden unwanted consequences, (3) refining the practice so that others can perform it, and (4) assigning a team to test it before rollout. If the further tests bring more admiration from the targeted stakeholders, then the leader directs the senior team to roll out the practice. In cultures of admiration, resolution is celebration.

Hence, leaders of these kinds of organizations have regular calls to identify achievements and to get to know them well so they can celebrate them in the coming-to-resolution meetings. (Sometimes leaders seed the organization with suggestions of ways of going the extra mile.) Senior team members advise on the nature of the rollout and on the level of training. The nature of the rollout determines the style the practice will convey. In developmental companies, senior team members tend to advise training employees to train others, thus developing those employees as experts in the practices as well as developing their training skills. In collegial organizations, leaders focus instead on raising levels of comfort with the new practice and engage in training with numerous feedback sessions and refinements on that basis.

Because this means of achieving the resolution to roll out new practices involves celebrating an outstanding action, the resolution practice conveys admiration. The training to train or the bringing of comfort to training conveys either a developmental style or a collegial one.

A famous instance of such a practice celebrated and then rolled out through training happened at the English department store John Lewis, which has a culture of developmental admiration. One Christmas Eve, a woman at one of the John Lewis stores had too many Christmas gifts to fit in her car. It was late, and she was obviously pressed for time. The John Lewis employee saw her distress, took off his tie, and tied her boot (trunk) shut. His manager happened to notice, congratulated the employee, and wrote up the case for the store manager. The rest was history, celebration, vetting, refining, and the roll out of instructions to all employees to spot customers in distress and identify something personal that they could give the customer along with the help. It is no wonder that John Lewis perennially leads in UK customer service.

Cultures of Zeal with Perfectionist or Pragmatic Style

We acknowledge Jim Collins (*Good to Great* and *Built to Last*) for making cultures of zeal the ones CEOs most desire. We have even known CEOs to change successful cultures and strategies so they could build a culture based on the mood of zeal. No doubt, zeal with a perfectionist or pragmatic style is great for operational excellence, but beware: it is not so great for innovation or for gaining the love of customers. Nevertheless, one of the good things about zeal is that once it becomes a shared organizational mood, it enables a leader to set up an arbitrary rule for reaching resolution, and so long as the rule does not conflict with the mission, the senior team will go along with it. (Indeed, the arbitrariness of the rule testifies to and conveys the team's zealous and disciplined devotion to mission.) So the real problem is how to get people into the mood of zeal.

For bringing zeal to an organization through a perfectionist conveying practice, we take a hint from one of Jeff Bezos's practices at Amazon, where the culture is one of zeal and perfectionism. To convey zeal, have members of your senior team write a one-page statement of their unit's mission, the goal for the year and the next five years, the approach to execution, and the single critical measure for evaluating everyone in the unit. Tell your senior team members that (1) you want them to write their statements as though they are the CEOs of their units, (2) you want them to go through the succinct reasoning that explains why the unit's mission is aligned to the overall company mission and achievable, and (3) you want them to have two trusted members of their team check the mission statement for its boldness. Bold is good. Writing such a document requires the synthetic intelligence to identify a unifying mission, the moral imagination to see how such a mission would affect the way people in the unit work, the analytic intelligence to figure out how to measure performance, and, finally, the careful, perfectionist reasoning to compose the mission statement succinctly. Writers will succeed in producing a good document only once they feel total zealous commitment to what they are saying. That is the secret behind brevity. Coach one-on-one and have them rewrite and review and revise quarterly.

A small variation to a Bezos-like mission statement will give you pragmatic zeal. Ask for a mission statement that starts with a quick summary of the past year's faults and achievements along with the leaders involved in both. The statement then identifies the mission for the next year and the trade-offs that the team will make to get there and avoid the previous year's faults. Ask them to write it in the blunt, transparent voice with which Warren Buffett writes his annual reports. Warren Buffett is the voice of pragmatic zeal.[14] (The senior team should already be reading his annual reports for that style of writing and reasoning.) The key to pragmatic style is the easy acceptance of fault and achievement as well as the pride in making difficult trade-offs.

Once you have those mission statements, you have the beginnings of the mood of zeal, at least among your senior team. (The senior team members become models for the rest of the organization.) As soon as the leader has a zealous senior team, the leader can use the bare-bones practice with a standard deadline for reaching resolution of any contested issue. As the deadline approaches, some zealous leaders like to freeze work, have the resolution meeting run as long as it takes (with no one leaving), or impose some other artificial structure for holding people back until they achieve resolution. With the mood of zeal, managers will accept artificial standards. Identify champions; have others advise, summarize, and decide.

For instance, one of our clients who has deployed a zeal culture with a perfectionist style declares a work freeze until the appropriate teams present an agreed solution to a problem. In zeal cultures, a delay on fulfilling the mission is always heartbreaking, and people will work and think tirelessly to overcome one. This client's approach produced near consensus quickly. At the other end of the scale, another client collected the best proposals from the appropriate teams, went off and discussed them with a couple of close advisers, and then declared the resolution. Zeal cultures give wide latitude for resolution practices so long as the resolutions support the mission and have strict, disciplined timetables.

Cultures of Joy with Pragmatic Style (and with Hints for Other Styles)

Gore and Morning Star are two of the best-known companies with a mood of joy. Gary Hamel has written about both. Malcolm Gladwell provides a short study of Gore when he discusses the founder's 150 rule (the company is composed of cross-disciplinary teams that have no more than 150 members).[15] As we mentioned earlier, Gore's joy comes with a style of opportunism. Morning Star has a mood of joy with a style of pragmatism. Our research shows us that the rare, *successful* megaproject teams are like these companies and have a mood of joy and a style of pragmatism. The team that built Heathrow Terminal 5 is particularly noteworthy.

Of the main positive moods we encounter, joy is the least common but the one most likely to have an admirable future because it offers a platform for people who lead good lives as improvisers, as described in chapter 2. All cultures of joy put a premium on members of teams knowing each other very well and knowing what each is good at doing. These teams make coming to resolution look like reaching an easy, magical consensus. Gladwell began to unravel the mystery by discovering the intricate deference structure of joyful cultures. There are four key elements in reaching a decision in a joyful culture with a pragmatic style.

First, these cultures are organizationally composed of smallish, cross-departmental, self-governing teams where everyone knows everyone else and where that knowledge leads them to help each other out. Compensation levels depend primarily on team success and then on levels of expertise. Each self-governing team makes promises to the overall organization, and, therefore, team members come to meetings to resolve issues in fulfilling those promises. Each team member is an owner of the team's promise, which requires focus on one's own work and that of the others. The team leader is mostly a facilitator. Decisions tend to get made by a majority vote, though normally the vote turns out to be a consensus.

Second, joyful teams have a deference structure. Each member of the team knows what the others are best at and defers to that expertise. Thus, team members must observe each other closely. We recommend the leader require each member of the team to identify another's outstanding performance—finding the most attractive opportunity (for opportunism) or the most brilliant trade-off (for pragmatism). Such write-ups go to peers, and then the team leader holds a weekly meeting to review and vote on who wrote the best evaluation. Since people are praising particularly skillful performances, they come to honor and then defer to skills and talents.

Third, teams, as self-governing organizations, work with ongoing promise management. The leaders of the organization set overall goals. Then team leaders negotiate appropriate promises with members of their teams and make their promises to the organization leaders. As managers monitor promises and hear reports of surprises in fulfillment, they will discover the topics they need to resolve in the next issue-resolving meeting. Typically, the topic will involve how someone is about to miss a promise and has no one offering a helping hand. That is the subject of the next team coming-to-resolution meeting.

Fourth, these small teams have the ethos of improv groups: they pick up when they see a member beginning to falter, and they pick up with the attitude of "yes-and"; they do that even if they are going to change direction. The leader plays a key role in conveying this improv way of acting in coming-to-resolution meetings. The leader can facilitate with a focus on getting a workable solution in the style of the organization—usually with joy organizations a perfectionist, pragmatist, opportunistic, or collegial style.

Whatever the style, the leader has everyone offer insights to resolve the issue. If, for instance, manufacturing is running late, how much additional time can sales renegotiate? How can engineering come up with a simpler, faster process? How can finance find a way to release some funds for temporary workers? Who can lend someone trained in manufacturing? Who can lend some people for cross-training? The leader might have to ask those questions in a pointed way to get people going. But once team members get engaged in team success, they make offers, or they use their knowledge of others' teams to suggest offers that those teams could make. Companies in other moods engage in these practices in emergencies. Joyful companies engage in them as a matter of business as usual, and that is how the leader conveys this picking-up-the-ball improvisational ethos in every coming-to-resolution meeting.

Much of the felt joy comes out of the relief everyone feels when someone picks up the ball just as another is about to drop it and then achieves a success. The more frequently teams run this "we have to find a helping hand" coming-to-resolution meeting, the more people will adopt picking up the ball in the course of their work. Then, the culture's coming-to-resolution conveying practice becomes a signature practice that manifests the culture's mood and style.

The Leader as Moral Artist

When you as a leader build a masterpiece organizational culture, you are a moral and aesthetic artist. You are designing aesthetically pleasing, dramatic, and economically valuable signature practices that will manifest your organizational culture's moral understanding of what matters and what counts as good. Is your organization changing the world? (Hope.) Is it increasing love? (Admiration.) Is it pursuing challenging missions to achieve extraordinary goals? (Zeal.) Are its members coming together and doing something together that would be impossible if each worked alone? (Joy.) In creating such an organizational culture, you are like the creator of *Star Wars* or *The Hunger Games*. You are like the creator Wallace Stevens describes in this chapter's epigraph. You are creating an artificial world that has moral consequences. It will provide you and your stakeholders with good lives or bad ones. To see this kind of creation in more dramatic detail, let us consider Ed Catmull.

After Catmull led Pixar to its immense success with *Toy Story*, he fell into a funk. Only when he realized that his purpose in life was to create the Pixar culture did he come into his own as a leader.[16] He discovered that he had to find a conveying practice that would become the signature practice of Pixar and, as such, excite its writers and directors and enable them to turn out imaginative success after imaginative success. In short, he had to create a signature practice that would create good lives for storytellers and illustrators to develop the Pixar stories and images that customers would make into parts of their own good lives.

The conveying practice that became a signature practice for Pixar was a coming-to-resolution practice with an imaginative, perfectionist twist. It had the main elements of a hopeful coming to resolution. It had truth-telling people able to take up both sides of the issue. It had people tuned into the writer's and director's project and not just their own preferred projects. But it left the resolution outside the meeting. In short, it is a rebellious variation on a theme that works for the kind of perfectionist artists attracted to Pixar. Catmull calls it the "Braintrust" practice.

The foundation of the practice was quite simple. The original creatives at Pixar—John Lasseter, Andrew Stanton, Pete Docter, Lee Unkrich, and Joe Ranft—had a pact to tell each other the truth about any work of art they engaged in. Out of that pact, Catmull developed the meeting he chaired where senior creatives, directors, and heads of story would review a work in progress every three months or so. The meeting has two premises, which Catmull reminds people of in every meeting. First, "early on, *all* [Pixar] movies suck." Second, "all directors, no matter how talented, organized, or clear of vision, become lost somewhere along the way."[17] With these reminders in place, Catmull plays a recent take of the film under discussion. Then the lead creative, John Lasseter, identifies what seems right and what does not ring true. On that basis, he asks others to elaborate on the elements that do not ring true and to suggest how they, looking from the director's particular personal perspective, would make a fix. They do not make suggestions about what they would do if it were their film, but rather, following the flow and feel of *the writer's and director's* story, they offer suggestions about what would make better sense from the latter perspectives. At the end, the film's producer gives the director a succinct list of the problems uncovered and the suggested solutions. It is then up to the director and story writer (often the same person) to adopt a solution or invent a better one.

Catmull identifies the genius of this meeting in its participants' lack of authority. They make suggestions. The director listens and comments. It is up to the director to make changes or not. But no one resolves anything in the meeting. When the practice works at its best, the director leaves the meeting knowing where the problem exists, having a desire to fix it, and carrying away a cache of suggestions.

A great suggestion is a great suggestion. But this framework inspires the creative perfectionists at Pixar to produce something better than anyone in the room imagined. For instance, the participants at the Braintrust meeting told Brad Bird, the creator of *The Incredibles*, that an argument between Helen and Bob Parr (Elastigirl and Mr. Incredible) made Mr. Incredible look like a bully and offered Bird several rewrites. Perfectionist that he was, Bird thought the script was already just right but acknowledged the problem. He then realized that he could change the impression of the scene by having Elastigirl stretch to the size of Mr. Incredible during the argument. In short, the Braintrust meeting inspires imaginative outperformance that resolves the issues, and that is what takes place after the meeting.

In developing your masterpiece culture, you will find yourself like Catmull: you are likely to have some practices that momentarily convey the mood and style you want. They are likely to involve coming to resolution, performance evaluation, handoffs, or celebration. Work with these practices. After you design those conveying practices for your company's mood and style, we advise you to try piloting them with your senior team and during the pilot to develop an ingenious Catmull-like twist that appeals to the particular kind of people in your organization and the particular kind of leader you are making yourself into.[18]

Notes on Deploying an Organizational Culture Change

We have spent most of this chapter describing the different common types of culture and the coming-to-resolution conveying practices appropriate to creating each type. We have mentioned the business focuses to which each mood-and-style configuration is most suited, and we have written about how leaders design, test, and refine conveying practices with their leadership teams and then create the opportunity for those practices to cascade throughout the organization. Now we provide suggestions on cascading and connecting your organizational culture with your masterpiece strategy and masterpiece style of leadership. The organizational culture is the glue that holds your masterpiece strategy (chapter 8) and masterpiece leadership style (chapter 9) together.

As we have noted, we recommend getting the conveying practices working first with the leader's senior team and then with her or his direct reports. Once they are working at that level, develop with senior team members a program for them and their direct reports to train people in their individual units to use the culture's conveying practices in their own coming-to-resolution meetings, performance evaluations, handoffs, celebrations, and any other more specialized practices (for instance, design freezes). In our experience, having the senior team and its direct reports do the training has two important effects. First, it sharpens the senior team's understanding of the practices and how they create the culture. Second, with the senior team and their direct reports leading the training, few in the company will doubt the importance of the new culture to the company.

There is one more matter to consider for deploying the new culture. Because people do not normally think in terms of practices and find them intangible, we find that it works best if the senior team uses promise management in getting people to adopt new practices. Ask for promises with completion due dates to prepare for a coming-to-resolution meeting and a promise with dates for holding it, debriefing it, and setting up the next one. Negotiate to ensure that people make promises that they can keep. Demand reports of happy or unhappy surprises in promise fulfillment. Give feedback with heartfelt emotions on the fulfillment so that everyone knows how important the change is. Track the promises and their completion. That is the simplest measure of the progress of the change.

Deploying new culture conveying practices effectively often requires telling the strategic story of how the organization is going to change its own or its industry's moral order, what moral risks the leader and the company will be taking, and how the company will win by taking such risks. We examine those moral-risk questions in the next chapter. It is not necessary to progress by telling the strategic story this way. People can move from resentment to hope or from fear to admiration, from arrogance to joy, and from resignation to zeal for the sake of producing a pleasing, productive culture. But believing that the cultural transition will make the world better supercharges the effort.

Last, make sure that the mood and style of the new culture harmonizes with your virtues as the leader. We take up that harmonizing in chapter 9.

Why Engage in the Hard Work of Cultural Artistry?

Why should you make your organizational culture into a masterpiece? Talk to a company founder you know. See how intimately the founder knows the company. See how the founder has created a personal identity out of the company. See how profoundly the founder loves life, the company, and the feast for the eyes that has been built. If you must, also check the founder's bank account. When you transform the culture of your company, even a company that you did not found, you gain the knowledge and wisdom of a founder. You gain the love the founder has for the creation.

Companies with distinctive cultures also perform well, so the paycheck will come, too. When you create your own organizational culture, you will be like Wallace Stevens's singer:

Then we
As we beheld her striding there along
Knew that there never was a world for her
Except the one she sang and, singing, made.

8   Masterpiece Strategy: Creating a New Moral Order through Morally Risky Commitments

This was a hateful decision, the most unnatural and painful in which I have ever been concerned. . . . It was a Greek tragedy. . . . The elimination of the French Navy as an important factor almost at a single stroke by violent action produced a profound impression in every country. . . . It was made plain that the British War Cabinet feared nothing and would stop at nothing.

—Winston Churchill, *Memoirs of the Second World War*

Masterpiece-creating leaders are masterpiece strategists. They do not focus primarily on increasing shareholder or stakeholder value. They focus on creating a new, admirable moral order for the company, its market, the industry, and the broader community. They know that in doing so they are likely to generate a competitive advantage recognized by a significant increase in shareholder value. For most of those who write about strategy, even those who focus on strategic innovation that goes beyond rivalry, business strategy comes down to finding a way to have a higher profit margin than competitors and then sustaining it until it becomes obsolete.[1] Succeeding at that within a moral order is no small feat, and it is one that we have helped leaders achieve.

However, influential strategy thinkers such as Richard Rumelt have known that the best strategists do something else. Rumelt has pointed out that the best strategists—Lou Gerstner and Sam Walton, for instance—changed the "perspective" or "basic philosophy" of their businesses.[2] That amounts to creating a new moral order. Our account of changes in moral orders driven by masterpiece strategists works out what we think Rumelt was trying to get at and what great strategists do behind their backs today. Masterpiece strategists work primarily with moral norms and then, on that basis, with financial value, operating models, processes, and new products and services. Moral orders are material to masterpiece strategists, and moral risk-taking is the masterpiece strategists' primary virtue and tool of execution. These claims are contrarian to the standard views of strategy, so here we move from commonly accepted accounts of strategy to seeing what masterpiece strategists do.

Strategic Thinking Leads to Changing Moral Orders

As we mentioned, business strategy usually means finding a competitive advantage over a firm's rivals: achieving a sustainable way to achieve a higher profit margin than competing firms. The business uses the surplus margin to satisfy owners (usually by increasing market-share or equity-share value), customers (by creating even better products and experiences), employees (by giving them more security or higher salaries), and other stakeholders. Generally, a business achieves its surplus margin in three ways: by offering higher-quality goods or services, such as Apple's iPhone; by offering lower-priced goods or services, such as Walmart's everyday low prices (achieved through managing a supply chain for a network of stores); or by understanding a niche better and offering a combination of cost and quality, such as Paccar, which supplies individual trucks (not fleets) to sole-proprietor truck drivers.

Traditionally, a strategist makes the advantage a lasting one in various ways, including by creating (a) legal protections, such as with patents; (b) information gaps, such as how Walmart selects locations and manages its supply chain; (c) positional advantages, such as first-mover advantages in industries where large capital investments are necessary or where network effects drive customer value (consider Meta); (d) high switching costs for customers, as with Oracle systems; or (e) a trusted, popular brand, such as Coca-Cola.

Lumpy Commitments
Underlying the making of competitive advantage are what the strategy thinker Pankaj Ghemawat calls "commitments"—large, long-term, specialized, and untradeable investments. Such commitments are "a few lumpy decisions involving large changes in resource endowments—such as acquiring another company, developing and launching a breakthrough product,

engaging in a major capacity expansion, and so on—that have significant, lasting effects on [a] firm's future menus of opportunities or choices." Ghemawat gives the example of Boeing's commitment to the 747. It required not only building the largest enclosed space in the world but also developing the know-how for designing and building such a plane.[3] Because its competitors made other commitments, Boeing could not sell this manufacturing capacity or skill. Thus, it had to focus virtually all its attention on making the 747 work. The lumpy commitment locked Boeing into a future course of action. At the same time as being a "lock in," such a commitment is also a "lock out" because then it is difficult for a company to seek other opportunities, which are too expensive to fund once the cash is spent on the lumpy investment.[4] As Ghemawat explains, such investments take time to pay off and, in addition to the commitment of capital and attention, require a commitment of time. Consider Coors's commitment to 10 years' elapsed time to cover the cost of achieving national coverage. Frequently and significantly, these commitments require a culture change.[5] Yet we argue here that the economic orientation of strategic thinking tends to obscure the moral dimension of lumpy commitments and the moral risks involved in making them. Still, strategic decisions that commit a company to a lumpy course of action usually involve a lumpy change in commercial principle and philosophy. That change usually requires the establishment of a new moral order to guide a new culture.[6] We believe that strategy theorist Richard Rumelt steers us in this direction.

Changing Commercial Philosophy

Rumelt notes that a simply good strategy applies strength against a competitor's weakness and that such application requires coherence and focus. However, the *most powerful strategies* create new strengths through "subtle shifts in viewpoint . . . [that] can create whole new patterns of advantage and weakness." Rumelt's lead example of such a subtle shift in viewpoint that amounts to a change in policy and philosophy is Walmart. When Sam Walton started out, the conventional wisdom was that "a full-line discount store needs a near population base of at least 100,000," and "decentralization is good": store managers "pick product lines, pick vendors, and set prices." Walton centralized the main elements of store management— product lines, vendors, and prices—and then treated each store as a node "in a network of computing and logistics." His basic unit was a network of

150 stores, each of which did not require a nearby population of 100,000. Thus, "*Walton . . . broke the old definition of a store. . . .* The network replaced the store." Kmart, Walmart's strongest competitor at the time, would have enormous cultural difficulties in centralizing. Rumelt likens this shift in perspective to the ones individuals have when they go through near-death experiences.[7]

Analyzing the shift of perspective and commercial philosophy makes us realize that it also involves a change in moral order. What counts as a *good* store manager, a *good* supplier, and even a *good* customer (lack of pickiness over local brands) changes as one moves from local stores to a network of nodelike stores. The change establishes a new mood, set of norms, habits, and the moral values that underpin these other elements.

Rumelt focuses his work on creating such changes in commercial philosophy. Every good strategy, he notes, includes a kernel that comprises a "diagnosis," a "guiding policy," and "a set of coherent actions." The diagnosis answers the question "What's going on here?" It is a judgment about the *meaning* of the facts, and it yields an intelligible story of the challenges facing the company. The best diagnosis brings a "radically different perspective to bear."[8] Part of the diagnosis is articulating the prevailing moral order. Lou Gerstner's diagnosis of the problem IBM faced is a good example. IBM had grown on end-to-end computing solutions. However, the information technology (IT) industry was fragmenting, with different providers specializing in desktops or larger computers or operating systems or applications or other elements and features. When Gerstner became CEO, IBM's senior team had already diagnosed that the industry situation called for IBM to fragment itself, and IBM was preparing to do just that. Gerstner looked at the same situation, noted the industry fragmentation, but saw that IBM was one of the few players who understood enough to advise IT departments on how to *integrate* all the various parts together. Gerstner's diagnosis looked at the same facts from a different perspective, that of how IBM had a distinct difference from the rest, which led to a new guiding policy (Rumelt's term), new signature practices, and a new style with its own moral order (our terms).

Diagnoses lead to "guiding policies." A guiding policy is a method for grappling with the current situation that reduces complexity by finding a source of competitive advantage. Gerstner's guiding policy was to draw on IBM's expertise to provide *customer* solutions, not just IT solutions using

IBM equipment.[9] Hence, Rumelt's "guiding policy" articulates a change in a moral order. In IBM's case, the old clarifying norm was thinking about the state of a company's IT as a whole; the grounding norm was the techie norm of computer systems builders; and the organizing norm was supplying a complete suite of IBM products to provide the company the systems it needed. The new clarifying norm was to think about the customer's situation in the market; the new grounding norm was thinking as an IT adviser coming up with the best system at the best price (not thinking like a techie); and the organizing norm was supplying an integration that offered a competitive advantage, not one that showed off the technical superiority of IBM equipment. What counted as doing morally good work at IBM changed dramatically.

The third element of the strategy kernel is taking "coherent actions" to execute the guiding policy. Because the hallmark of coherent actions is a series of painful trade-offs, these actions often tend to lose their coherence in being taken. Rumelt's best example of a success case is Franklin Roosevelt's handling of World War II with all the trade-offs he had to make. The two most famous trade-offs were having US industry supply the Soviets before US troops were ready for battle in Europe and focusing the war effort first on Germany, even though Japan had attacked the United States.[10] In our terms, making significant trade-offs involves taking moral risks—that is, taking actions considered controversial, even shocking, at the time they are taken. The taking of moral risks may come through far-sighted reckoning, as Rumelt suggests, or by practically wise sudden interventions (consider Churchill and Calais), which respond to competitive challenges facing the organization. The coherent execution of a guiding policy is usually both planned and evolutionary, intentional and emergent.

In what sense are the moral risks leaders take in making trade-offs moral? First, the leader takes a morally shocking action with the understanding that the current moral order needs to change to *preserve* some of its most morally crucial aspects and achieve a practical success. Gerstner faced a moral anomaly. IBM's end-to-end thinking about IT was a good thing and had driven the computer revolution. But competition left him with the seeming choice of trying to hang on to that thinking as a manufacturer with diminishing returns or giving it up completely to focus on manufacturing different components. There was no right moral answer. However, Gerstner preserved the rightness of IBM's developing an end-to-end view by taking the shocking step of making IBM an IT advisory company, which led to a *shift* in the moral order; the action that was formerly shocking—say, of advising a client to purchase another provider's goods—would become at least an acceptable, if not a morally good, action for leading a good life.

The Masterpiece Creator's Practical Wisdom

In strategy formation and execution, masterpiece-creating leaders are closer to the tradition of inventing strategy by practical wisdom: attending to one's coping and adjusting. The morality of moral risk-taking is an extension of the practical wisdom leaders must exercise constantly in their non-lumpy actions, which are usually driven by practical skill. We can see this by looking at how practically wise leaders embrace and manage standards.

Practically wise strategists know that every practice—including any commercial practice—has its *internal standards of excellence*: its goal and what counts as well-done and poorly done work. Practitioners must subject themselves to the authority of those standards maintained by either management or the community of practitioners or by both. Practices also have *external standards of excellence*—why the practice is good for the broader community. The material rewards of good practice depend primarily on achieving that external standard of excellence. So practitioners must submit themselves to judgment on that external ground as well on internal grounds. In learning the practice, practitioners must cultivate at a minimum the moral virtues of honesty, diligence, temperance, and fortitude. In working with other practitioners and accepting or rejecting their judgments, practitioners must also cultivate the virtues of justice, courage, and generosity.[11]

Those virtues do not dwell strictly within the confines of a single practice such as manufacturing or purchasing or accounting. They extend to the whole business, especially to making and executing strategy. Strategy's internal good (making the organization survive) and external good (making the organization valuable to the community) are tightly intertwined, but even here they can come apart. Operational excellence is an internal good that easily comes into conflict with the external good of providing desirable products and services. Internally focused managers ask, "Is this expensive product tweak necessary?" Consequently, strategists must cultivate the virtue of vigilance and remain alert to when the two moral goods (what is morally right for the organization and what is right for the community) are

out of balance and then rebalance them or create a new balance.[12] Therefore, strategists need to be alert enough to notice when the firm has gone
off track and then act to get it back on the track. Commitments—lumpy
strategic decisions to create a new moral order and a new way of doing
business—are essential when the internal and external goods come apart.

For instance, in the 1990s circus directors had to maintain the integrity
of the basic circus acts—acrobatics, animal acts, comedy, and so forth—
while at the same time ensuring that circuses entertained audiences. In
other words, directors had to balance the excellence of their organizations
with the commercial success of selling their service to those who appreci-
ated it. However, with the increasing concern for animal rights, audiences
came to find animal acts distasteful, and circus success was in jeopardy. Of
course, ending such performances meant engaging in the morally shocking
practice of ending both careers and a traditional, well-established practice
that was part of the circus identity. Some thought that small modifications
might work. But the founders of Cirque du Soleil took the moral risks of
eliminating animal acts completely (as well as conventional clowning) and
emphasizing drama and acrobatics.[13] The trade-off of giving up both animals and clowning was easier for Cirque du Soleil because it was a new
company, but its success would force other circuses to do the same and
accordingly end careers and traditions.[14] It also changed what was good.
The organizing norm changed from multistage amusement to narrative
order. A new moral order displaced the old order of circus entertainment.
(Indeed, in this unusual case it might replace the old order.)

Lumpy Commitments, Moral Risk-Taking, and the Making of a New Moral Order

Balancing excellence with success—namely, holding together the internal
goods of practices and the external goods of the organization—is challenging. It requires ongoing moral reevaluation as a key part of strategy making. When moral reevaluation requires a change in the underlying moral
order, as is the case with lumpy commitments, leaders take significant
moral risks. The path that moral risk-takers blaze has a pattern. First, there
is a small moral risk in identifying the anomaly (frequently manifested as
discord between internal and external goods) and trying to get others to
take it seriously. Second, proposing what will cut through the anomaly and

seeking finances to fund the change increase moral reputational risk. Third, the moral risk-taking becomes highly risky and peaks with the moral risk-taking of creating a distinctive organization that can address the anomaly. Sometimes the third moral risk is enough to shift the community's normative order, but when it is not, fourth, moral risk-taking continues in delivering a product or service that changes the moral order of the market, industry, or broader community. We bring out this pattern with the well-known example of Anita Roddick, fill in the grainy detail with the example of Julia Robertson, and then show how, with the same pattern, things can go badly with the example of Andrew Fastow. We start with Anita Roddick.

Anita Roddick and the Body Shop: Founding a New Moral Order through Moral Risk-Taking

Anita Roddick's main moral-risk-taking action was, like Gauguin's, a personal betrayal that she committed for the sake of establishing growth as the organizing norm of the Body Shop.[15] We show how this moral risk-taking worked by going through the four essential elements of masterpiece strategy formation and deployment.

First, Taking the Moral Risk of Committing Oneself to Understanding and Resolving an Anomaly

Masterpiece strategists start by noting and taking hold of a moral anomaly, whose destructive power the strategists see as quite significant for the market, industry, or broader community. An anomaly is something morally extraordinary, a discontinuity or a breakdown where there is no right thing to do. Typically, in commercial circumstances, the moral anomaly would break the prevailing connection between the organization's operational excellence and its commercial success. Though most people ignore or minimize anomalies, masterpiece creators do not. They see the anomaly in its own distinctive terms. Moreover, they recognize the moral dimension of the anomaly in that they sense they will have to take currently shocking actions to respond to the anomaly adequately and thereby, with luck, establish a new moral order.

According to Anita Roddick, in the 1970s the "beauty business" had a moral order consisting of a grounding norm of encouraging women to seek physical attractiveness, a clarifying norm of seeing beauty strictly as *youthful*, and an organizing norm of inspiring women to "feel dissatisfied with their bodies" and making "miracle claims" of enabling youthfulness.[16] (Recalling chapter 1, Booker T. Washington hesitated to support Madam Walker because he thought she subscribed to this moral order.[17])

In the 1970s, women became more autonomous, and the science of aging made the industry's self-interested propaganda obviously fallacious.[18] However, the growing awareness of false dealing did not drive change in the moral order, and that anomaly—autonomous women's awareness of the lies did not change the order—captivated Roddick. Spotting this anomaly and recognizing its moral potential would be, in Rumelt's words, the diagnosis of the situation. There was no obvious right thing to do: either go along with the deceit or futilely decry it.

In response to the anomaly, Roddick discovered that women all over the world had for centuries been caring for their skin by using natural ingredients. Drawing on these centuries of self-care would form the core of her solution to the anomaly.

Second, Taking the Moral Risk of Advocating and Seeking Financing for a Solution to the Anomaly

The leader increases moral risk in trying to convince others that the anomaly poses a serious risk and that the leader is committed to managing it. Most people ignore anomalies because they are, well, anomalous! If people do not ignore them, they normalize them by simply viewing them as the way things are and always will be. Women just want to look good. They do not care about the rest. Thus, we normalized the awareness of lies in the beauty business. Masterpiece creators such as Roddick instead see danger and insult in the anomaly and because of this perception appear to be wild fanatics, deluded doomsayers, or scaremongers who want to frighten us to gain power. Roddick repeatedly called the beauty business deceitful. Having a wacky idea might be fine, but embracing it suggests a bit of fanaticism, and pushing us to invest in it for our own good crosses a moral line, not necessarily into evil but certainly into the morally dubious. We have a small but lumpy moral risk.

By imagining and investigating anomaly-trumping scenarios, the leader comes to see the sort of offering and organization that can respond to the anomaly and tame its disruption. Again, in Rumelt's language, this is the development of a guiding policy. Roddick wanted to make purchasing beauty products an act of fun, compassion, and frugality.[19] That became her clarifying norm. Her grounding norm, which her research on women around the world gave rise to, was that of *women knowledgeably taking care of* their bodies. The new organizing norm was that of a caring, small-is-beautiful, family business.[20]

To make a go of the Body Shop, Gordon and Anita Roddick had to give up their family hotel and restaurant business and seek a bank loan. These were primarily financial risks. However, when Anita Roddick, the radical attacker of the beauty business, sought her first loan from a bank, the bank rejected her. Gordon, her husband and business partner, put together a proper presentation, dressed as a nonconfrontational businessman (along with his professionally attired wife), and secured the loan. Having Gordon was a bit of moral luck here and, as we shall see, even more so later.

Third, Taking the Moral Risk of Establishing an Organization with the Abnormal Moral Order Required for Resolving the Anomaly

Once a masterpiece-creating leader sees the way forward to resolve the anomaly, the leader takes stock of the virtues that enabled the understanding of the anomaly and the development of the solution. These virtues are necessary going forward. Most people dwelling in the current moral order will see boundary-breaking virtues as excessive, even as vices. But because the leader has them to such a high degree, the leader can hold on to the anomaly. To succeed, the masterpiece-creating leader must create an organization where these virtues in their excessive form will become norms around which signature practices will develop. Roddick's virtues were her capacity to drive fun, compassion, frugality, and "good trade" all together. Roddick implanted her clarifying and grounding virtues along with the family-business feeling in her first store. She attracted customers, but no one in the beauty business cared.

Accordingly, Roddick encountered a new anomaly: the beauty business could happily give her a small-is-beautiful niche and not change at all. Leaders in the industry could simply grant that there was a small customer base for an oddball product. To shift the norms of the industry, the Body Shop had to adopt the organizing norm of a high-growth enterprise. She took the mild moral risk of raising the issue with Gordon and the rest of her family. They got her point but held firm to a family-business norm—no expansion until success was clear. So, when Gordon was out of town, Roddick took the shocking moral risk of selling half the company to Ian McGlinn for £4,000 to open a new store.[21] Her betrayal of Gordon's trust was both immoral and compounded by treating the family business with fiduciary irresponsibility. However, she had twofold moral luck. When Gordon returned, he saw his rebellious wife running a growth business—shocking—but in response he adopted her vision of growth, forgave her, and became her "rock." Had Anita Roddick slackened on growth and the second shop failed, the forgiveness would likely not have lasted. With successful growth, Gordon's and the employees' sense of complicity increased. From 1976 to 1990, the Body Shop grew from one shop to 600 and had the largest overseas presence of any British retailer.[22] Roddick's moral risk-taking certainly replaced the moral order of the old family-business nature of the Body Shop. She changed the organizing norm of her business.

Fourth, Taking Moral Risks to Shift the Wider Moral Order

The masterpiece-creating leader takes moral risks to create an organization that can drive the resolution of the anomaly, which means turning the power of the organization's new moral order to the task of resolving the anomaly in the broader context of the industry or market. In taking on the anomaly, the masterpiece-creating strategist transforms the anomaly's destructive power and harnesses its constructive potential. The masterpiece-creating leader breaks market, industry, or broader community moral norms by taking initially shocking actions to harness the anomaly. With the luck of practical success, the leader adjusts the reigning moral order by making the formerly shocking action highly valued or at least acceptable. Thus, the masterpiece-creating leader protects the organization as it becomes synonymous with the new way of evaluating things.

Roddick continually challenged the industry on the grounds of deceitfulness, animal testing, impurity of product, and cost. Her stores were the consummate challenge to the industry's norms. In her stores, women could experience their autonomy in trying out products and having fun doing so. They experimented with their own skin care. Compare that to the industry's highly controlled customer sampling. Of course, Roddick took the moral and financial risk that people would see the Body Shop as an ineffectual place where they could use skin-care products and cosmetics for free. Just as Jobs did with iTunes, though, Roddick took the moral risk of trusting her customers, and her risk paid off. She displaced the industry's

moral order with a clarifying norm of compassionate, frugal fun in purchasing, grounded in a norm of knowledgeably taking care of oneself, with
both growth and in-store sampling and experimentation as the organizing norms. The industry had to adjust. Sephora, recently Ultra Beauty, and
many small boutiques dwell in Roddick's moral order. Virtually all cosmetic
companies imitate Roddick's stand on animal testing. Figure 8.1 illustrates
how Roddick took moral risks to change the moral orders of both the Body
Shop and then the beauty business with the growth of the Body Shop.

We turn now to a more granular account of moral risk-taking in the
process of strategy making and execution by drawing on Julia Robertson's
change of the recruitment industry's moral order. The same basic elements
of the change apply.

Julia Robertson Creates a Masterpiece That Changes the Moral Order of Recruitment

This case exemplifies a strategy composed of a series of moral risk-takings.
It covers Julia Robertson's transformation of the recruiting industry as she
moved from being the managing director of Tate to being Group CEO of
Impellam in 2013 and then changed the moral order first within Impellam
and second within the industry by 2017 (with the help of some comple-
mentary forces). By that point, she had made Impellam a masterpiece.

The Initial Moral Order

In the 1990s and early 2000s, the employee-recruitment industry had zeal
as the mood behind its grounding norm of getting people into seats quickly
so that employers could flexibly staff up and down according to demand.
The clarifying norm of the industry was clever calculativeness in getting
people into seats at low cost. Its organizing norm was a style of street smartness, where players admired each other's commercial prowess, coolness,
and nerve. It was this sleight-of-hand style that Julia Robertson discovered at the beginning of her association with the industry. Attracted by a
newspaper advertisement for a job offering £100-a-week wages, Robertson
left her first job at Dun & Bradstreet for a national recruitment business,
Atlas Staff Bureau. "Nice girls like you don't go into recruitment," her boss
warned. Sure enough, when she opened her first pay packet, she found
that the basic wage was £40. Earnings of £100 per week were possible with

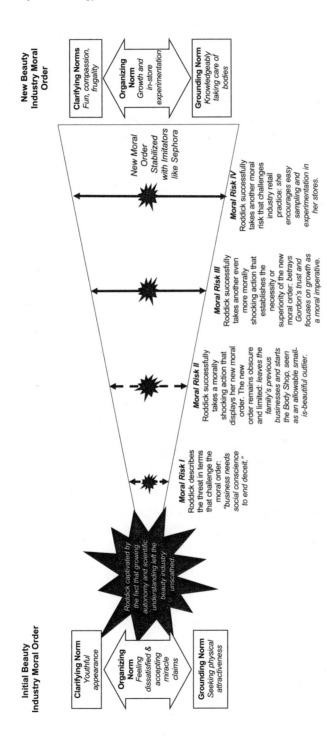

Initial Beauty Industry Moral Order

Clarifying Norm *Youthful appearance*

Organizing Norm *Feeling dissatisfied & accepting miracle claims*

Grounding Norm *Seeking physical attractiveness*

Roddick captivated by the fact that growing autonomy and scientific understanding left the beauty industry unscathed.

Moral Risk I
Roddick describes the threat in terms that challenge the moral order: "business needs social conscience to end deceit."

Moral Risk II
Roddick successfully takes a morally shocking action that displays her new moral order. The new order remains obscure and limited: leaves the family's previous businesses and starts the Body Shop, seen as an allowable small-is-beautiful outlier.

Moral Risk III
Roddick successfully takes another even more morally shocking action that establishes the necessity or superiority of the new moral order: betrays Gordon's trust and focuses on growth as a moral imperative.

New Moral Order Stabilized with Imitators like Sephora

Moral Risk IV
Roddick successfully takes another moral risk that challenges industry retail practice: she encourages easy sampling and experimentation in her stores.

New Beauty Industry Moral Order

Clarifying Norms *Fun, compassion, frugality*

Organizing Norm *Growth and in-store experimentation*

Grounding Norm *Knowledgeably taking care of bodies*

Figure 8.1

How Anita Roddick changed the moral order of the Body Shop and the beauty industry. Vertical lines show the new moral order displacing the original one as moral risks are taken one after another.

commissions on sales, but she was nowhere near that. In her mind, the £100 per week had been a promise, and so she experienced her "first recruitment industry scam."[23]

As a matter of corporate organization, successful recruitment companies in the past and present combine two modes of operating. One mode tends to focus on particular kinds of workers or professionals and therefore provides specialized workers in distinct disciplines, such as secretaries, office assistants, warehouse workers, chefs, kitchen workers, events workers, and hospital workers as well as professionals and paraprofessionals in IT, finance, law, the sciences, and so forth. These businesses are mostly transactional, and frequently the same recruiter both makes the sale to an employer and recruits the temporary or permanent employee. The other form of organization is the managed-solution business where an employer contracts with a recruiter over multiple years to manage the ebbs and flows in multidisciplinary staffing. This form has multiple contractual variants, but it is common for the managed-solutions provider to be associated with many specialized recruiters and to go out to others on the open market as needed. Following this norm, Impellam consists of two large, managed-solutions recruitment companies and many smaller, specialized recruiters, all with their own separate brands.

Impellam came into existence in 2008 with the merger of two diversified recruitment businesses, Carlisle Group, PLC, and Corporate Services Group, PLC. These two companies were unlike each other, and an earlier CEO of Carlisle Group, Richard Bradford, had wanted to moderate industry moral norms and so had purchased Tate, the anomaly in the industry, to do so.

Lady Virginia (Ginny) Tate founded Tate as a specialty recruiter primarily for secretaries. She ran the business like no other recruiter. She walked the floor of Tate and would often say to a tired recruiter, "You are doing important work." She took care not only of her recruiters but also of the secretaries Tate recruited. She had many impeccable standards of dress and behavior for both her staff and her secretaries and thereby gave them confidence and pride. She would even develop customized standards for the secretaries sent to each of her main types of clients: dress and act this way for this fashion house; dress and act that way for that accountancy. Tate had a culture where recruiters, temps, and employers admired each other and celebrated that admiration at least weekly. Given the industry's lip service to taking care of all involved, Tate won multiple industry awards. But Tate was self-consciously a boutique business and hence not a threat to the large recruiters. Indeed, no one except Julia Robertson thought that a Tate style of recruiting could work in the rough-and-tumble, aggressive deal-making world of big recruiting.

Robertson found her way to Tate, but only after she had an epiphany in her first few weeks at Atlas, where, in her words, she learned everything about "how *not* to do it."[24] Robertson felt the conviction that she could find a way to do recruitment without the scamming sleights of hand. She says now that she has spent her whole working life proving that people in recruitment could be trusted and that their work was something they could take pride in for the good it does to the workers, their employers, and the recruiters themselves. That it should take so long to prove it (37 years) shows the old moral order's strong hold over people in the industry.[25]

When Robertson went to work for Ginny Tate in 1996, she saw one aspect of the way forward. She came to call it "high-road recruiting": the recruiters took care of and went the extra mile for their temp employees—for instance, coaching and directing a nervous temp all the way to the employer's door. Using Ginny Tate's tools and standards, the recruiters also taught the temporary employees to go the extra mile for employers. And Ginny Tate worked only with employers who would treat their temps well. Recruiters in general thought such customers were rare. Thus, the model held no real competitive threat. Nevertheless, Julia Robertson wanted to find a way in which she could have a large-scale recruitment business where recruiters "look themselves in the mirror at the end of each day and answer yes to the question, 'Are you happy with how you made your money today?'"[26] When Tate and her husband, Sir Saxon Tate, decided to move away from the business, they asked Robertson if she would take it over and sell it. Robertson said that she would be happy to and promised the sale would be for the highest multiple yet attained in the specialty recruitment business. With that promise, she showed herself ready to take moral and financial risks to advance the business into the top ranks.

To fulfill her promise, Robertson took the moral risk of advancing what seemed like an irresponsibly risky idea. She created a watertight guarantee: if for any reason an employer was dissatisfied with a Tate-recruited employee, Tate would pay back the fee and replace the employee free of charge. If a permanent appointee proved unsatisfactory within the first 100 days, Tate would repay the client 110 percent of the fee. People in the industry thought Robertson was morally and financially irresponsible because with this guarantee she would likely destroy everything Ginny Tate had built, as the company would certainly veer toward bankruptcy. However, the guarantee worked, and Robertson kept her promise when she sold Tate to Carlisle.

Julia Robertson Faces the Moral Anomaly and Invents a Resolution

Robertson then became responsible for the Impellam Group's UK operations in 2008, and Impellam went through a series of rationalization and cost-cutting efforts. Those efforts lowered morale, but the changing economy and media attention lowered morale even more. With the "gig economy" growing, more and more professionals were becoming temporary workers. That meant increasing numbers of educated people became temps, and they witnessed and decried the low-trust, aggressive, scamming, sleight-of-hand practices. Academic writers began writing about how the standards for treating temp workers were out of touch with wider business standards and that the recruitment industry encouraged those low standards. Most starkly, Erin Hatton wrote in 2011:

> The temp industry has been much more than just a symbol of the degradation of work. It has been an active player in the drama. First, the temp industry's business is literally to sell degraded work: The temp industry provides American employers with convenient, reliable tools to turn "good" jobs into "bad" ones (and bad jobs into worse ones). But the temp industry has also operated on another, equally important level—in the cultural arena, where battles over "common sense" about work and workers take place. The temp industry's high-profile marketing campaigns have had a powerful impact on this cultural battlefield, helping establish a new morality of business that did more than sanction the use of temps; it also legitimized a variety of management practices that contributed to the overall decline in Americans' work lives.[27]

For Hatton, temporary work was an indignity, and ramping up the business was evil.

By 2014, the broadcast news media started focusing attention on the recruitment industry. Stories claimed the industry inflated profits by levying charges on unwitting workers and passively deceiving workers who did not demand and therefore receive benefits due them.[28] The Corporate Services Group, one of the two merged companies that had become Impellam, had well-publicized difficulties with fraud dating back to the late 1980s and 1990s. As the media were increasingly calling out recruiters for such behavior, Robertson faced a clear moral anomaly in which the recruitment industry's aggressive deal-making standards were falling out of harmony with the wider community's standards.[29] She saw that there was no moral solution that could make sense within the industry of big recruiting. Conducting a radical reform all at once would lead to internal wars that would cripple the industry and those—the temp workers and employers—the industry served. That was wrong. Consequently, she saw that the recruitment industry would treat the problem as one for public relations, and she believed that treatment was also immoral. She knew in her heart that she wanted to scale Tate and that doing so would resolve the moral anomaly, but she also saw clearly all the reasons that strategy would not work. She let three intuitions of what might work guide her: first, scale promise making; second, scale Tate's high-road practices; third, scale good profits and cut the scamming, sleight-of-hand financial practices. As Robertson saw the industry's potential death in the face of intense media scrutiny and new, high European Union standards, she stuck to her intuitions.[30]

As early as 2008, the large recruitment companies such as Manpower, Adecco, and Randstad started emphasizing in their annual reports that they were not only in the business of providing their clients fairly priced staffing to manage the ebbs and flows of worker demand but also of creating better lives for the temporary workers and better working environments for their own employees. But these reports were a public-relations matter. Because managers and staff in the industry shift firms frequently, the Impellam team, which regularly acquired team members from both large and small competitors, knew that until 2017, despite public words, aggressive, sleight-of-hand practices continued across the industry. However, Julia Robertson started driving the change in moral order intensely in the struggling Impellam in 2013 when she accepted the group CEO position there. She unhesitatingly took her first moral risk.

Julia Robertson's First Lumpy Act of Moral Risk-Taking: Termination Makes Promise Management a Grounding Moral Norm

In the prevailing moral order of the recruitment industry, promises were the prelude to an aggressive deal. Each party sought the promise that could slyly extract the greatest gain, and frequently one or the other wound up unhappy. Negotiators regularly took advantage of asymmetries of information, so suspicion was endemic, and the tricky promises were excused as inevitable given the rough-and-tumble world of recruiting.

In this setting, Robertson mandated *internal* promise management, where teams made explicit promises to their leaders and where the leaders made explicit promises of performance to Robertson. "When all 3,000 of our people make and keep their promises every day, we will be the world's most trusted staffing company," she said.[31] Robertson faced resistance because the street-smart leaders saw her as undermining their own high evaluation of themselves for aggressive deal making (which included deceitful promise making) and as raising the moral evaluation of dutiful (spiritless) promise keeping. Robertson's promise management was especially distasteful because she required that if a person saw failure to fulfill likely, that person was to renegotiate right away rather than craftily shift blame. This management style went against all common sense in the industry.

The quarter after Robertson mandated promise management, two brand leaders missed their promise for the quarter by huge amounts and with no warning or renegotiation. Others missed by lower amounts. To deal with this poor performance according to the new moral norm being established, Robertson chose a widely admired manager who was not taking promises seriously and was missing his numbers. She terminated him kindly but quickly *and made sure people knew why*. Given the prevailing moral order in the industry, the termination looked overly harsh, even immoral. Without the popular leader, the brand could have performed very poorly, and that would have made Robertson's action look like a mistake. With that perception, she would also have faced more outright rebellion as others refused to manage their promises and dared her to terminate them. However, the shock to the system given by the termination was sufficient and brazen enough (think Madam Walker) for Robertson to make her point, and the fired manager's brand suffered no significant loss of performance. Thus, termination and its successful aftermath sent the message reverberating throughout the organization. Promise management was not just a good idea or a prudent practice at Impellam; it had moral force. Violating it meant termination with the reasons made clear. As time went on, making responsible promises and keeping them displaced the grounding norm of merely getting people into seats as quickly as possible.

Julia Robertson's Second Lumpy Act of Moral Risk-Taking: Termination of the Heir Apparent Makes the High Road a Clarifying Norm

Robertson took the term *high road* from Erin Hatton's book. She saw that it applied to how Tate recruiters and Tate temporary employees behaved.

Robertson wanted her recruiters and employers to respect her temporary workers as highly dedicated to their work. She wanted them to take care of workers who took pride in their work and went the extra mile for the employers' customers. She would treat her own recruiters in the same way and expect them to go the extra mile for the employers, all in the spirit of the Tate guarantee.[32] She would provide high-road workers to high-road employers. She frequently gave as an example of a high-road worker someone delivering a meal to a patient in a hospital: the high-road worker would talk to the patient, describe the meal, tuck the patient in, or arrange the items on the patient's table. A high-road employer sought to create a great place to work with high levels of both employee and customer satisfaction. In contrast, low-road employers saw workers as costs or liabilities. These employers sought and received cheaper, low-skilled, undedicated workers and wanted them to follow routines that would get the work done as quickly as possible.

Robertson's two brands that had descended from Tate (Tate for specialty and Guidant Global for managed services) already worked this high-road way. To make the transition easier at Impellam, Robertson had an idea of how to move in the high-road direction while raising profits and not losing market share because high-road employers were hard to find. Robertson had noticed that Impellam's managed-services businesses did not go out of their way to seek workers from Impellam's own specialized businesses, and indeed, the managed-contract businesses were using large numbers of workers from competitors. Most of the £1.6 billion that Impellam managed services spent went to non-Impellam staffing. So, with the traditional strategy of applying a strength (working with partner companies that had high-road workers) against a weakness (working with nonaligned companies that had varying kinds of workers), Robertson mandated that the managed-contract businesses work with Impellam brands to enable them to find the best person for the job. Though the heads of managed-service brands saw this requirement as an infringement on their independence, the financial logic was indisputable. Robertson sweetened the demand by making sure her specialist brands had high-road temporary workers. In this way, she drove regular profitable growth in the UK specialized-service brands and in Impellam overall.

Given Robertson's embrace of the high-road strategy, everyone wondered whether she would have the courage to take the next logical step of stopping Impellam from serving low-road clients. As a start, she developed a basic tool for analyzing and ranking employers according to their profitability and their high-, middle-, or low-road status. She then mandated that her brand leaders would have one chance to transform low-profit, low-road customers. If the brand leaders could not move them out of the low-road status, the brand leaders would have to let the contract lapse. She also mandated that brand leaders consult informally but regularly with high-profit, low-road clients to provide them with ideas for moving to a high-road practice, such as providing training, allowing workers greater latitude for decision-making and job crafting, providing performance feedback, and offering regular coaching.

Brand leaders had to complete the analysis of their clients for quarterly meetings, and the entire leadership team reviewed them. Early on, many of her leaders fudged their analyses and claimed that almost all their clients were high road. Robertson interrogated them. The resistance to Robertson and her moral authority was fierce. In fact, the most charismatic brand leader—the one some thought would fill Robertson's role when she left— boasted that she had placed temp workers with a client that she considered gangsterish. Yet because this client was lucrative and paid bills quickly, she designated the client a high-road profitable one.[33] Others followed her example. Robertson could not afford to lose all those resisting her moral-order changes. To everyone's surprise, though, after a robust discussion of the issue, she accepted the resignation of her heir apparent. Seeking a high-road client list was not just a prudential or public-relations tactic for Robertson or the new Impellam. The departure of the putative future leader showed it was a moral matter for Robertson and Impellam.

Ultimately, under Robertson's leadership Impellam brand managers started letting contracts with low-road employers lapse. Robertson called such actions "liberating."[34] However, at first the moral risk-taking of letting the future leader go nearly failed, and Robertson had to work closely with the new leader to settle staff and recover losses in growth. Only a leader steeped in the business could have turned the brand around. It was a narrow escape. If the termination had backfired, she would have faced a team that would fight her or fall into resignation and let profits sink.[35] However, this high-road ethos became the clarifying norm at Impellam. It replaced cunning calculativeness. Next: finding a tough chief financial officer (CFO).

Julia Robertson's Third Lumpy Act of Moral Risk-Taking: Waiting for the Right CFO to Make Seeking *Good* Profits an Organizing Moral Norm

Robertson knew that changing the moral order required more than making Impellam a high-road company grounded in promises. She had to make it a high-performance growth company as well. Her strategic objective was to grow enough to lead the industry in the high-road direction, and she wanted to demonstrate strategic success primarily through a higher share-price growth than experienced at similarly sized companies in the industry and secondarily through higher growth than experienced by the large players. However, she set an even higher goal. Impellam's growth would come from "good profits," not from financial engineering or other aggressive financial practices. Good profits came from high-road clients who paid for high-road workers and did so repeatedly. Robertson labeled non-good profits as "gray profits."[36]

Robertson took a substantial, lumpy moral risk in identifying and then mandating the elimination of Impellam's aggressive, or "gray," financial practices. As we have already seen, these practices were standard in the industry. Most of her brand leaders and their brand CFOs were proud of their competence in deploying them and coming up with variations. A few examples of the practices should suffice. Swedish derogation allowed that if a recruitment firm hired an internal worker who then worked at a client site, the client did not have to pay the temporary worker at parity with permanent workers at the same site. Similarly, in line with European law, temps accumulate holiday pay, but at many companies they receive it only if they request it, and few did. Likewise, client invoices might include provisions for sick leave that frequently went unused, but the recruiter did not return the unused money to the employer.

Against fierce resistance from some of her brand leaders, Robertson demanded that they curtail gray-profit practices. The risk of eliminating these aggressive commercial practices was a moral risk for three reasons. First, brand leaders felt immorally betrayed by her, especially because she focused so much on gross profits, which the aggressive practices produced. Second, her blanket rejection of practices that were common in the industry seemed morally crude and an insult to the skills that the brand leaders had refined and were proud of as a form of excellence within the industry. Third, her blanket injunction also undermined their ability to make subtle judgments in individual cases.

Her reluctant brand leaders were not the only resisters. Many of the finance executives that Robertson inherited when she became CEO had been trained during times when gray profits were celebrated even when they strayed into the criminal.[37] Brand leaders and their brand-level financial executives could easily resist Robertson's mandate by inventing ever new gray profits. Robertson needed an aggressively effective (Machiavelli's virtù) CFO who understood accounting and the industry completely and who could therefore go through each brand's financial accounting and call out and eliminate gray profits. Such CFOs were rare in the industry; nevertheless, she had promised good profits to the board and therefore faced the additional moral risk of not fulfilling that promise. In the end, she found the CFO she needed. That CFO's financial rigor shocked (as Machiavelli's leaders do) the brand leaders and the financial executives into compliance. Seeking morally good profits became an organizing norm that replaced street smartness. Replacing street smarts with morally good profits yielded a huge change not only in the company but also in the industry.

Within a few years, Robertson had clear evidence of the financial success of her strategy. Impellam had returned to growth and by June 2016 had a high compound annual growth rate above 20 percent across three years and an EBITDA (earnings before interest, taxes, depreciation, and amortization) / net-fee income (the industry equivalent for sales) that was at or better than its peers' EBITDA profit ratio. In December 2016, Robertson was presented with a lifetime achievement award in recognition of her work. By June 2022, Impellam's share price had grown 34.33 percent since December 2012.[38] Of the competitors the City (London's financial community) recognizes, only Hays at 38.31 percent came out a little ahead. Impellam dramatically outperformed its other peers, Michael Page (12.67 percent), SThree (6.41 percent), Gattaca/MatchTech (–72.66 percent), and Staffline (–83.53 percent). At the same time, Impellam had moved from being fifth-largest recruiter in the United Kingdom and seventeenth largest in the world to being *the largest* in the United Kingdom (the home of Hays) and the twelfth largest in the world by 2021.

Bonus Moral-Norm Change: Virtuosity

The terminations over promise management and over the high-road ethos as well as the rigorous execution of good-profit principles were Julia Robertson's main, strategic acts of moral risk-taking. The grounding norm changed from just getting people into seats quickly to managing promises; the clarifying norm went from cunning calculativeness to the high-road ethos; and the organizing norm went from street smartness to good-profit seeking. As is frequently the case with such risky norm change, Robertson saw an additional, unexpected, beneficial norm change. Her most like-minded recruiters observed her moral risk-taking, and the best among them lived with Impellam's overarching commitment to be "trusted in equal measure by customers, our teams, and our investors." These recruiters became, in Robertson's term, "virtuosos."[39] Following in her moral-risk-taking footsteps, they would bend and even break conventions to build trust and to show new, better ways of behaving. In 2017, she realized that she was creating a culture of virtuosos who were highly skilled recruitment artists well versed in balancing client, temporary worker, and employee needs for the good of each. To strengthen the culture, she regularly celebrated virtuosity.

The Industry's Change in Moral Order

By 2017, Robertson had most people in Impellam managing promises, using high-road practices, and seeking good profits. One brand still resisted, but it represented only a small blip on the radar after the storm that Impellam had been through. Then a remarkable thing happened. Famous for its low-cost process orientation, the second-largest recruitment company in the world, Adecco, genuinely adopted a new vision. Gone was the sole emphasis on efficiency and in its place was "making the future work for everyone."[40] In 2017, Adecco adopted practices for empowering people and producing value for workers, clients, and employees. Manpower had a little earlier made such noises, but until Adecco made its switch, few took Manpower's marketing seriously. In 2017, former Adecco and Manpower workers who came to Impellam claimed that both companies were changing. People at Impellam noted that the marketing language of Adecco and Manpower was so close to Robertson's language that no one doubted that leaders in those organizations had clearly learned from her. Under Robertson's leadership, Impellam had changed the moral order of the industry.

Robertson had created a masterpiece and changed the industry, but as with all masterpieces she had to keep creating and adjusting. In response to digital competitors, she acquired Flexy, which had a popular digital job-matching platform. Robertson could then offer different levels of service starting with purely digital transactional service and moving up to the kid-glove service of her top, high-road recruiters. In this way, she developed a mix of the genuine high-road service and its digital imitation. She expects that the true value of her high-end masterpiece will show itself yet more clearly and profitably as people migrate toward it within the Impellam offerings. Accordingly, Julia Robertson's Impellam is working to change the moral order of the industry further. In figure 8.2, we represent the change Robertson accomplished by 2017.

Robertson herself has read Nietzsche and thinks that the Nietzschean good life of brief habits where people go from engaging in one short story and then on to the next captures the good life of temporary work and our age. Consequently, she is developing practices to make that good life real for her workers—for instance, by providing ways to help temporary workers get steady income, portable benefits, and discounted professional-development courses.

As we look back, it is easy to think mistakenly that the moral risks Robertson took were likely to come out favorably because she was on the right side of history. It did not seem that way at the time. To show how moral risk-taking in the face of an anomaly is genuinely risky and can go wrong, we turn to the case of Andrew Fastow, Enron's former CFO whose financial inventiveness played a lion's share in undoing Enron. It looked as though he, too, was on the right side of history. The temptations Fastow faced and the mistakes he made could have undone any of the leaders we have described—Churchill, Walker, Roddick, and Robertson.

Bad Moral Luck: How Moral Risk-Taking Turns Evil and How to Ward Off the Evil

The headline is that when a leader takes moral risks in the face of a moral anomaly, two things can go wrong: The proposed resolution of the anomaly might not be powerful enough. Or the dark side of the anomaly that the leader sought to resist might seduce the leader. The Fastow story includes both.[41]

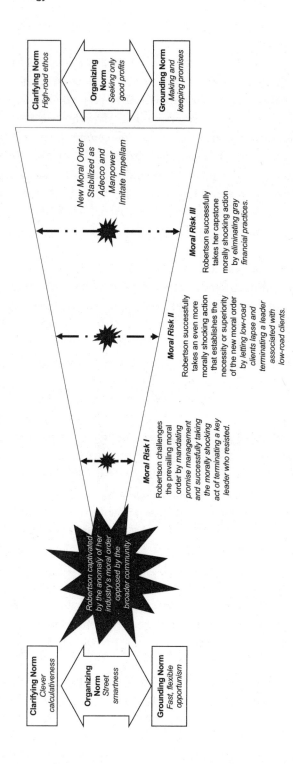

Figure 8.2

How Julia Robertson changed the moral order of Impellam and the staffing industry. Vertical lines show the new moral order displacing the original one as moral risks are taken one after another.

Initial Moral Order

Without analyzing the changes in the financial moral order in the United States during the 1980s and 1990s, we can confidently say that the grounding norm of this order was using Generally Accepted Accounting Principles (GAAP) to give a view of a company that approximated its economic reality. We can also confidently say that the clarifying norm involved continuous learning about and amending the GAAP to accord with the best understanding of companies' economics. The organizing norm that held the other two norms together was taking pride in transparent disclosing where the disclosures should give (at least sophisticated) investors a good, reliable view of the company.

Moral Anomaly and Its Resolution

In the mid-1980s, Andrew Fastow saw that the new notions of marking-to-market and fair-value earnings lost their direct tie to cash flow and now flowed from rules of thumb along with some US Securities and Exchange Commission rules for estimating the marking to market and fair value. For him, this was an anomaly that dramatically increased what he called the "gray area," the range where financial rules and standards were ambiguous, conflicting, or nonexistent. Yet Fastow saw the gray area as a space of opportunity for creative CFOs and their professional advisers. He also saw the obvious danger of completely speculative evaluations of earnings, which he considered enormously tempting and enormously deplorable. Fastow saw that the old moral order could not manage the instability of the fair-value and mark-to-market rules and that a new order would have to replace it. He thought that he could manage this anomaly of earnings freed from cash flow by following the accounting and other financial rules *devotedly* and *scrupulously*.

So his response to the anomaly was to ground his actions according to the norm of the new rule-of-thumb (not cash-dominated) economic reality while employing a clarifying norm of creativity and organizing these two norms by scrupulous rule following. Accordingly, what had been the cash-dominated economic reality became the rule-of-thumb economic reality; continuous learning became creativity; and pride in reliable disclosure became rule following. In the new moral order he was bringing about, he stopped asking the key question of disclosure, "Would a reasonable person under normal circumstances behave this way?" Clearly, one might also argue that scrupulous, even devoted, rule following is too weak a norm and, hence, that Fastow's resolution of the anomaly was too weak. If so, his project could not succeed. Just following rules would not curb creativity enough. So while simply following rules scrupulously might well have been too weak a solution from the start, it certainly did not appear so to Fastow, numerous other CFOs, accountants, and others. In any case, this new moral order started developing.

First Lumpy Moral Risk

In establishing this new order, one of Fastow's early signal cases of moral risk-taking came in 2000 before he became CFO. Enron was seeking to acquire a pipeline worth $1 billion. Fastow saw this purchase as a classic case where Enron would make the purchase through an operating lease, which would keep the acquisition off the balance sheet. Such an operating lease lowers the cost of capital and makes additional capital available. Most importantly, however, while the actual cash flow would be the same, Enron would show earnings on paper increased by $50 million each year for 10 years. Though dodgy because of their off-balance-sheet nature and lack of reflection of any change to the economic reality of the firm, such operating leases became common. Fastow said in his interview by Quinton Mathews in late 2020 that by that year there were at least $1 trillion worth of such acquisitions.

However, in 2000 this acquisition ran into a problem. Two days before the close of the deal, the legal team discovered that the pipeline company had purchased a company that Enron had a partial interest in, and the rules regarding operating leases required that the lessor have no ownership in the leased asset. As Fastow put it, if Enron owned even a screw in the pipeline, it could not legally use the lease for the purchase. Fastow called the lawyers, accountants, and investment bankers into a room to figure out what to do. Someone—he does not name who, and it might have been Fastow himself—came up with the idea of using an operating lease to take over the holding company instead of the physical asset and adding in a simple clause allowing the lessor to use the assets of the holding company. The accountants, lawyers, and investment bankers needed 24 hours to check out this idea's feasibility. The next day, the accountants said that such an operating lease broke no accounting rule. The lawyers said that they found it violated no legal rules. If they moved forward, Enron would invent the first operating lease of an intangible product. The investment bankers were delighted and said that they would start selling such leases.

Here was an early triumph growing out of the new moral order of developing rule-of-thumb representations of economic reality plus creativity (replacing continuous learning) plus rule following (replacing disclosure). Fastow became famous for such deals and earned a CFO of the year award in the early 2000s. Thus, he and his fellow leading-edge CFOs were on their way to displacing the old moral order, in particular its organizing norm of reliable disclosure determined by the answer to the question "Would a reasonable person under normal circumstances behave this way?" The success of the investment bankers in selling this new operating lease for intangible assets drove a Gestalt shift in the way finance people looked at things. The CFO of the year award shows that many leading-edge CFOs started dwelling in the new order.

Second Lumpy Moral Risk and Seduction by the Dark Side of the Anomaly
Even in 1999, Fastow engaged in contemplating the LJM deal that eventually led to the Enron bankruptcy. In this case, Kenneth Lay, chairman of Enron, and Jeffrey Skilling, CEO of Enron, asked Fastow to set up his own investment fund independent of Enron with the intention to use it to help Enron get deals done more quickly. By using the fund, Lay, Skilling, and Fastow estimated that they could more quickly drive $400 million in earnings, which would be about half the Enron earnings in the year.

The legal problem was clearer in this case. How could Fastow run a so-called *independent* investment fund that would operate for Enron's sake without an obvious and unjustifiable conflict of interest? The intention behind and the structure of the fund manifested the conflict to anyone who looked. However, conflicts of interest are not illegal. They must be *sensible*, and they do require board approval as a sense check.

As time went on, Fastow put the lawyers and accountants to work to find a way to set up such a fund that broke no rules. Together they produced a structure that technically abided by the laws and allowed the board to approve the conflict of interest. Again, we have representing rule-of-thumb economic reality as the grounding norm plus creativity as the clarifying norm plus rule following as the organizing norm. Counterintuitively, the flows of cash with the special new fund violated the old moral order's cash-flow norms much less than Fastow's innovative operating lease. With the investment fund, profits would genuinely come in more quickly. In the operating lease deal, off-balance sheet bookkeeping simply made the numbers look better. The creativity of such a fund for quick acquisition was obvious. The rule following was supposed to keep the creativity from going too far. One board member, sensitive to the old financial moral order, asked Jeff Skilling what the biggest risk was of approving this relationship with the investment fund. Skilling answered honestly that the biggest risk was the *Wall Street Journal* risk: that a reporter would discover the deal and write about it. Though the deal was legal, it stank. The stench came from this transaction's violation of whatever remaining force the aging organizing norm of reliable disclosure still had: Would a reasonable person interpret the fund as independent?

In his interview of Andrew Fastow in 2020, Quinton Mathews speaks with the voice of the reasonable person: "Regardless of all the legal structure put in place, this transaction amounted to plain lying deceit." The clarifying norm of creativity had become so seductive that it made scrupulous rule following into special pleading and undid the grounding norm of representing even rule-of-thumb economic reality. Fastow became seduced by the danger he had earlier identified and wanted to limit. Why? With the fund, Lay, Skilling, and Fastow could ingeniously double the company's income. The board discussion turned to what it would do if a *Wall Street Journal* reporter got ahold of the story. The board members foolishly thought that Enron could dissuade the writer from publishing the story simply by having the writer meet with Enron's lawyers and accountants.

As we know, a *Wall Street Journal* writer found out about the fund and wrote the exposé, the government sued, and a federal grand jury indicted Fastow on October 31, 2002. Fastow pled guilty to two counts of wire and securities fraud (lying) and agreed to serve a 10-year sentence. To receive a reduced sentence, he became an informant and helped federal authorities in the prosecution of other former Enron executives. The court sentenced him to six years at Oakdale Federal Correctional Complex.[42]

Fastow calls his actions a combination of "genius and evil." "Genius and evil" describes a leader who gets seduced by the dark side of the moral anomaly (in this case unleashed creativity) whose danger the leader has set out to remedy. The audacity and genius of following rules to create an "independent" fund was so great that it outshone any memory of the old standards of disclosure. Fastow's, Lay's, Skilling's, and the board's focus was purely rule following. If such a fund could technically be "independent," then economic reality would be whatever you could imaginatively make it into. To some extent, Fastow could justly blame the GAAP. Following the old disclosure norms, as Mathews conceded, would require putting enormous numbers of footnotes in financial documents, making them nearly unreadable. (However, that line of argument only shows that the old normative order was inadequate, not that Fastow's new one was right.)

Based on this account of Fastow, it is easy to see what the seduction would have looked like for the other moral-risk-taking, masterpiece-creating leaders we have discussed. Churchill could have responded to Hitler's ferocity by unceasingly bombing German civilians in the hopes of never having another world war. Again, it would have been Hitler's fault. The *miracle* of regrowing hair could have seduced Walker into looking for ways to drive women to make huge sacrifices to pay huge prices for her treatment. She very likely could have maximized her own wealth without looking to make sure her agents and clients developed their own financial independence and fashioned themselves into masterpieces. Likewise, skin-care-product users' desire for magic results could have seduced Roddick into making her own magical claims about the results of autonomy and pure, natural products. After all, it would be the fault of today's women for not listening to Roddick when she proclaimed the deceit. Robertson could have used profits from the recruitment-industry standard manipulations for investment in high-road care for recruits. What if she had had a brilliant, creative Andrew Fastow working for her when she wanted to move to good profits? The point is that any leader who sees the anomaly for what it is will also see the audacious moves either to advance the anomaly's danger or to block it. That audacity is itself the lure that opens the space for self-serving special pleading. Thus, we have the evil of the leader who falls for the attraction of the dark side of the anomaly after fighting it and holding it at bay.

Masterpiece-building leaders must not, in the face of their own audacious insights, lose track of what the moral risk-taking is for and how members of the old moral order would judge the action taken in the face of the anomaly. If Fastow had asked how he was reducing the threat of the anomaly of stated earnings coming untethered from real cash flow, he would have hesitated. If he had asked how members of the old moral order would judge his actions, he would have stopped. He could have easily inferred that he was increasing the threat of wild creativity and that members of the old moral order would see him as deceiving people. Churchill engaged in this form of reasoning when he asked about the bombing of civilians, "Are we beasts?"[43]

To check moral risk-taking, Fastow himself recommends that companies use automated natural language processing to read the emails of top executives and find out when tension levels are rising. That rise would be an indicator that the executives are about to take a questionable moral risk. Therefore, Fastow advises that with the triggering of the indicator, a corporate officer investigate. Fastow's idea is a high-tech version of determining when the executives are acting with fear and trembling. When they are acting with fear and trembling, ask if the risk-taking is resolving a moral anomaly or advancing its dark side. Ask how severely the old moral order would judge the action.

These two lessons suggest a more important one. When a masterpiece-building leader takes moral risks for the sake of resolving an anomaly, the leader is acting as a moral legislator. That requires looking far and wide at the consequences of the risky actions being taken. Churchill was always looking at the consequences of his actions because they would extend beyond World War II. That is why he sketched out the terms of mutually assured destruction. Bezos and Roddick looked at retail broadly. Robertson looked at labor of all sorts. Fastow, it seems, kept his vision glued to the world of corporate finance but did not look at the economy or business world as a whole. In his recent interview, he seems to have changed that scope of interest.

So, What Do Masterpiece Strategists Do and Why?

Masterpiece-creating leaders gain competitive advantage by changing the moral orders of their organization, industry, or wider community to create admirable good lives for people within those communities. Masterpiece builders are sensitive to the moral aspects of misalignment between an organization's internal and external goods: excellence and success. These builders then identify the danger in a developing misalignment or moral anomaly. They search for a response. Identifying dangerous anomalies, speaking of their danger, and finding a way to avoid the danger requires high levels of truth seeking and saying. Indeed, these actions require the ancient art and warrior-like courage of *parrhesia*—speaking truth to power.

To speak truth to power and maintain trust, leaders must cultivate and manifest their virtues—Bezos's famous relentlessness, Roddick's compassion, Robertson's developmental nurturing. Masterpiece-creating leaders can further mitigate risk and build trust if they listen for difference, as Bezos famously did in developing his high-speed delivery and easy-return systems. Then to change moral orders, masterpiece strategists must take lumpy (following Ghemawat's usage) moral risks, where these leaders might end up condemned as immoral. That move requires a refined moral imagination. Masterpiece-building leaders mitigate moral risks by following the practical wisdom that embodies Rumelt's application of strength against weakness. However, at bottom, masterpiece-building leaders are primarily moral leaders who give people a new sense of right and wrong that enables a community to overcome its moral anomaly.

Because there are many masterpiece builders and, we hope, many more to come, we can anticipate that they will bring sensitive moral diversity to a world that increasingly faces the insensitivity of tribal moral fanaticism: my tribe's current sense of what is right is final; all others are and do wrong. Masterpiece builders replace fanaticism with admiration of moral difference. Consider again Nietzsche's Genoa.

9 Turning Your Style of Leadership into a Masterpiece

We want to be the poets of our life.
—Friedrich Nietzsche, *The Gay Science*

No, I never heard it at all
Till there was you
—Meredith Wilson, "Till There Was You"

Getting Your Footing as a Leader

Masterpiece-creating leaders must cultivate a personal style of leadership that draws admiration from others, encourages the cultivation of good lives among followers, and, on that basis, fosters acceptance of and complicity in the moral risks the leader takes. This kind of self-cultivation goes against five of the current, common maxims about leadership today. Before we get to those maxims or the details of cultivating a leaderly style, we want to turn to the first step a masterpiece-creating leader (and, indeed, any leader) must take. Taking this step means that you can no longer go along with the flow. We call it "establishing your footing as a leader." On what does a leader stand? Or even better: What form of discourse and thinking is peculiar to a leader, whether a masterpiece creator or not?

Our term *footing* indicates that certain ways of speaking and acting establish the basic stance of particular roles.[1] We constantly find that managers do not know how to occupy the cognitive space of leadership. They are constantly looking for ways to get around the risks of *standing for* the organization and its mission *as a whole*, of personally taking responsibility for its success or failure, and of speaking in a way that owns up to that risk.

We scorn Louis XIV's hyperbole, "L'etat; c'est moi," but there is an element of truth in it: leaders' good lives involve maintaining and advancing the goodness of the organizations they lead. Jocko Willink and Leif Babin call this stance "extreme ownership" of the organization, its activities, and the activities' outcomes. Ben Horowitz agrees.[2] We see extreme ownership as the leader's footing. It is just the first step of leadership. But this footing is difficult to maintain. There is always the risk of falling into authoritarianism, narcissism, and self-aggrandizement. More commonly, managers see what the organization as a whole needs but hesitate to take the responsibility— put their heads on the block—to achieve it. They want to lead by rational persuasion, not by risk-taking. In that, they lose their footing.

For instance, in one of our consulting engagements, a chief information officer (CIO) saw that an outsourced IT unit responsible for collecting the company's revenue would fail and needed replacement. He insisted that the company faced a significant risk that it might not be able to collect its revenue for three-quarters of a year. That consequence would be financially devastating. His report to the CEO was purely in the mode of analytical persuasion, as if writing a consulting report: the situation is such and such, and the company ought to minimize risk by insourcing part of the outsourced team and renting IT capacity from another provider. But he never took the footing of a leader. He never said, "This risk is huge, and if you give me the budget, I will deal with it by insourcing and renting IT capacity from another; I will keep our cashflow safe." Because he did not speak from that leaderly footing, the CEO did not take the CIO seriously and, in fact, saw him as trying to accumulate more internal power. The difference is stark. The CIO acted only as an adviser, leaving the responsibility for making decisions, including the decision about technical details, to the CEO. The CIO did not take ownership of what would happen on his watch.

Leaders have a sense of ownership of the whole enterprise under their responsibility, including its future. The CIO took ownership only, at best, of spotting a problem. He did not respond to the problem with an "Oh my God, never on my watch; I have to fix this" urgency or insight. Worse, he did not even take this step imaginatively when prompted. The CEO asked him, "What would you do right now if you were the CEO here?" The CIO responded, "I would gather a senior team to discuss and evaluate the proposal I just made." In short, he advised the CEO to do what he, the CIO, was doing: shift his own ownership to a team. Even in the face of a potential financial loss that would devastate the company, the CIO looked for a team to come to agreement so that no one would be fully responsible for the decision. No wonder the CEO took the CIO's response as grandstanding or a power grab (running an insourced team). Anyone with the footing of a leader—who may not even be a manager—must take responsibility for preventing the breakdown.

In today's world, the best perspective for advising the leader is the leader's perspective—gained by assuming the leader's footing. We will assume that our readers, going forward, will take that footing. We believe it is a critical step to having a good life as a leader. However, we recognize that leaders are receiving contrary advice from authoritative sources. We turn to the popular, indeed beloved, maxims about leadership today and explain why we think they impede masterpiece-creating leadership, though they may help leaders lead in today's eternally returning, postmodern normal order.

Widely Held Leadership Maxims and Why We Disagree with Them

We had fed the heart on fantasies,
The heart's grown brutal from the fare
—William Butler Yeats, "The Stare's Nest by My Window"

These widely held maxims are crisply set out in *The Handbook for Teaching Leadership* (2012).[3] They represent a postmodern decadence that Nietzsche feared. Nietzsche wanted us to become free spirits who broke from the herd instead of sophisticated, flexible members of a postmodern herd. The five maxims that move us in the latter direction are: (1) Leaders do not depend on formal authority but influence others. (2) Leaders need to recognize and advance the personal and professional styles of their followers. (3) As leaders drive change, they must express, acknowledge, and care for their own and others' vulnerabilities. (4) Leaders need to share leadership with their team. (5) Anyone can lead.

We disagree with all five. First, when leaders are admirable, followers follow out of admiration. Sometimes followers admire rank. Influence is not the core of leadership. Many who influence—for instance, celebrities or writers of customer reviews—are not leaders. Second, leaders do not lead by developing their senior teams, though they can do that. Leaders make difficult, morally risky decisions that most others would flee from having to make. If we admire a leader who takes a morally risky action, our admiration is likely to keep us loyal to the leader and hence feel complicit in the moral risk-taking. And when the risk pays off, followers feel relieved as though they were full participants in the risk-taking. (Of course, leaders can also care for and mentor their followers, but that is not a requirement for admiration and therefore not of leadership.) Third, acknowledging vulnerabilities might work for a particular kind of leader, but leaders become admirable by taking risks that accord with the leader's particular admirable style, whether it is autocratic or empowering, resolute or open-minded, ruthless or gentle. Fourth, sharing leadership is ceding leadership. A leader who tries to share moral risk-taking falls into indecisiveness, fearful fantasies of betrayal, firefighting, and then failure. We advise that leadership team members should speak with the ownership of a leader so that they show an understanding of leadership, but that does not happen when the leader shares leadership. The leader can, of course, delegate, but "sharing" is too vague an action. Fifth, few people have the emotional resilience to take moral risks regularly and therefore lead. Consider the lonely footing of the leader. As Churchill said, only the few who are leaders at the top will deserve to have their heads cut off with failure.[4] Without facing that just desert, they are not leaders building masterpieces.

These maxims are the voice of the herd seeking the herd to lead. Be aware that the voice of the herd on leadership sounds extremely commonsensical, compassionate, and pragmatic, but it only enables a form of leadership that does not create masterpieces by taking moral risks. It is the peculiar leadership of being sensitive to and following the herd. Jay Conger shows this predilection as he explains why managers find it hard to become leaders: "One of the common dilemmas facing participants who return from formal [leadership] programs is the lack of reinforcement for exhibiting the leadership behaviors taught in the program. . . . The attitudes and styles of superiors are a critical factor in the transfer of learning. . . . [L]earning on the job is largely dependent on his or her superior's support."[5] This statement represents cloistered thinking. Real-world leading happens in the absence of support. The leader does what is right, not what superiors coax the leader to do; handholding would stand in the way of cultivating leadership. Given the need for post-program support, it is likely that such "leadership" programs did not get their participants to find their footing as a leader, take stands, tell truth to power, and so forth. If the program did include such training, it would also raise the expectation that such actions would face resistance. Cloistered thinking assumes that the rough-and-tumble world should become more like the cloistered training program. Of course, the leaders that emerge could lead from within the cloister, which in actual business life means sticking close to what the herd thinks. No admirable masterpiece is to be made there.

Jeffrey Pfeffer makes similar points about bringing out in potential leaders the morally difficult things leaders must do:

> The first and maybe most pernicious problem is that thinking on leadership has become a sort of morality tale. There are writers who advocate authenticity, attention to employees' well-being, telling the truth, building trust, being agreeable, and so forth. A smaller number of empirical researchers, contrarily, report evidence on the positive effects of traits and behavior such as narcissism, self-promotion, rule breaking, lying, and shrewd maneuvering on salaries, getting jobs, accelerating career advancement, and projecting an aura of power.[6]

What the herd praises as moral is different from the effectiveness that is in fact admirable in the world. As Scott Adams of *Dilbert* fame tells us, "Leadership requires a deep and innate sense of evil. . . . The essence of leadership is getting people to do things that they know isn't in their self-interest."[7] Pfeffer and Adams sound like Machiavelli on virtù: expediency wins. We endorse taking morally risky actions, but we also claim that leaders do live morality tales too. They find moral anomalies and overcome them with morally shocking actions. There is a moral register that captures the good and bad of masterpiece-creating leaders. The register runs from noble and courageous to ignoble and cowardly, not from authentic and vulnerable to deceitful and irresponsible or from friendly and good to mean-spirited and exploitative. Leaders who take moral risks to create masterpieces have an owner's footing, a broad vision, courage, and a noble sense of care.

How to Develop an Admirable Leadership Style

So, if masterpiece-creating leaders lead by inspiring admiration, what do they do beyond moral risk-taking? These leaders refine their admirable styles as they take moral risks. They develop a leadership style that encourages them to take moral risks and thereby achieve admiration for a moral achievement. Such a life is the good one Nietzsche describes as giving style to one's character.[8]

Seven steps lie at the heart of creating and constantly revising your leaderly style. (1) Identify in story form how you became who you are; in short, develop your foundational story, and (2) truthfully identify the virtues you exhibit in the story. A foundational story that reveals virtues is compelling enough to draw initial admiration. (3) Examine your current leaderly situation to determine its challenges and how, counterintuitively, your *very own leaderly virtues* generate the challenges. Frequently, those challenges will add up to a moral anomaly. (4) Following that difficult examination, find a popular but disappointing poetic way to characterize your virtues and your situation so that you can distance yourself from your own virtues. (5) As you distance yourself from your virtues, note the new ones that arise and identify a poetic image that crystallizes them. (For instance, "I was previously a model of strength and persistence, like Joe Fraser, but now I am facing a situation that forces me to cultivate the elegant agility of Mohammed Ali.") (6) Use that image to cultivate your new admirable, leaderly style, usually while taking a moral risk. (7) Once the new story of the development of your new style is clear, tell it. It is now a legendary story because it shows you taking a moral risk and shows others how to lead in the organization. Following these principles well requires two additional basic disciplines.

Once leaders accomplish their initial work on foundational stories, virtue analysis, and developing a poetic image that distances them from the fundamental narrative, then they can start asking tough questions about their leadership. At the end of each day, they should ask: *What did I do wrong today? What went surprisingly well?* Regarding something that went wrong, did the leader suffer the mishap for lack of skill or weakness of will, or did the leader act according to her or his own style? Is the style the source of what went wrong? When our virtues are the source of the challenges we face—when, for instance, our mode of working hard lets others slack off— then we need to adjust our leaderly style. In contrast, if a misdoing came from a simple weakness, then the leader simply needs more practice and perseverance. If a misdoing came while leading according to the leader's style, then the leader must reflect on whether the style needs adjustment. Looking at something that went surprisingly well, a leader asks the same sorts of questions: Did the surprise come from poor anticipation? Or did the leader act outside the style? If outside the style, why? Does the action suggest that the style has become unsuitable?

Masterpiece-creating leaders are consequently always questioning their leaderly styles. These leaders are asking daily whether they need to change their styles by developing distancing poetic images and then new attractive ones. In short, this time of "long practice," as Nietzsche calls it, does not look for quick behavior modifications but for new habits relevant to making leadership into an admirable masterpiece.[9]

This sort of self-questioning and reflection derives from the Stoic tradition of coaching, exemplified by Seneca's coaching letters to Lucilius.[10] The aestheticization of it with popular dramatic characters comes from our Nietzschean interpretations of cultivating a style. You might ask if self-coaching is possible. Yes, it is. The Stoic Roman emperor Marcus Aurelius appears to have done so; Seneca also writes about how he does it.[11] It requires more honesty and more critical self-evaluation than many can achieve, but it is doable. Indeed, once you become sensitive to your style, you become sensible to trends and events that might make it irrelevant, and you will begin to adjust it on that basis. For instance, you might see that bloggers' and podcasters' attitude-laden accounts are displacing the discourse of truth-seeking explainers.[12] Out of this daily self-questioning and reflection alongside moral risk-taking, the leader develops a new legendary story, which the leader will use to answer the question, "How does one lead in this organization?"

Are we simply describing an old-fashioned charismatic leader of the sort described by Max Weber?[13] We give a negative answer in the next chapter. For now, though, we spell out the steps to cultivating an admirable leadership style with a single case study based on our own work with a CEO and end this chapter with a summary of the common steps taken to develop a masterpiece leadership style.[14]

The Case of Jessica

Develop Your Foundational Story

Like most other stories, a foundational story starts with who you were before your life-defining event with its challenge, and then the missteps you took in trying to overcome the challenge, how you finally overcame the challenge, and who that success made you into.

Jessica's parents were UK lawyers who were left-leaning, public defenders and not very wealthy.[15] However, they valued education and put Jessica in an intellectually challenging private school filled with wealthy students. Jessica loved the intellectual challenge and was regularly at the top of her class. She was competitive, and she came to want the things her wealthier friends had. Her parents saw her transforming into the sort of upper-class British person they despised.

In response, after she completed primary school, they moved her to a middle-class school with much less intellectual challenge. Jessica brought all her competitive intellectual drive with her, but when she outperformed her fellow students, things went badly for her. Her fellow students started harassing her verbally and then physically. As a young teenage girl, she felt in danger and had no friends. At first, she tried to befriend those who bullied her least. But that only led to those people getting bullied. She then devised the strategy of not excelling and not showing her intellect so much. She would purposefully make mistakes in the classroom and on tests. She still wanted to be the top of the class but just barely. Though she kept reading and studying hard in the evenings and late at night, she stopped talking about studies, grades, or universities. She acted as though she had the same aspirations as her fellow students, and they came to accept her. She even gained the friendship of the girl who had bullied her the most. Her middle-class manners delighted her parents as well; however, they did not really trust her and, according to Jessica, prevented her from interviewing at Cambridge.

Jessica learned to succeed by hiding her talents, doing just a little better than others, acting as though she cared about what most others cared about, keeping her ambitions secret, and working on things she loved when others would not notice. Ultimately, she did all this with goodwill, thinking that it was a matter of community spirit and what other successful people did. Later, as a manager, she was both calculating and hard working. She let her team perform with mediocrity while she would spend nights and weekends redoing her team members' work and figuring out ways for them to excel. Her hard work enabled her to put herself in the right place at the right time for promotions. But, in correcting others' output, she felt oppressed by the team she led. She went from being a chief counsel at a company to being a CEO of a small company within a group and then to being the CEO of a group of companies. That was when we started working with her. Over the years, she had honed the skill of patiently hiding her intellect. But she occasionally would respond to a hare-brained idea with the brutality of an intellectual assassin, taking it and its proposer apart.

Identify the Virtues Revealed by the Foundational Story

People today do not think in terms of virtues very much, but we think they are important, so we start our work in analyzing leaders' virtues by going over the four classical virtues (courage, fairness or justice, temperance, and prudence or wisdom) and the three Christian virtues (hope, faith, and love). They are still the most recognizable virtues in our postmodern North Atlantic worlds.[16] (When we work with others in non-Western parts of the world—China, for example—we develop with them a list of suitable, culturally specific virtues. Recently in China, we drew on the Confucian virtue of duty and explored more recently developed entrepreneurial virtues.[17])

In examining the virtues exhibited in a foundational story, it is important, first, to identify only the main ones. Once clients and client teams get the hang of identifying the main virtue behind an action (for instance, the courage of standing for an unpopular position or the persistence of trying over and over although everyone thinks the task impossible), they then look behind every action, even inconsequential ones, and soon find themselves claiming to have every virtue possessed by the culture. Stick with the *main* virtue that drives the *main* action of the story. In identifying virtues, it is also worth noting that there are clear ones that people can recognize that they are cultivating because they take pride in them, but there are also hidden virtues that come out only in moments of stress or unusual circumstances. In the latter cases, we tend to say, "I did not know I had that in me." Jessica's clear virtues, evinced by her foundational story, were hard work, calculativeness, deceptive modesty, and a generous bonhomie that meant she did not want to overshadow others or hold them to the same standards she held herself to. Her hidden virtues came clear in her moments of assassination: sharp intelligence, directness, and justice.

Clarify the Leaderly Situation and the Challenges Generated by Your Virtues

People admired Jessica for her hard work, generous spirit, high performance, and care for her team (which she occasionally disrupted in her moments as an assassin). (Note that with these admirable ways of acting, Jessica fulfilled many of the current, common maxims regarding successful leadership.) This style, with its combination of clear virtues, worked well while she was chief counsel and then the CEO of a small company in the group. But when she became the CEO of a group of companies, she simply no longer had the time to raise the level of everyone's work in the evenings and on weekends. And by then, her extra work included joining her subordinates' management meetings, helping them craft directives, and handholding as they executed those directives.

To make matters worse, when managers reporting to her saw that she would generously do or redo their work, they slacked off, took long weekends, and designed sloppy meetings. Consequently, Jessica felt even more oppressed by them and all the work she had to do. She felt that she was giving everyone else a good life but depriving herself of one. She stopped admiring herself. This circumstance was a small moral anomaly. She had developed her virtues to give herself a good life, and now they were depriving her of one. Any of her typical moral actions would have made matters worse.

Identify a Popular and Disappointing Poetic Image to Distance Yourself from Your Virtues

Through long practice and daily work with her foundational story and her virtues, we helped Jessica see that she could not turn the corner by relying on her well-cultivated virtues, which only added up to offering more generous support to those reporting to her. Her individual company leaders needed to see what she saw, and that meant she would have to exercise her sharp intelligence and do so directly but without the assassin's edge. She did not want to be a bully. Accordingly, she set up strategy review meetings, asked piercing questions, and started proposing jaw-dropping possibilities. Her companies' performance started improving. But she still felt terribly oppressed. She had not increased either her own admiration of herself or her team's admiration of her. Working long hours and handholding in meetings become attractive only in the sunlight of admiration of oneself by others and by oneself.

Foundational stories and virtue analysis give the storyteller enormous insight and self-awareness, but they do not give the storyteller something in themselves to *hate* and something new to *love*.[18] When the story is no longer providing a good life, the leader must poetically reinterpret her or his foundational story. The leader needs to find an expressively dramatic, poetic way she or he can both see the attraction of the current virtues and nevertheless create distance from them. At one point, one of us had to tell himself that he was Polonius, a tedious explainer. Who was Jessica? After searching for someone in popular culture whose circumstance were like hers, we announced to Jessica early one morning that she was the famous lonely librarian from the 1957 Broadway show *The Music Man*. She pointed out how rudely sexist our comparison was, but we had her trust by then. We asked her then if she knew the story, and she did not.

We told her the story of Marian the librarian, who with modesty works extremely hard at the library. She has grown up to believe that if she does her job, treats people with fairness and kindness, does not expect too much of anyone, then good things will happen for her. But they do not. She is lonely and sees only increasing work for the rest of her life. Marian is also probably the smartest person in the town. When a con man arrives there to sell musical instruments and create a town band (that would, he promised, learn to play using the "think method"), he captivates all the residents. Marian quickly sees that he is a con man and no musician. She even sees that he engages in small acts of kindness simply to make the confidence game work. Even so, when he treats her brother with uncharacteristic kindness, she suddenly falls for him. She knows that this con man will leave her, but she also wants to tell him that she feels love for the first time and that it is all around. She famously sings "Till There Was You."[19]

Jessica was Marian. She was mostly still hiding her intelligence, mostly displaying a kind of modesty and politeness, working night and day, handholding and substituting in meetings, while others left early and performed sloppily. She expected deep down that there would be a reward for all of this but had found none and felt oppressed. Worst of all, she could not even robustly enjoy her love for the group of companies to which she devoted herself. So we told her that unless she saw herself through our eyes for a moment and then changed, she would end up like the lonely librarian. That was something she could picture and hate. We also gave her another image, a film line, and a story for her moments of assassination. She was then like Clint Eastwood from the spaghetti Westerns: "[God] hates idiots."[20] Jessica wanted to be neither Marion nor Clint, and we would go through end-of-day reviews pointing out where stylistically she fell into being one or the other.

Why is it important to come up with a poetic rendition of yourself that distances you from yourself? It is extremely hard to give up on virtues that you feel proud of and that have brought you to your successes in life. Most people do not make this transformation. Masterpiece-creating leaders do.

Note New Virtues and Identify a Poetic Image to Crystallize Them

Jessica would not give up her modesty; however, she could stage herself as someone who would bring incisive thinking joyfully. She started complimenting the managers who attended her meetings. She took their proposals and statements and refashioned them into brilliant gems, while giving them all the credit. She would design meetings to discuss widely contrasting strategies to ensure debate. As she experimented with these changes, we struggled to find a popular-culture icon that Jessica could love and that captured the new ways she was trying to behave. (We have found that we cannot use Shakespeare and Milton as sources for poetic character types, so we have turned to Marvel comics.) For Jessica's new poetic image, one blazing Marvel comic hero after another fell. It turned out that Jessica had made both hiding her intelligence and even her hard weekend work too much a matter of her masterpiece style as a leader to fit with the heroes. Iron Man works weekends but never hides his intelligence. Captain America is modest but not a fiercely blinding light. Jessica Jones is deceptive but too bitter. Black Widow is too much of an assassin.

We finally left the Marvel world and hit on Babette from the great film *Babette's Feast*. That could be Jessica's image of herself. Babette is a leading Parisian chef who flees the revolution and assumes a disguise as a household chef in Denmark. At the end of the movie, she uses all her saved money to create a feast that takes the guests through personal transformations from fear and suspicion to exuberance and love. That feast became the basis for Jessica's management and her all-important weekly review meetings.

Cultivate the New Style (Usually with Moral Risk-Taking)

With that image in mind, Jessica made each of her meetings into a feast. She was the enchanting hostess. Guests (her team) feasted on her brilliant ideas and engaging questions. This way of acting brought together her modest, calculative deceptiveness with her sharp intellect, her sacrificially hard work with her bonhomie. Jessica had to bring her team to see things as sharply as she saw them; she needed them to put in the hard work to get things done. She accomplished this by creating sumptuous meeting topics and complimenting and recrafting what her team members said to make their words remarkable. By this means (and this was the most notable change), she drove them to diligent, arduous work, which they did out of a desire for more compliments and more goodwill. Jessica had to work hard to craft such meetings. It was like Babette's feast at least three days per week, but the work did not seem so hard because she admired herself in doing it, and they admired her.

As is normally the case, a leader's transformation of her or his own style in the face of deep challenges requires that the leader take moral risks. Just as Bezos's moral risk-taking ended up transforming him from someone saving the orderliness of retail with an online everything store to the primary promoter of hyperconvenient transactions, so Jessica's transformation happened alongside her own moral risk-taking. To resolve her own moral anomaly of not having a good life, she had to send away two of her smartest, most talented, highest-revenue-generating managers who were taking advantage of her. She took the risk that their leaving might sink her two most profitable brands and cost her the respect and admiration of others. However, Babette-like, she helped these two brand leaders understand that they loved an older way of working that each could sustain in a small business but not in a growing one like hers. When the rest of her team saw them leave with goodwill, it seemed almost magical. It was also clear that the old way of working that included early stop times, relaxing weekends, sloppily designed meetings, and unfulfilled commitments was gone; cleverly crafted growth was the agenda. Jessica's new style enabled her to face another problem that the overworked librarian in her could not have faced.

Digitalization was destroying a key component of the customer intimacy her companies competed on. Within her feastlike meetings, Jessica, along with her team, crafted the careful closing of still highly profitable branch offices in order to gain resources to compete digitally. She even purchased a digital company that could eat her main businesses alive. All these actions were morally risky in so far as they changed what was the right thing to do in her companies: she transformed the grounding, clarifying, and organizing norms. The grounding norm went from leading a relaxed work life to joyful diligence. The clarifying norm went from focusing on branch profits to focusing on the company profits. The organizing norm went from cultivating intimate customer service to cultivating a range of services. Also, by drawing on her enchanting, joyful style, she brought together people with opposing frames of reference—those who create strong personal relationships and the new digerati—and had them finding reasons to work with and support each other. Her managers felt deeply complicit in making good her daring actions.

Tell Your Legendary Story

Jessica could leave behind her foundational story and now could tell the legendary story of herself as a leader. The legendary story is the one that not only shows how the leader leads but also what leadership in general looks like in the leader's organization. Now Jessica tells her story about someone who learned the hard way to become a wonderful hostess who brings joy to her meetings. Telling people how she operates as a hostess makes her no less admirable to them. They feel even more connected to her. She reminds her management team of her management style when they drift from it. She tells it as part of her hiring of new managers. While other managers' leadership might not deliver the same sumptuous meetings Jessica delivers, her managers lead in her mold by creating joy and seeking opportunities. Her managers follow her out of admiration for her virtues and respect for the moral risks she takes in driving the businesses she oversees.

Jessica's leads in the style of Babette, a magically enchanting hostess, in a truly tough, highly competitive, even paranoid industry. No one would expect such a leadership style to work there, but when a leadership style is a well-performed masterpiece, its power is enormous: it draws admiration from almost all who experience it. But maintaining this power takes work. Every evening Jessica goes through the introspective questions: Where did I produce joy today? Where did I fail? She constantly recrafts herself to bring out her style even more sharply.

Jessica's is a masterpiece of leadership based on Nietzsche's most famous good life. But is it a good life? Jessica admires herself. Her team and the customers admire her as well. The owners of her group admire her for pulling off what should be impossible. Her profits outshine competitors. The change in leadership style also had the unintended consequence of helping Jessica change her relations with her wider family. She has brought joy to her parents as well. They take pride in and support her son's ambitions to attend Oxford. Creating an admirable style as a leader draws admiration from family even when the leader's style yields little time for family. Jessica is a postmodern leader who follows none of the postmodern herd's maxims. We certainly do not promise that all admirable leaders' styles will create such a coherent life, but so long as they make their leadership and their organizations into their masterpieces, they will have a good life. Jessica created an organizational culture of joy with a style of opportunism. It perfectly suited her leadership style and the kinds of moral risks she undertook.

Steps for Making Your Leadership a Masterpiece

To sum up, whether you are seeking a mentor, as Seneca's Lucilius did, or seeking to self-mentor, as Marcus Aurelius and Seneca himself did, you will find yourself pushing yourself through changes like Jessica's. Table 9.1 summarizes the essential steps and actions to take in developing and cultivating your leadership style as a masterpiece. The essence is turning your foundational story into a legendary story.

Bringing Together the Masterpiece Culture, Strategy, and Leadership Style

Leaders can never complete working on their leadership style. When answering your daily questions, you will find that even your legendary style is not up to some situations you face (perhaps, because of a new moral anomaly). Then you must go through the process of creating a new legendary story by treating your current legendary story as though it were a foundational story. In sum, we never complete our second nature. As with culture and strategy, it is another instance of what Shakespeare editors call continuous copy (where the writer continually revises even published works).[21] As with Shakespeare's plays, there are masterpieces but no final authorized versions.

Note, too, that while our example of Jessica shows a masterpiece-building leader who brings joy and creates a culture around her, we have helped leaders cultivate styles very different from Jessica's—for instance, ruthless zeal. As we warned earlier, do not take pride in having the herd's virtues, and do not accept the herd's account of leadership. The herd does not enable masterpiece creation. Remember Machiavelli's point that in most situations it is better to be feared than to be loved.[22] Also, remember Jessica's

Table 9.1
Summary for Cultivating One's Leadership Style as a Masterpiece

Step	Action	Example
1. Develop your foundational story.	Identify the story of the event that made you who you are: include who you were, the challenge faced, the missteps, the resolution, and who you became.	Jessica's story of hiding her light during school hours and succeeding through hard, though disguised, work.
2. Identify its virtues.	Get clear about your main virtues, both nice and not-so-nice ones. Identify hidden virtues that only occasionally reveal themselves.	Jessica's clear virtues were diligence, calculativeness, deceptive modesty, and good-natured generosity. Her hidden virtues: sharp intelligence, directness, and justice.
3. Clarify your challenges and how your virtues generate them.	Ask yourself: What are you struggling with? What or who do you regularly find challenging? What feels oppressive? Are you facing a moral anomaly? How are your virtues generating the struggle?	Jessica's diligence, generosity, and care for her team led them to slack off; she no longer had the time to make up for that slack. She faced the anomaly that the virtues that once gave her a good life were now taking it away.
4. Identify a popular and disappointing poetic image to distance yourself from your virtues.	Crystallize your sense of how your virtues generate your challenges by finding a popular-culture figure who does the same and from whom you want to distance yourself. (Such distancing is extremely hard.)	Marian the librarian from *The Music Man* depicts a lonely, oppressed, and selfless hero who has Jessica's virtues and whom Jessica could dislike.
5. While distancing yourself from your current virtues, note the new ones that arise and identify a poetic image that manifests them.	When you distance yourself from the virtuous actions that bring defeat, alternative virtues will appear. Attend to them and find a popular-culture figure who exemplifies them. Having such a figure in mind makes the change you want achievable.	In drawing back from doing others' work, Jessica used her intelligence to create sumptuous meetings that made others think new thoughts, work with new diligence, and shine. She was like Babette in *Babette's Feast*. Babette modestly and joyfully created dinners that made others shine.

Table 9.1 (continued)

Step	Action	Example
6. Cultivate the new style.	As you cultivate your new style and overcome the challenges your old virtues created, you will find yourself taking moral risks to overcome a moral anomaly.	Jessica took the risks of removing leaders and purchasing a competitor that could destroy her main business. She replaced relaxed work hours, a focus on the branch, and strictly high-touch service with joyful diligence, a focus on the whole company, and multiple levels of service.
7. Tell your legendary story.	People will want to accord themselves with your admirable leadership style. Tell your story. Burnish it and retell it.	Jessica admires how she manages joyfully and tells her story, while joyfully insisting that others accord themselves with it. Telling the story strengthens connection with her managers.

leadership, where the admiration of Jessica comes much closer to love than to fear. Work to make sure that the moods and style of your culture suit your leadership style, as Jessica did. The moral order you strategically create will follow from your leadership style and the nature (mood and style) of your masterpiece organization's culture. Jessica's artfully enchanting virtue as a leader played directly into the culture of joy and opportunism she cultivated, and her virtues and culture drove the moral risk-taking that led to a moral order grounded in joyful diligence with a clarifying norm of increasing company profits and an organizing norm of constantly developing a range of services. We turn now to ask whether what we have done in this book is simply revitalize charismatic, heroic, top-down leadership.

10 Is Masterpiece-Creating Leadership a Return to Heroic Leadership?

We possess art lest we perish of the truth.

—Friedrich Nietzsche, *The Will to Power*

Summary of the Argument

This book takes a major part of its inspiration from Jacob Burckhardt's insight in *The Civilization of Renaissance Italy* that city-state rulers—princes, condottieri as despots, and leaders of republics—treated their states as works of art, masterpieces, of their own creation. The other part of our inspiration is captured in the epigraph of this chapter. It tells us that we need the art of organization creators lest we perish from the truth of postmodernity's eternal, agile return of the same.[1] We say that today's small-business leaders and mold-breaking leaders of such large businesses as Amazon, Google, Netflix, and the Body Shop treat their organizations as works of art. We say, too, that even leaders of businesses between the small and mold-breaking ones would like to do the same but only make the attempt half-heartedly. This book is out to help them create masterpieces with full hearts. The lessons apply to all who lead teams and can adjust styles of working to do what is right for customers, colleagues, suppliers, owners, or other stakeholders.

What makes an organization a masterpiece is that it has an admirable moral order—a distinctive character. From the leader's example, the business develops a distinctive right way to deal with customers, colleagues, managers, subordinates, suppliers, and owners. We repeatedly compare the moral order of Amazon with its relentless work ethic, its raising of the bar on performance expectations with every hire, and its frugality, on the one hand, with Google and its promise of psychological safety and lavish benefits and perks, on the other. The good life at Amazon is one of relentless, hard-driving accomplishment. The good life at Google is dreaming up new products and services in a protected Xanadu. The treatment of colleagues and employees in each could hardly be more different.

With this picture of the two morally distinct and admirable organizations, we find one of our other sources of inspiration: Nietzsche's postmodern thinking. Nietzsche invented the postmodern world in which we live and in which we cannot take anything, not even ourselves, fully seriously—nothing is above criticism. Although we cannot easily be righteous within such a world, we can admire ourselves in four broadly different ways that give us four good lives: (1) the life of cultivating a style by replacing one's first nature with one's second nature; (2) the life of "brief habits" where one gets captivated by a life project, gets sated by it, and then gets captivated by another—the captivation with each full of wonder; (3) the life of risk where, win or lose, experience is wonderfully vivid; and (4) the life of improvisation, of navigating through and turning each mishap into graceful beauty. Masterpiece leaders cultivate their own style and cultivate the same for their masterpiece. Of all the leaders we report on in this book, Madam Walker best captures that definition.

The point of Nietzsche's four good postmodern lives is that although they might be meaning poor (not strongly attached to traditions that matter), they are wonder rich. Hence, if a broad range of others admire us, we can admire ourselves and our lives. As part of our admiration, we promote ourselves and our good lives when we have them so that others can appreciate and share in them. While John Ruskin simply claimed point blank that the business leader created an organization that gives those in it good lives, today's postmodern masterpiece organizations enable good lives in two ways. First, these organizations enable style cultivation (for leaders), brief habits (for project workers), and improvisation in supporting moral-risk-taking leaders. Second, they give their customers a platform for becoming opinion leaders who promote themselves in the evaluation of the organization's products and services. With their celebrations, many organizations give their employees similar platforms.

Nietzsche inspires this book in another way as well. To help us picture our postmodern world as a whole, he turns our gaze to the palaces lining the streets of Genoa—a resplendent Italian Renaissance city. As in Venice,

Genoa's palaces are distinctly beautiful and recall for us the different, competing moral codes that created their beauty. Should an early-modern leader seek to be loved or feared, a little of each, or something else entirely different? Each sentiment brings with it a different moral code. Accordingly, for us in our world, as businesses establish different moral orders, we can enter a postmodern world of moral pluralism that lives in admiration of most organizations rather than in resentment of different moral tribes. Helping business leaders to create such an admiringly livable postmodernity is this book's ultimate goal. That goal stands against our current direction, captured brilliantly by Don Sull, of ceaselessly inventing more convenience, more efficiency, more safety, and more flexibility for taking up increasing numbers of options.[2]

But are leaders really free to create masterpieces? Are not such creations, at least for big businesses, rare matters of luck? Is not business about fulfilling needs and acting on necessity? After all, only the paranoid survive. Do we not leave free design to artists and political leaders? No. There is more freedom in a business leader's actions than most suppose. Since the ancient Greeks, people have thought that business is about taking care of needs and dwells in a realm of necessity. Such thinking, however, covers over the nature of business's most primitive act: transactional exchange.

In contrast, the best exchanges are ones where the business sells something that comes from the heart of all those in the business. Think of all the exchanges that happen in business today. How many of them can be described as coming from the heart of those selling the product or those making the product? The number is low. Simple transactions rule the day. However, the Romans invented exchange as an emancipation, as when you sold something that had been in the family for years and seemed an essential shaping force of the family. Such selling liberated the commercial activity of the West. But we—except for the rare Steve Jobs, who decided to package each Apple product as if it were a rare jewel—have lost touch with the emancipatory exchange. However, leaders can bring it back and on that basis design their businesses with admirable distinction. One of us was surprised to discover that GM assembly-line workers really love the cars they produce. Nothing about the way the exchange happens would bring that sense home. What if GM designed its organization and sales to make it clear that each car was something that a team loved? How would GM package the sale? How would GM make the sale individualized? What would the narrative voice of the sale say? We have a hint of the answer. GM moved in that direction with Saturn. What if other businesses were to do the same. The freedom to redesign is huge.

So, once it is clear there is room to create a masterpiece, how does a leader do it? In answering that question, we draw on our other main inspiring voices: Niccolò Machiavelli and Bernard Williams. Machiavelli proposed that the only way to establish a secure, stable state in which the more common virtues (love, justice, wisdom, hope) could thrive was through aggressive effectiveness, virtù: the capacity to take uncomfortably single-minded, even ruthless, effective actions to get things done. We draw on the philosopher Bernard Williams and his discovery of moral luck to develop our claim about masterpiece-creating leaders. They encounter moral anomalies—situations where there is no right thing to do within the prevailing moral order—and then find a way to cut through and resolve them by taking morally shocking (under the prevailing order) actions that become examples of a new moral norm or that give moral force to a previously prudential norm. Our examples in the book include Winston Churchill, who established brutal realism and ruthlessness as the moral order for waging World War II; Madam Walker, whose betrayal of her benefactor and mentor Annie Malone enabled her to emphasize the magic for Black American women in regrowing their hair and thereby making themselves individual masterpieces in the Jazz Age; Ray Dalio, who fired both his thinking partner and the person he treated like a son to make Bridgewater an idea meritocracy; Anita Roddick, who deceived her husband and acted with financial recklessness in order to make growth an absolute for the Body Shop; and, finally, Julia Robertson, who conducted shocking terminations to transform the recruitment industry into one that took good care of recruiters, temps, and its clients. All exhibited forcefully our form of Machiavelli's virtù: moral risk-taking in the face of a moral anomaly.

Beyond luck, successful moral risk-taking requires exercising moral imagination and listening for difference. It requires intervening directly in people's emotional lives. It requires the capacity to build trust. And, finally, it requires disciplined truth seeking and saying. But simply accepting the necessity of moral risk-taking for creating a masterpiece is the hardest step a masterpiece-creating leader must take. It requires going against the grain in a deeply uncomfortable way even when the moral risk is not anywhere as large as Bezos's, Roddick's, or Robertson's.

Take the case of an entrepreneur who left a large video game company to start up his own small video game company. He hired mostly people who felt mistreated at their previous large companies, and in the new culture of hope with perfectionism, most of his hires were contributing brilliantly. But one was not and so was dragging the others down. What was the entrepreneur to do? In conversation, his senior team advised that because the employee had been mistreated at her previous job, she should receive a long-term performance-improvement plan where he, the CEO, would act as her coach. This suggestion might be a normal, big-company solution. All the documentation that performance-improvement plans require protects the large company against lawsuits and masks any inadequate coaching the employee has received so far. But in a small start-up racing to get its first product out the door and with no spare people, the entrepreneur wondered if it made sense to establish a performance-improvement process.

Together with the entrepreneur, we considered Reed Hastings at Netflix. Hastings took the moral risk of doing away with such plans. He ensures that feedback comes regularly at Netflix, and when an employee nonetheless underperforms—that is, when the manager determines not to pay above-market rates for the person—the manager negotiates a generous, agreeable severance settlement. Hastings believes such a process is less costly and more effective than running performance-improvement processes.[3] Our entrepreneur realized that the Reed Hastings approach was right for his company but suffered deeply over it. He seriously wondered if he was a "Nazi," as he put it. Moral risk-taking does not come easily.

Leaders find it hard to follow Reed Hastings, and in our experience, we see that they need to develop moral imaginations to steel themselves with the courage to take moral risks. The literary critic Lionel Trilling made the term *moral imagination* famous in the 1950s.[4] A moral imagination is one where you look at something aberrant, such as an object or behavior, and develop a believable, contextualizing story to show that a morally valuable understanding might well lie behind the strange object or action. Then the person with a moral imagination accedes to that account as the grounds for action. Philosophers have developed the notion further to argue that moral reasoning is inherently imaginative so far as it depends on the use of metaphors. To be morally imaginative, notes Mark Johnson, is to sharpen our power of making distinctions, envision new possibilities, and imaginatively trace their implications.[5]

Trilling succinctly showed what a moral imagination can be by drawing on a moment from *Huckleberry Finn*. In the middle of the night, Huck looks down at a town and, seeing several houses with lights on, observes to his companion, Jim, that those lights mean that the people there are taking care of the ill. In this way, he gives a satisfying reason for the aberrant lights. He then senses an affinity between those lights and the lights in the night sky.[6]

Consider, too, how the brilliant novelist and essayist David Foster Wallace showed his moral imagination in his commencement address to the graduates of Kenyon College in 2005. He set a scene. He is driving home after a tough day. He is in bumper-to-bumper traffic and surrounded by fuel-guzzling SUVs, Hummers, and V-12 pickup trucks. To the audience's delighted applause, he described the rant going on inside his head about the ugly drivers in their "disgustingly selfish vehicles." And then he said there is another way to think about this. Those SUV drivers have been in horrible accidents and have vowed to be safer. The Hummer that just cut him off is trying to get a young child to the hospital. And so forth. A moral imagination reevaluates the aberrant and troublesome by means of a morally restorative account. David Foster Wallace is sure that the second account is better for his interpersonal relationships in constituting a good life.[7] Of course, a moral imagination can reveal evil as well. When after searching you come to find that there are no circumstances under which you would engage in a troubling, aberrant activity or that the only circumstances when you would do so simply do not obtain, then you are seeing something evil. Famously, in this way, Huck Finn discovers that he cannot abide slavery. Using the moral imagination yields a thoughtful, trustworthy judgment of good and evil.

How would such acts of moral imagination help the entrepreneur with the underperforming, previously mistreated employee? Is her underperformance because her skills are inadequate or because of laziness or another weakness? Or does she find the culture of carefully developed perfectionism not suited to her sense of herself and the good life she is trying to cultivate? Is the start-up company culture just another form of the oppression she has already suffered? The entrepreneur imagines both accounts, looks for hints in her behavior, and then makes his judgment accordingly. In our experience, much underperformance comes from cultural mismatches. In this case, perfectionism simply did not suit this entrepreneur's troubled employee. Exploring the situation with such an imagination helps the entrepreneur to act with fear and trembling, yes, but also without self-recrimination or remorse.

Developing a moral imagination is a step toward listening for difference.[8] The leader with a moral imagination sees something anomalous or annoying and asks, "Under what conditions would I engage in that activity? Could the behavior I am observing come from such conditions?" The questioning takes place all within a single moral order, but in listening for difference, the leader goes beyond that order. The leader starts similarly by identifying something anomalous or disharmonious. It is usually something that the leader might overlook as a passing abnormality. Listening for difference, then, the leader asks what different ways of morally evaluating life the anomaly could point to.

When cultivating the skill of listening for difference, we read older literature and watch older films, note what appears odd, and then try to produce a moral order that makes sense of the oddity as though the oddity were the centerpiece of moral conduct. In our experience, leaders become good at this skill only when they practice it with customers to develop innovations. To help leaders who want to create masterpieces get a feel for listening for difference, we have them meet customers and suppliers who are not like them. However, we must get them out of their own heads and hearts, and so we have warm-up exercises before customer meetings. We have leaders identify what seems odd in the speeches of their predecessors or in the speeches of their up-and-coming younger colleagues and then ask what these leaders see if they take it that differences are of crucial importance. We look for people whom the leaders already admire and feel comfortable thinking about. In one case, in working with a leader who had led his electric and gas utility through privatization, we had him note what was truly unusual in a conversation he had with his new mergers-and-acquisitions specialist. The specialist was one of the few people who had come from outside the utility industry, and at a particular moment in a conversation recommending an acquisition, he had said, "At £300 million, the power plants are as cheap as chips." At first, our leader trivialized the expression as simply an expression to bring urgency to the conversation and underline the cost. "But what," we asked, "if that statement is the heart of the presentation?" Our masterpiece-creating leader came to see that the mergers-and-acquisitions specialist was telling him that investing is an art and that although the financial projections were sound, this purchase struck a positive chord for reasons too numerous to put in a spreadsheet or a report. When such moments occur, you must check and then act fast. These practical insights were so powerful that our leader opened the space for the acquisitions specialist to become the company's next, highly successful CEO, who in turn changed the organization's moral order.

In all our examples, we have leaders dealing with people as fully emotional, rational beings. Masterpiece-creating leaders engage directly in their employees' moods, and learning to do so is one of the hardest changes to make. The leader must develop the courage to say, "You seem to be in a bad mood. What's up?" Most leaders can say something when they see a team member suffering significant grief or depression. But most leaders do not inquire into lighter negative moods because they assume that moods are private and will pass. But moods are contagious and when not managed cause enormous emotional wear and tear. We recommend beginning team meetings by simply requesting that the members, one at a time, say what mood each is bringing to the meeting. Such a practice gets everyone speaking, and even those who claim to be in a better mood than they are start faking it until they make it. Of course, if someone acknowledges the negative mood, then it is good to try to change it before the primary business of the meeting takes place.

Changing a mood starts with the understanding that moods are rational and that we can change them by shifting the moody person's understanding of what is going on. Sometimes it is a matter of understanding the trigger. If the trigger is a false assumption, bringing that out will change the mood. If the assumption is correct but lives in a larger context where it is not so important, then showing that low importance changes the mood. The second way to shift context is simply to act as though you are in another mood. And, finally, there is the act of shifting the context by understanding the story the moody person is telling about the general situation and then shifting that whole story. Simply having the person tell his or her story opens other possibilities for interpretation and shifts the mood to one of curiosity and then wonder. Telling such stories is a simple form of what the masterpiece-creating leaders do daily regarding their own leadership styles. Implicit in understanding profound differences, speaking directly to people about their emotions, and allowing oneself to become captivated by moral anomalies is the discipline of seeking truth and speaking it to those in power.

Masterpiece creation generally requires that people develop a sense of absolute responsibility to speak out whenever they see a way to make the situation better. With that responsibility to speak out comes the additional responsibility carefully to compose the truth that will be spoken so that others can listen to it. Teams that adopt these practices have a powerful sense of wonder that comes with truth seeking and delight that comes with composing thoughts well and thereby helping others out.

When we speak with leaders, the typical examples of truth seeking and saying involve reporting on revenue or profit figures from various regions, reporting on the status of a complex project, reporting on levels of customer happiness, or recounting the findings from a researcher who spoke at a conference or who published online. Such reports are matters of collecting mostly standard data, drawing its implications (for instance, exceeding or missing targets), and finding some accompanying details to make the reports interesting to the audience. Unfortunately, philosophy has gone down the same road with its typical cases of speaking truth: "Snow is white." "The cat is on the mat." These are, indeed, cases of truth seeking and saying, but they are weak in disclosure and poor in meaning. They do not have the wonder or joy of the rich, illuminating cases. Of course, we need to pass around true statements, but such statements should not be the exemplary cases of truth saying.

The story of Einstein's development of the theory of general relativity highlights exemplary truth seeking and saying. Initially, he started looking for a new truth that would bring electromagnetism and gravity together into a coherent new picture. The finding of such a truth is an aha moment. It is the truth of discovery. Then comes the truth of verification, which can take numerous shapes but gives confidence that the aha was about something real, not a delusion, not a form of phlogiston. Of course, we will make mistakes. Truth seeking itself does not promise that an ultimate truth will be found, even if there is such a thing. Nevertheless, once you have uncovered a new truth—that is, once you have found out through persistent and possibly uncomfortable inquiry *why* revenue is growing, *why* the customers like the product, *why* the sales force is underperforming—then you will want to compose your account of it so that you show both your truth-seeking virtue and your care for your audience.

The first thing masterpiece-creating leaders do based on these claims about the importance of truth seeking and saying is to change their status-reporting meetings. Turn the horses around. Give the most time to the new and especially surprising truths uncovered or getting uncovered. Ask, "What surprised you in doing the project?" Spend the minimal time necessary on the privative truths in reports of status and so forth. Get back the wonder of truth saying. Bezos did it by having his senior team members write short, six-page memos (no PowerPoints) about the new important things they were seeing. "We don't do PowerPoint (or any other slide-oriented) presentations at Amazon. Instead, we write narratively structured six-page memos. We silently read one at the beginning of each meeting in a kind of 'study hall.' Not surprisingly, the quality of these memos varies widely. Some have the clarity of angels singing. They are brilliant and thoughtful and set up the meeting for high-quality discussion. Sometimes they come in at the other end of the spectrum."[9] Bezos wanted reasoned insights. He wanted Einstein's truth of discovery. He did not want data collected into bullet points. Of course, we have observed that requiring such writing (and thinking) frequently produces grumbles and resistance: "I have not had to write like that since high school, and I hated it then." Masterpiece creators push through such grumbles.

Two refreshing quotations reinforce the importance of keeping truth seeking and saying front and center. Thomas Carlyle, the father of heroic leadership, writes: "First recognize what is true, we shall *then* discern what is false; and properly never till then."[10] Paraphrased: do not surrender to feel-good posturing; genuinely figure out with your interlocutor what each of you sees as true and why. Remember that seeking truth is superior to being right. And Nietzsche writes: "Truth is a woman" who will not allow herself ever to be won.[11] Rephrasing this metaphor in a nonsexist way, we can say that Nietzsche is advising us to approach looking for truth as a suitor—in good humor—and as a fallibilist whose vision is perspectival, based on a cultivated second nature. Indeed, we should think that the perspectival, second nature is surprisingly the source of our having any truth at all.[12] We need the taken-for-granted in order to have a stable ground upon which to conduct the vetting that will confirm something as true. Of course, we will likely never have all the truth, but that just means that masterpiece creation always continues.

Searching for the truth and speaking the truth will lead the masterpiece creator to moral risk-taking. To address the anomalies that masterpiece creators uncover in their truth seeking, masterpiece leaders deploy shocking practices and make their followers complicit in the deployment of those practices, and when the practices are successful (partly through luck), the leaders and followers turn those shocking practices into a new moral order. Churchill is a clear example. With the incalculably risky sacrifice of his own troops and his allies' troops, he created the moral order of total war against Nazism. Walker is another example. To create the feminine self-promotion of the 1920s—making oneself a masterpiece—she had to take the incalculable risk of betraying the woman who had helped her reshape her life.

This truth seeking and saying and moral risk-taking—both of which are essential for masterpiece creation—cut against the current moral norm of maintaining psychological safety. Psychological safety does not inspire the cultivation of unconditional responsibility or the courage to take a stand and a moral risk. Under the influence of the ethos of psychological safety, leaders, managers, and employees usually hesitate to take risks for what seems like the good reason of not having others' support. In chapter 2, we speculate on how Google has brilliantly managed the acrobatic act of maintaining psychological safety by making managers desperate for truth. In place of Google's acrobatic act, however, we encourage developing a Shakespearean warrior spirit—taking on outsize odds as Henry V did at Agincourt—and cultivating the courage necessary to take the risk and overcome the odds.

Developing an organizational culture, a moral-order-changing strategy, and an admirable leadership style are the key elements of masterpiece creation. The leader works on all three at the same time to create a complete masterpiece. In this review, however, we describe them individually and point to the interconnections.

The masterpiece-creating leader creates a pervasive unified organizational culture that has a particular mood and style. The mood tells people what matters—threats (in fear) or breakthroughs (in hope)—and the style says what kind of action is most highly valued in response to what matters—getting it perfectly right (with a perfectionist style) or making a brilliant trade-off (with a pragmatic style) or opening a new opportunity (with an opportunist style). To establish a new culture or strengthen an old, a masterpiece-creating leader designs and implements conveying practices. These practices are widely engaged in or observed throughout the organization, are dramatic, and provide clear financial and operational value when performed well. Typically, such practices are specialized forms of coming to resolution, performance evaluation, handoff, or celebration. Masterpiece-creating leaders work like artists to design practices, test and refine them with their senior teams, and then have them percolate down.

Masterpiece-creating leaders create competitive advantages by shifting the moral orders of their organizations, industries, and sometimes communities. A moral order has grounding norms, clarifying norms, and organizing norms. In the case of the recruitment industry that Julia Robertson entered, the grounding norm was getting temp employees into seats as quickly as possible; the clarifying norm was cost-saving calculativeness; and the organizing norm was pride in street smarts. Though a shift of only one of those grounding, clarifying, or organizing norms could shift the moral order sufficiently to obtain a competitive advantage, Julia Robertson is exemplary because she replaced each of the moral norms with three signal acts of moral risk-taking. She imposed promise management—people dutifully making and keeping promises—and terminated a star brand leader who did not comply. In her organization of admiration and development, such an act of termination was unthinkable, but its force established promise making as a grounding norm that would replace just getting people into positions as quickly as possible. Likewise, she established "high-road" practice as the clarifying norm: recruiters, temp employees, and clients would go the extra mile to help each other and the end customers. Again, it took the shocking termination of her heir apparent to establish this as the clarifying moral norm of Impellam in place of cost-saving calculativeness. Finally, she hired a rigorous CFO to go through financial reports painstakingly to find and then eliminate all the scheming, street-smart ways of earning money outside of high-road practice. She found that practices such as paying temp employees holiday benefits only if they asked for them were endemic. Robertson replaced the organizing norm of pride in street smarts to pride in making morally good profits from high-road practices.

To achieve the change in her company's moral order and then expand it to cover the industry, Robertson had to institute a war-room practice where her brand leaders together examined their numbers weekly. Thus, while maintaining a mood of admiration, she shifted the organization's style from development to pragmatism. Although she did not abandon her developmental, nurturing leadership style, she put it in tension with her organization (a discordia concors) and had to redefine development within her own organization as stretching brand leaders to become virtuosos at balancing the concerns of temps, recruiters, and clients.

Making an organization a masterpiece rewards leaders because in the process they are creating an organization that suits, stretches, and evolves their personal leadership style. Masterpiece-creating leaders understand themselves in terms of the stories of their accomplishments and virtues. Those accomplishments and virtues make the leaders who they are. They know, too, that their stories and virtues can become traps. In what superficially seemed like a successful organization, Jessica, our modest, hardworking leader, saw that her management team was taking advantage of her hard work to slack off. This happens regularly. People easily fall into taking advantage of the virtuous among them. The wise leader's team looks to the leader to solve all tough problems. The nurturing leader's team begins to seek unnecessary handholding. The courageous leader's team waits for the leader to act. Hence, leaders must become clear about their foundational stories (the way they overcame events and thus fashioned themselves) and then through daily inquisition uncover when the virtues of that story no longer serve. They then develop a poetic image of themselves that allows them to distance themselves from themselves and then find a new image to embrace as they uncover new virtues. In our account of Jessica, she went from the oppressed librarian from *The Music Man* to the joyful feast creator Babette from *Babette's Feast*. (Jessica created operational meetings that were like feasts.) In doing so, she transformed her organizational culture from admiration with a style of collegiality to a culture of joy with a style of opportunism. And as such changes require changes in strategy, she took the moral risks of removing highly profitable managers, closing profitable offices, and purchasing a dangerous competitor to set up a moral order with a grounding norm of joyful diligence, a clarifying norm of profitable growth of the whole rather than of each branch, and an organizing norm of providing a range of customer experiences rather than only high-touch service with every customer. Thus, in masterpiece organizations, culture, strategy, and leadership styles are intertwined, draw admiration, and enable good lives. As leaders create increasing numbers of masterpiece organizations, we will find ourselves in a world of multiple admirable moral orders. We may embrace only one, but we can admire others while condemning, we hope, only a few.

Have We Re-created Authoritarian, Charismatic, Top-Down Leadership?

Today's management thinking is all about empowering people throughout the organization. Leadership, we are told, happens in conversation with multiple parties, not just a conversation led by a formal leader. Leadership bubbles up; it is distributed, as the business-school jargon has it. We disagree with such a view because it misunderstands the most critical feature of leadership: the taking of moral risks to reform moral orders. We have suggested, therefore, that leaders—those we conventionally understand as formal leaders—face the challenge of turning their organizations and leadership styles into masterpieces through moral risk-taking. Such moral risk-taking happens all over an organization but is manifested most clearly and in its largest dimension from the top. Because moral risk-taking does not arise from a vote or consensus, it seems autocratic. Because followers feel complicit, the leadership appears charismatic. Although all these claims are correct, they miss what is truest about postmodernity's masterpiece-creating leaders and what sets them apart from modernity's authoritarian, charismatic leadership.

For brevity's and authenticity's sake, let us turn to the source and strongest advocate of authoritarian, charismatic, heroic leadership, the Victorian Era's Thomas Carlyle. For Carlyle, the flow of history continually depends on, as a Victorian would say, great *men*. They (he includes women) are the ones who take us out of confusion to reality.[13] He provides, in the clearest way, the essential core of thinking about heroic, hierarchical, autocratic, charismatic leadership in writing about kingship *loosely* understood. (His two lead examples, Cromwell and Napoleon, were in fact not kings.)

> We come now to the last form of Heroism; that which we call Kingship. The Commander over Men; he to whose will our wills are to be subordinated, and loyally surrender themselves, and find their welfare in doing so, may be reckoned the most important of Great Men. He is practically the summary for us of *all* the various figures of Heroism; Priest, Teacher, whatsoever of earthly or of spiritual dignity we can fancy to reside in man, embodies itself here, to *command* over us, to furnish us with constant practical teaching, to tell us for the day and hour what we are to *do*. He is called *Rex*, Regulator, *Roi:* our own name is still better; King *Könning*, which means *Can*-ning, Able-man. . . . The Ablest Man; he means also the truest-hearted, justest, the Noblest Man: what he *tells us to do* must be precisely the wisest, fittest, that we could anywhere or anyhow learn; . . . that were the ideal.[14]

We can hear echoes of Plato's philosopher king and of the church fathers on Christian magistrates. We can also plainly hear the gendered, classicist assumptions. However, Carlyle gives us the core insights about the heroic, top-down leadership that remains in place today. The leader in the ideal case is all-knowing. We can think of the owner-managers of small businesses who have weathered numerous storms, know their customers and suppliers personally, and can name each member of their teams. Today, we see this in the top practitioner who leads certain medical teams. In any organization where the primary challenges are technical—think of fire crews, military units, police units—such a technically all-knowing leader makes sense.

No one in Queen Victoria's England, however, could have been so wise as to rule the British Empire as a philosopher king. Carlyle knew that, but he thought we needed such an ideal. Only with such hero worship, where we see the spark of divinity in our "brother," could we continue seeking truth and honor other moral norms. Under that circumstance, we would have reason to believe that there is truth and goodness on earth.[15] How much damage Carlyle's ideal leader has caused, we do not know. Carlyle's great-man theory motivated thinking that gender, race, and IQ yielded "great men." But Carlyle's account goes deeper than those reductive barbarisms as he seeks to explain why we follow a leader. He wants to identify the leader's charisma (we use the term following Weber).

Leaders, he says, have divine charisma: "Whatever man you chose to lay hold of . . . and called King,—there straightaway came to reside a divine virtue." Carlyle then goes on to give us the source of the divine virtue: "There is no act more moral between men than that of rule and obedience. Woe to him that claims obedience when it is not due; woe to him that refuses it when it is! God's law is in that."[16] Why obedience? If someone draws us out of confusion and shows us the right thing to do and does it regularly—as does the knowing person—then we feel awe. Within modernity (not postmodernity) and before it, our response to awe was obedience. Obedience was the bedrock and ethical micropractice that grounded heroic leadership.

Our masterpiece-creating leaders are not know-it-alls, nor is obedience their due. Their achievements depend on moral luck guided by sensitivity to a mysterious moral anomaly and by their perspectival, fallibilist truth seeking, moral imaginations, and practical wisdom. To identify the ethical micropractices that our masterpiece-creating leaders depend on and sustain in their leadership, we return to the philosopher Bernard Williams, who introduced the concept of moral luck. For Williams, our responsibility for the effects of our actions (or the lack thereof) stems from our involvement with others.[17] We are so profoundly connected with each other in our community that if we harm someone, even unintentionally, we are morally responsible. Given that insight alone, we could imagine the involvement we have with each other to be a low-grade responsibility for the welfare of immediate neighbors and no more. However, we can see that Williams likely thinks it is more, and we definitely think it is more, particularly if we return to his related notion of *gratitude*.

In the Gauguin case, we give Gauguin a pass for abandoning his family because of the gratitude we feel for his great art, which changed us for the better. This gratitude has a moral character because it offsets moral wrongs, just as choosing the lesser evil would. Starting from the Gauguin story, that gratitude we feel toward Gauguin extends more broadly to Western culture, which made Gaugin's painting possible, and to Eastern cultures for inspiring him. Similarly, we are grateful not only to those scientists who made the COVID-19 vaccine possible at such short notice but also to science at large and the modern, global institutions that underpin science. Our community is wide, not just our immediate neighborhood. Our involvement in it, while not precisely defined, covers a potentially extensive range.

Accordingly, this involvement with a broad community raises the question of its nature. Is the involvement fully expressed in the minimal mandate to feel friendly warmth and do no harm? In the world Williams tells us we inhabit, we think the mandate cannot be so thin, and his account of gratitude tells us more. If gratitude makes us complicit and offsets simple as well as large-scale moral wrongs, then it is not something that we feel only in extraordinary circumstances. Indeed, for most of this book we have been saying that moral risk-taking and small changes in moral orders happen regularly. We raise the level of customer care so that past actions are now wrong. We tell people something that is important but that might injure their spirits. Moral risk-taking happens on the level of micropractices, and when we are successful, feelings and expressions of gratitude happen there as well. That is the nature of our involvement with each other and with larger communities. That is why admiration is key. Obedience is not our master. We are living in a noncloistered gray area where we seek to become worthy of gratitude.[18]

Can we bring ourselves to believe that a world built on gratitude is the world we live in?[19] To do things worthy of gratitude, people must do something that goes beyond following moral norms. They must take micro-moral risks, such as pushing their neighbor out of their comfort zone, creating bridges to neighbors who are quite different from them, spotting and telling uncomfortable truths. In such a culture, neighbors ask themselves in the evening whether they challenged their own or someone else's emotion too strongly or not enough, invaded a privacy or did not go far enough, spoke truth too bluntly or too softly, evaluated too fiercely or too sweetly, pushed too hard or too little. In short, they are exercising a mild version of the interrogation that goes with developing one's leaderly style into a masterpiece. These skills are valuable when moral norms change, which happens when people live any of Nietzsche's good lives: refining a style, entering and leaving brief lives, taking risks, or improvising.

Why do we admire such lives? We do so because we feel gratitude for the wonder they bring us, and we admire masterpiece creators as paragons who bring wonder in their successful moral risk-taking and in the new lives and new moral orders they create. Masterpiece creators produce moments of admiration and gratitude in a world where otherwise we can criticize everything.

Where does this leave us in comparing old-style heroic leaders with masterpiece-creating leaders? The most profound worry about top-down, heroic, authoritarian, charismatic leadership, no matter how refined it is, is that it treats nonleaders as obedient order takers. Obedience is the core practice on which older heroic leadership depended and supported. Our masterpiece-creating leaders are like the older heroic leaders in that they need positions of authority to act for whole organizations and therefore to change the moral order of those organizations. But the analogy stops there. For all their similarities, heroic leadership and masterpiece-creating leadership are rooted in different worlds. Our masterpiece-creating leaders do not expect obedience. Authority gives them added responsibility, not privileges. They do not ask for sycophancy but put their heads on the block. They are not so much heroic as worthy of admiration so far as they take moral risks guided by moral imagination and practical wisdom. They are not know-it-alls. They depend on luck for their success but nevertheless assume full responsibility for the consequences, whether good or evil. Their moral risk-taking might seem authoritarian because they must act without consenting votes and without full understanding behind them. But they do not require obedience. They expect gratitude and admiration if they succeed and condemnation with some leniency if they fail. Gratitude is key. It is a fantasy to believe we can overcome the economy of obedience with anything less than an economy of gratitude. Authenticity, compassion, vulnerability, empathy, candor, and consensus seeking are hobbles. Let Yeats guide us. Do not feed on those fantasies. Our hearts will become brutal herd hearts. Let us open our hearts to courageous, truth seeking and moral risk-taking and then to the economy of gratitude that follows.

Are we not too demanding when we ask leaders to aspire to the greatness of masterpiece creators? How realistic is such an expectation? True, leaders such as Churchill, Walker, Bezos, Dalio, Roddick, and Robertson are hard acts to follow. Does our thesis apply to more ordinary leaders, those who are humble enough to know that, although they may not be a Churchill, Walker, Bezos, Dalio, or Roddick, they are nonetheless well intended and determined to become good leaders? We think it does. These more ordinary leaders face moral anomalies that require moral risk-taking whenever they make improvements that will produce even slight changes in the moral order. They will have to terminate those faithful employees who cannot make the change. As the moral philosopher Martha Nussbaum remarked in an interview, one does not have to be King Agamemnon to face moral conflict, just as one does not have to be Othello to experience self-inflicted tragedy.[20] Tragic, dramatic, or high-profile cases remind us—all of us—of what "we know and do not acknowledge."[21] Any leader who tries to effect an organizational cultural change will break with the norms of the old culture and will face some sort of moral risk.

Let us take our moral risks as Churchill did. Though he directed the bombing of civilians, he also regularly worried about whether the bombing was going too far: "Are we beasts?"[22] That worry and our response to it count as the best preventions of evil. Kierkegaard concluded similarly. He expected that his knights of faith would experience "fear and trembling" at the unethical content of their acts (Abraham sacrificing Isaac).[23] Churchill's physical sickness after giving the Calais order would count as such trembling.[24]

We will have better leaders if they genuinely understand that moral risk-taking is at the core of their role, and so we recommend leadership training that develops conscience, practical wisdom, and what Rowan Williams, the former archbishop of Canterbury, aptly calls "a tragic imagination."[25] "The tragic imagination," he notes, "insists that we remain alert to the possibility that we are already incubating seeds of destruction; that our habitual discourse with ourselves as well as with others may already have set us on a path that will consume us."[26] There are no guarantees or reassurances that moral failure will not come about when one takes moral risks.[27] As the example of Andrew Fastow shows, our very capacity to identify moral anomalies and respond to them will always also tempt us to fall for the seduction of the anomaly. Masterpiece creators are always in a moral struggle. What is critical is that these leaders do not refrain from asking themselves each day, along with the other questions about style, the perennial Socratic question: "Am I doing the right thing?"[28]

Our Call to Action

We are grateful to all leaders and scholars whose insights we draw on in this book. We hope that what we have offered will help you to create masterpieces of business and scholarship for which others and we will express grateful admiration. Toward that purpose, we end with an exhortation. Manage moods; manifest your virtues; listen for difference; seek and speak truth; find anomalies and take moral risks to resolve them; build a culture with a positive mood and a clear style; organize your moral risk-taking to change your company's and industry's moral order; and continuously work on the masterpiece that is your style of leadership. May you create and maintain your masterpiece as a beautiful city-state and dwell in admiration steeped in gratitude, and may people sing your song forever.

Acknowledgments

Charles thanks his formative university teachers, Lionel Trilling, Ann Douglas, Steven Knapp, Thomas Barnes, Joel Fineman, Joel Altman, and, of course, Bert Dreyfus. He thanks Fernando Flores, Chauncey Bell, Luis Sota, and Chris Davis for introducing him to management consulting. His former business partner, Maria Flores Letelier, taught him how to run a business. Professors Bobby Calder and Don Sull taught him how to write on business. Special thanks go to Billy Glennon, CEO of VISION, who collaborated with Charles and gave him the stage to test many of the lessons explored in this book. Special thanks to Reena Sequeira, Anna Fidler, and Joanna Bielecka, who stood front and center in workshops and then in coaching leaders on the book's claims. In addition, the VISION LinkedIn site posted several short blogs that included the nascent ideas that now find mature expression in the first five chapters of the book. Sean Kelly of Harvard and B. Scot Rousse of Pluralistic Networks have acted as outside thought partners. Special thanks also go to Chris Davis, who codeveloped and cowrote chapter 7 with the other authors. Chris's company Stratam has taken the lead in helping clients make their cultures into masterpieces. Charles thanks his diverse clients over the years. Their stories form the threads that make up the fabric of this book. For their editorial support, Charles thanks Christopher Michaelson of the *Journal of Business Ethics*; David Musson, former senior editor at Oxford University Press; the anonymous reviewers for the MIT Press; and especially editors Phil Laughlin and Ginny Crossman of the MIT Press. Last, Charles thanks his coauthors and his family, Nancy and Adam.

Matt's view on the importance of the anomalous to human existence was first inspired by listening to the great existential phenomenological psychiatrist R. D. Laing speak while at Durham University in the late 1980s. Matt is grateful to the late David Kleinman at Durham for introducing him to Laing and for broadening his appreciation of what it might mean to be a psychologist, to the late Bert Dreyfus for their conversations until Bert's untimely passing in 2017 and for introducing him to Charles Spinosa, and to Charles for many years of searching inquiry and learning. From his time at the University of Essex, Matt thanks Steffen Böhm for introducing him to Lacanian thought in the context of business, Patrice Maniglier for supporting his exploration of Heidegger and Alain Badiou, and Mark Wrathall, Katharina Kaiser, Joseph Rouse, the late Mari Ruti, and B. Scot Rousse for ongoing conversations about Heidegger, practices, and the self. Matt is grateful to the psychoanalyst Anthony Stadlen for practical supervision in Daseinsanalysis. Matt also thanks colleagues and clients Michael Samuels, David Hindson, Stewart Oades, Bill Torbert, Karen Ellis, Bridget McIntyre, Paul Hirst, Chauncey Bell, Guillermo Wechsler, Fernando Flores, Richard Bradford, and Julia Robertson. Finally, Matt thanks his coauthors and his family—Alison, Jacob-Juriaan, Nina-Marit, Lucas, and Anna.

Haridimos owes a great deal of his training in philosophy to Richard Whitley's pioneering epistemology course at the Manchester Business School when he was a doctoral student. At Manchester, Stafford Beer introduced him to cybernetic and systems thinking, which took off for him later through his encounter with complexity science. Fascinated by Karl Weick's aphorism "complicate yourself," Haridimos has long sought complex ways of understanding in management and organization studies, a search that has taken him to virtue ethics, process philosophy, phenomenology, Wittgenstein, and pragmatism. His encounters with the late John Shotter, Bert Dreyfus, and Charles Spinosa were important for shaping his thinking from Wittgensteinian and Heideggerian perspectives. Although not a philosopher, he cannot help but see everything, especially leadership, from a philosophical angle. Haridimos is grateful to his coauthors for their unfailing intellectual stimulation and excellent cooperation. His wife, Efi, and his daughters, Maria Anna and Fotini, have been an unfailing source of support, for which he is grateful.

Notes

Preface

1. Robert Jackall has it both ways: leaders "establish different frameworks," "occupational ethics," "specific situational moralities," and "moral rules-in-use" but corporate ethics are narcissistic forms of helping friends and hurting enemies. Jackall's leaders have the morality of courtiers in corrupt Renaissance courts. Thus, corporate leaders' morality making is based on their "self-images and temperaments," not on their hard-won understanding of what is true about customers and employees and therefore the right way to treat them. In short, Jackall's managers are "narcissistic" self-aggrandizers. We agree that Jackall's findings cover organizations trapped in shared organizational moods of resentment, resignation, fear, and arrogance. We say a little about such moods in chapter 7, but only a little because no masterpiece organization can remain trapped in any of those moods. See Robert Jackall, *Moral Mazes: The World of Corporate Managers* (Oxford: Oxford University Press, 1988), 4, 35, 192, 203–204.

2. Lucius Annaeus Seneca, "On Providence," in *Seneca: Dialogues and Essays,* trans. John Davie (Oxford: Oxford University Press, 2008), 3–17.

3. Ernest Gellner, *Conditions of Liberty: Civil Society and Its Rivals* (London: Penguin, 1994), 97.

4. John Milton's classic expression of the thought is, "And perhaps this is that doom which Adam fell into of knowing good and evil, that is to say of knowing good by evil." See John Milton, *Areopagitica*, in *Areopagitica and Other Writings*, ed. William Poole (London: Penguin, 2014), 111.

5. Quoted in Martin Heidegger, "The Question Concerning Technology," in *The Question Concerning Technology and Other Essays*, trans. and ed. William Lovitt (New York: Harper & Row, 1977), 34.

6. Martin Heidegger, "The Word of Nietzsche," in *The Question Concerning Technology and Other Essays*, 64.

Introduction

1. Jacob Burckhardt, *The Civilization of the Renaissance in Italy* (New York: Barnes & Noble, 1999). In the academic literature, Donna Ladkin has seen the importance of the aesthetic in understanding and evaluating leadership. See Donna Ladkin, "Leading Beautifully: How Mastery, Congruence and Purpose Create the Aesthetic of Embodied Leadership Practice," *Leadership Quarterly* 19 (2008): 31–41. Whereas Ladkin adopts a Platonic aesthetic, we draw on a Renaissance one with more disharmony. We also note earlier work on aesthetic leadership and organizations that focuses on artfulness, aesthetic sensibility, the treatment of employees like creatives, and so forth but does not bring out, as the rulers of Italian Renaissance did, the crucial nature of moral risk-taking in creating masterpiece organizations. See, for example, Antonio Strati, *Organization and Aesthetics* (London: Sage, 1999); the collection of articles in Majken Schultz, Mary Jo Hatch, and Mogens Holten Larsen, eds., *The Expressive Organization: Linking Identity, Reputation, and the Corporate Brand* (Oxford: Oxford University Press, 2000); and Rob Austin and Lee Devin, *Artful Making: What Managers Need to Know about How Artists Work* (Upper Saddle River, NJ: Financial Times, Prentice-Hall, 2003). Pierre Guillet de Monthoux comes close to the importance of moral risk-taking in *The Art Firm: Aesthetic Management and Metaphysical Marketing* (Stanford, CA: Stanford University Press, 2004).

2. Niccolò Machiavelli, *The Prince*, in *The Essential Writings of Machiavelli*, ed. and trans. Peter Constantine (New York: Modern Library, 2007), 5–100.

3. Niccolò Machiavelli, *The Discourses*, ed. Bernard Crick, trans. Leslie J. Walker, SJ, (Harmondsworth, UK: Penguin, 1970), I.45, pp. 221–222.

4. On the issue of Machiavelli's morality, we side with Isaiah Berlin in seeing Machiavelli as embracing pagan morality with its values of "courage, vigour, fortitude in adversity, public achievement, order, discipline, happiness, strength, justice, above all assertion of one's proper claims and the knowledge and power needed to secure their satisfaction [virtù]," while setting aside the Christian values of "charity, mercy, sacrifice, love of God, forgiveness of enemies, contempt for the goods of this world, faith in the life hereafter, belief in the salvation of the individual soul being of incomparable value." See Isaiah Berlin, "The Originality of Machiavelli," in *Against the Current: Essays in the History of Ideas*, ed. Henry Hardy (Princeton, NJ: Princeton University Press, 1955), 58. We also agree with Berlin that Machiavelli embraced pagan virtues for the sake of state building without rejecting the idea that Christian virtues might well lead to Christian salvation. As Machiavelli said, he loved Florence more than his own soul (Berlin, "The Originality of Machiavelli," 68). Accepting that there were two incompatible moral systems (and implicitly that there could be more) is what Berlin says makes Machiavelli frightening (*erschreckend*) (72, 84). In contemplating a multiplicity of incompatible moral systems, Machiavelli anticipates both Berlin and us.

5. In *The Discourses*, Machiavelli writes: "The virtue of the builder is discernible in the fortune of what was built, for the city is more or less remarkable according as he is more or less virtuous who is responsible for the start. The virtue shows itself in two ways: first in the choice of a site, and secondly in the drawing up of laws" (I.1, p. 102). Following up, he says, "Laws make [men] good" (I.3, p. 112).

6. One of Machiavelli's most original achievements was to see that the success of the Roman Republic depended on a grand discordia concors, strife between the Senate and the people. See Machiavelli, *Discourses*, I.4, pp. 113–114.

7. See Jeff Bezos, *Invent and Wander: The Collected Writings of Jeff Bezos* (Boston: Harvard Business Review Press, 2021), and Brad Stone, *The Everything Store: Jeff Bezos and the Age of Amazon* (London: Transworld, 2013).

8. There has been some development here. The United Kingdom has launched an MBA-style course for small and medium-size enterprises. See Jonathan Moules, "A Mini-MBA Course Designed to Transform British Business," *Financial Times*, June 2, 2021, https://www.ft.com/content/a67ab910-b53e-4eeb-9e5a-c055d435cb65. Oxford has established family-business courses. See "Transforming Family Businesses: Choosing Your Path," Saïd Business School, Oxford University, n.d., https://www .sbs.ox.ac.uk/programmes/executive-education/campus-open-programmes/trans forming-family-businesses-choosing-your-path/download-brochure. The Institut euro-péen d'administration des affaires (INSEAD) has a similar program. See INSEAD, "Entrepreneurship & Family Business Programmes," n.d., https://www.insead.edu /executive-education/entrepreneurship-family-business. See also Universität Leipzig, "MBA in Small and Medium-Sized Enterprise Development," n.d., https://www.wifa .uni-leipzig.de/fileadmin/Fakultät_Wifa/Sept_Center/Dateien/MBA_Downloads /2021_MBA_Broschure.pdf.

9. Here we are supplying what we consider to be the commonsense distinctions among the various kinds of norms that are relevant to the arguments in this book. Philosophers speculate about the nature of the differences between "moral norms" and "conventional norms." Much of the debate goes to the ontological nature of morality (what kind of being does it have). Is morality from God, from reason, from nature, or merely from heightened convention? We leave that issue aside. Our view comes from our interpretation of Bernard Williams, who claims that the norms people follow to have a good life are as moral and intertwined with the norms people have for not mistreating others. For more on the debates, see Edouard Mach-ery and Stephen Stich, "The Moral/Conventional Distinction," Stanford Encyclope-dia of Philosophy Archive, Summer 2022 ed., June 8, 2022, https://plato.stanford .edu/archives/sum2022/entries/moral-conventional/. Moreover, though we leave "aesthetic norms" under the heading of "conventional norms," we point out that moral norms generally come with associated aesthetic norms. It is surely not a coin-cidence that the modern subject's norm of autonomy came with an appreciation of novels and biographies with central characters figuring out what to do in everyday

life or with the bold, vivid, human figures of Renaissance art. Likewise, the ancient world's high moral evaluation of contest gets readily figured forth in epics filled with both warriors' exploits and speeches contesting against other speeches. Arguably, in our postmodern time, when people no longer see themselves in such resonant traditions, they find their expression of themselves in the thrilling, safe, peak moments of video games. We make these remarks about the association of aesthetic norms with moral norms because we expect that as leaders create morally distinct, admirable organizations, their organizations will also develop their own admirable aesthetics. Consider, again, the palaces lining the streets of Genoa or Venice.

10. Stone, *The Everything Store*, 61.

11. For examples of these moral differences, see Machery and Stich, "The Moral/ Conventional Distinction."

12. Stone, *The Everything Store*, 20–21, 61, 85.

13. In making this claim, we are leaning on Bernard Williams, "Postscript," in *Moral Luck*, ed. Daniel Statman (Albany: State University of New York Press, 1993), 251–258.

14. See Alexis de Tocqueville, *Democracy in America and Two Essays on America*, trans. Gerald E. Bevan, with notes by Isaac Kramnick (New York: Penguin, 2003), and Robert D. Putnam, *Bowling Along, Revised and Updated: The Collapse and Revival of American Community* (New York: Simon & Schuster, 2020).

15. High-design companies have mold breaking as a normal activity. As such, they are a category of their own, and leaders of these companies do not see themselves as servants of stakeholders. Consider great Italian companies such as Olivetti (founded 1909) and Illy Caffe (1933), the car company owner-designers Agnelli and Pininfarina, and Coventry car industry figures such as Captain Sir John Black and William Lyons. For academic studies, see Antonio Strati, "Beauty of Responsible Management: The Lens and Methodology of Organizational Aesthetics," in *The Research Handbook of Responsible Management*, ed. Oliver Laasch, Roy Suddaby, Peter B. Gustavson, R. Edward Freeman, and Dimi Jamali (Cheltenham, UK: Edward Elgar, 2019), where Strati writes on Olivetti. See also de Monthoux on Wagner in *The Art Firm*.

16. In fact, this is not quite what Friedman said. Though the title of the article misleads, Friedman is quite clear that he is thinking in terms of property law and that the senior managers are agents for the owners and should fulfill the owners' desires, which are only *generally* to make money. See Milton Friedman, "A Friedman Doctrine—the Social Responsibility of Business Is to Increase Its Profits," *New York Times*, September 13, 1970, https://www.nytimes.com/1970/09/13/archives/a -friedman-doctrine-the-social-responsibility-of-business-is-to.html.

17. In our usage of the term *anomaly*, we are inspired by Charles Spinosa, Fernando Flores, and Hubert L. Dreyfus, *Disclosing New Worlds: Entrepreneurship, Democratic*

Action, and the Cultivation of Solidarity (Cambridge, MA: MIT Press, 1997), which in turn was inspired by Thomas Kuhn's notion of anomalies, laid out in Thomas Kuhn, *The Structure of Scientific Revolutions* (Chicago: University of Chicago Press, 1970). For Kuhn, anomalies were puzzles that the current resources of science could not solve. Their solution required a new paradigm of key concepts and practices for doing science, such as moving from Aristotelian to Galilean physics to understand the trajectory of bullets. *Disclosing New Worlds* and works published after it speak about anomalous marginal practices that some leaders, activists, or artists felt puzzlingly obliged to engage in on certain occasions but that the dominant culture trivialized. A simple example was the disposal of worn-out objects. It was trivial but important. By clinging to this oddness, King Gillette made "disposability" an essential part of his famous product, the disposable razor blade, and, with that, disposability has become a dominant feature of things. Moral anomalies are irresolvable puzzles under one moral order (as in Kuhn's paradigm) but are generally resolved by drawing on a morally shocking marginal practice (and thus like the anomalies discussed in *Disclosing New Worlds*). Of course, there are also practical and conventional anomalies for which no action that is conventionally or practically right will produce a desired conventional or practical outcome. Henry Kissinger, Francesca Gino, and Joseph L. Badaracco Jr. write about them persuasively. See Henry Kissinger, *Leadership: Six Studies in World Strategy* (New York: Penguin, 2022); Francesca Gino, *Rebel Talent: Why It Pays to Break the Rules at Work and in Life* (New York: Dey St., 2018); and Joseph L. Badaracco Jr., *Defining Moments: When Managers Must Choose between Right and Right* (Boston: Harvard Business School Press, 1997).

Chapter 1

1. The details of this account of Churchill in 1940 come primarily from Andrew Roberts, *Churchill: Walking with Destiny* (New York: Viking, 2018), 187–230, 494–574, supplemented by Winston Churchill, *Memoirs of the Second World War* (Boston: Houghton Mifflin, 1959), 274–333.

2. For more detail on the Churchill case and the change in moral norms that he instituted, see Charles Spinosa, Matthew Hancocks, Haridimos Tsoukas, and Billy Glennon, "Beyond Rational Persuasion: How Leaders Change Moral Norms," *Journal of Business Ethics* 184 (2023): 589–603, https://link.springer.com/article/10.1007/s10551-022-05149-3.

3. Churchill, *Memoirs of the Second World War*, 333.

4. Quoted in A'Lelia Bundles, *On Her Own Ground: The Life and Times of Madam C. J. Walker* (New York: Scribner's, 2001), 230, 231. At the time of the speech, Walker had about 10,000 sales agents (Bundles, *On Her Own Ground*, 179).

5. Bundles, *On Her Own Ground*, 49.

6. "Tuskegee University," Wikipedia, last edited December 14, 2022, https://en.wikipedia.org/wiki/Tuskegee_University.

7. Bundles, *On Her Own Ground*, 121.

8. Quoted in "Helena Rubinstein," Wikipedia, last edited November 16, 2022, https://en.wikipedia.org/wiki/Helena_Rubinstein.

9. Bundles, *On Her Own Ground*, 61.

10. Bundles, *On Her Own Ground*, 68, 124–136.

11. Bundles, *On Her Own Ground*, 178–179.

12. Bundles, *On Her Own Ground*, 60–61, 65.

13. "Annie Turnbo Malone," Wikipedia, last edited October 27, 2022, https://en.wikipedia.org/wiki/Annie_Turnbo_Malone.

14. Bundles, *On Her Own Ground*, 64–66, 86–91.

15. Quoted in Bundles, *On Her Own Ground*, 65.

16. Bundles, *On Her Own Ground*, 60.

17. Bundles, *On Her Own Ground*, 81–82, 89.

18. Bundles, *On Her Own Ground*, 88.

19. Bundles, *On Her Own Ground*, 137–139. Note in chapter 8 the similar challenge to growth that Anita Roddick faced.

20. Bundles, *On Her Own Ground*, 138–139.

21. "Annie Turnbo Malone," Wikipedia.

22. Bundles, *On Her Own Ground*, 184–187, 236–243, 274, 186, 117, 269–270.

23. Bundles, *On Her Own Ground*, 198, 221, 233, 235, 210.

24. Erica L. Ball, *Madam C. J. Walker: The Making of an American Icon* (Lanham, MD: Rowman and Littlefield, 2021), 72, xii, 75–93, 95–96.

25. Ball calls Walker an icon rather than a masterpiece: "Madam Walker must be considered an American icon"; she "ultimately created and embodied new ways of being for black women in the United States" (*Madam C. J. Walker*, xii). Ball's account of Walker's "self-fashioning" is like ours. However, Ball focuses more on the development of Walker's celebrity and the way she used advertising to shift moral views regarding how Black American women could make themselves beautiful (*Madam C. J. Walker*, 41, 49–56). We focus on the moral anomaly Walker faced and how in overcoming it she transformed conventional self-promotion into fashioning the self as a masterpiece and then making it so that such self-fashioning (at least for

the 1920s) was the destiny of "every woman of pride" (quoted in Ball, *Madam C. J. Walker*, 55).

26. Bundles, *On Her Own Ground*, 279, 280, 16. A'Lelia Walker was clearly celebrated in the fictional character Adora Boniface in Carl Van Vechten's best-selling and controversial novel *Ni**er Heaven* (1926).

27. Ball, *Madam C. J. Walker*, 121.

28. Nancy F. Koehn, Erica Helms, Katherine Miller, and Rachel K. Wilcox, *Oprah Winfrey* (Boston: Harvard Business School, 2009), 14.

29. Koehn et al., *Oprah Winfrey*, 15.

30. Oprah Winfrey works hard and spends a lot of money to keep private those parts of her life that she draws on in her revelations. She controls the narrative. Consequently, writing her biography is difficult. But Kitty Kelly has much evidence that Winfrey gives accounts that will appeal to her audience rather than show what really happened. Winfrey's cousin Katharine Carr Esters has this to say about the revelation of sexual abuse Winfrey used to get early national attention: "That story helped launch Oprah and make her what she is today. I don't hold with telling lies, but in this case I forgive Oprah because she has done so much for other people. Maybe this was the only way for a poor child to succeed and become rich. . . . Her audiences may believe her stories. Her family does not" (quoted in Kitty Kelley, *Oprah: A Biography* [New York: Three Rivers Press, 2010], 37). Esters excuses this act of moral risk-taking. We discuss later Nietzsche's good life through giving oneself a style. Oprah Winfrey, according to Kelly's account, fits it to a tee. Her life is artifice inextricably mixed with nature.

31. Robert C. H. Chia and Robin Holt, *Strategy without Design: The Silent Efficacy of Indirect Action* (Cambridge: Cambridge University Press, 2009).

32. Thus, we distinguish our claim from the literature that treats corporate assholes, jerks, psychopaths, narcissists, borderline personalities, and schizophrenics. On the latter, see, for instance, Paul Babiak and Robert D. Hare, *Snakes in Suits: When Psychopaths Go to Work* (New York: Harper Business, 2006); M. E Thomas, *Confessions of a Sociopath: A Life Spent Hiding in Plain Sight* (New York: Broadway Books, 2013); Kevin Dutton, *The Wisdom of Psychopaths: What Saints, Spies, and Serial Killers Can Teach Us about Success* (New York: Scientific American and Farrar, Straus and Giroux, 2013); Michael Maccoby, *The Productive Narcissist: The Promise and Peril of Visionary Leaders* (New York: Broadway Books, 2003); Bill Eddy, *5 Types of People Who Can Ruin Your Life: Identifying and Dealing with Narcissists, Sociopaths, and Other High-Conflict Personalities* (New York: Penguin, 2018). Masterpiece creators take shocking actions in response to moral anomalies. Shocking responses to everyday problems might come from various sources, including those cited here.

33. Stone, *The Everything Store*, 83–85.

34. Ray Dalio, *Principles* (New York: Simon & Schuster, 2017), 34.

35. Anita Roddick, *Body and Soul* (New York: Crown Trade, 1991), 217, 86.

36. Phil Knight, *Shoe Dog* (New York: Scribner, 2016), 364.

37. See Dalio, *Principles*.

38. See William D. Cohan, *Power Failure: The Rise and Fall of General Electric* (New York: Allen Lane, 2022).

39. Robert Slater, *Jack Welch & the G.E. Way: Management Insights and Leadership Secrets of the Legendary CEO* (New York: McGraw Hill, 1998); Jack Welch, with Suzy Welch, *Winning: The Ultimate Business How-to Book* (New York: HarperLuxe, 2005); Roddick, *Body and Soul*.

40. Reed Hastings and Erin Meyer, *No Rules Rules: Netflix and the Culture of Reinvention* (New York: Penguin, 2020).

41. Consider Robert I. Sutton, *The No Asshole Rule: Building a Civilized Workplace and Surviving One That Isn't* (New York: Business Pluss-Hachette, 2010).

42. See Walter Isaacson, *Steve Jobs* (New York: Simon & Schuster, 2011), 117–124. Isaacson is blunt: "Was all of [Jobs's] stormy and abusive behavior necessary? Probably not, nor was it justified" (123–124). In an added afterword written 10 years after the original biography, Isaacson notes that he came to see that Jobs's nastiness, his brutal honesty, was key to his success. But Isaacson thinks this shocking behavior a matter of intertwined personality traits rather than moral risk-taking: "The issue is not simply whether we can balance respect for a person's achievements with disapproval for their flaws. The more complex issue is whether the achievements and the flaws are connected. . . . If Steve Jobs had been predisposed to be kinder and gentler, would he have had the passion that allowed him to bend reality and push people to realize their full potential? A person's good traits and bad traits are often intertwined like a double helix. It may not be possible to pluck out the unpleasant strands and be left with the same whole cloth" (580–581).

43. Kevin Roose, "Pursuing Self-Interest in Harmony with the Laws of the Universe and Contributing to Evolution Is Universally Rewarded," *New York Magazine*, April 2011, http://nymag.com/news/business/wallstreet/ray-dalio-2011-4/.

44. See Ronald A. Heifetz, *Leadership without Easy Answers* (Cambridge, MA: Harvard University Press, 1994); Robert K. Greenleaf, *Servant Leadership: A Journey into the Nature of Legitimate Power and Greatness* (Mahwah, NJ: Paulist Press, 1977); James MacGregor Burns, *Transforming Leadership* (New York: Grove Press, 2003); Herminia Ibarra, *Act Like a Leader, Think Like a Leader* (Boston: Harvard Business Review Press, 2015); Bill George, *Discover Your True North* (Hoboken, NJ: Wiley, 2015); Robert Kegan and Lisa Laskow Lahey, *An Everyone Culture: Becoming a Deliberately*

Developmental Organization (Boston: Harvard Business Review Press, 2016); and Jim Collins, *Good to Great: Why Some Companies Make the Leap and Others Don't* (New York: HarperBusiness, 2001).

45. See Peter Gronn, "Distributed Leadership as a Unit of Analysis," *Leadership Quarterly* 13 (2002): 423–451, and Mollie Painter-Morland, "Systematic Leadership and the Emergence of Ethical Responsiveness," *Journal of Business Ethics* 82 (2008): 509–524.

46. Michael Beer, Russell Eisenstat, Nathaniel Foote, Tobias Fredberg, and Flemming Norrgren, *Higher Ambition: How Great Leaders Create Economic and Social Value* (Boston: Harvard Business Review Press, 2011).

Chapter 2

1. Since we are followers of Hubert L. Dreyfus, readers might expect us to elucidate many of Heidegger's arguments. Except for Heidegger's views of postmodernity, we leave his thinking in the background. Along the way, though, we cite articles where we have explained his arguments, advanced his phenomenology, and drawn implications.

2. For clarity's sake, we see that what counts as the humanities evolves and has divergent interpretations at any one time. We expect that our interpretation is easily recognizable and that its account of how people are diverges from the dominant accounts in the social sciences.

3. The humanities consisted of grammar, rhetoric, poetry, history, and moral philosophy, and humanists were people who taught and made contributions in these areas. Machiavelli would not have been more than a student of the humanists because he did not write in Latin or Greek or make appropriate contributions. He posed his virtù (aggressive effectiveness) against the humanists' classical and Christian virtues.

4. Bernard Crick, introduction to Machiavelli, *The Discourses*, 59, inside a fuller account of virtù, 57–60.

5. James Hankins, *Virtue Politics: Soulcraft and Statecraft in Renaissance Italy* (Cambridge, MA: Harvard University Press, 2019), 451.

6. Hankins, *Virtue Politics*, 459–460.

7. We pointed out earlier that moral risk-taking requires a kind of leadership that blends genders. In this regard, Machiavelli seems an odd predecessor. There is no doubt that for Machiavelli virtù is exemplified by men more often than by women. However, Machiavelli gives one clear case of a woman exercising virtù. For the record, we set it out:

Some conspirators who were citizens of Forli, killed Count Girolamo, their Lord, and took prisoner his wife and his children, who were little ones. . . . Mistress Catherine, as the countess was called, promised the conspirators that if they would let her go to the citadel, she would arrange for it to be handed over to them. Meanwhile they were to keep her children as hostages. On this understanding the conspirators let her go to the citadel, from the walls of which, when she got inside, she reproached them with killing her husband and threatened them with vengeance in every shape and form. And to convince them that she did not mind about her children she exposed her sexual parts to them and said she was still capable of bearing more. The conspirators, dumbfounded, realized their mistake too late, and paid the penalty for their lack of prudence by suffering perpetual banishment. (Machiavelli, *The Discourses*, III.6, pp. 418–419)

In light of this passage, we believe that virtù is not strictly masculine. For an argument describing a nonmasculinized virtú, see Michelle Tolman Clarke, "On the Woman Question in Machiavelli," *Review of Politics* 67, no. 2 (2005): 229–255. For feminist scholarly inquiries into Machiavelli, see Maria J. Falco, ed., *Feminist Interpretations of Niccolò Machiavelli* (University Park: Pennsylvania State University Press, 2004), and Gerry Milligan, "Masculinity and Machiavelli: How a Prince Should Avoid Effeminacy, Perform Manliness, and Be Wary of the Author," in *Seeking Real Truths: Multidisciplinary Perspectives on Machiavelli*, ed. Patricia Vilches and Gerald Seaman (Leiden, Netherlands: Koninklijke Brill NV, 2007), 149–172.

8. Hankins, *Virtue Politics*, 431.

9. Joseph L. Badaracco Jr., *Managing in the Gray* (Boston: Harvard Business Review Press, 2016); Gary Saul Morson and Morton Schapiro, *Cents and Sensibility: What Economics Can Learn from the Humanities* (Princeton, NJ: Princeton University Press, 2017); Robert Solomon, *A Better Way to Think about Business* (Oxford: Oxford University Press, 1999); Oliver F. Williams, ed., *The Moral Imagination* (Notre Dame, IN: University of Notre Dame Press, 1998). Williams's book focuses on good lives and sees moral norms for peaceful interaction thoroughly intertwined with norms for a good life. But the contributors generally write as though we live in the modern rather than the postmodern world.

10. Others, such as those in the critical management studies movement, draw on the humanities but do so in the ancient fashion to portray business as devoted to instrumental thinking and necessity.

11. Haridimos Tsoukas, "Leadership, the American Academy of Management, and President Trump's Travel Ban: A Case Study in Moral Imagination," *Journal of Business Ethics* 163 (July 2018): 1–10, https://doi.org/10.1007/s10551-018-3979-y; Antonino Vaccaro and Guido Palazzo, "Values against Violence: Institutional Change in Societies Dominated by Organized Crime," *Academy of Management Journal* 58, no. 4 (2015): 1075–1101; Muel Kaptein, "The Moral Entrepreneur: A New Component of Ethical Leadership," *Journal of Business Ethics* 156 (2019): 1135–1150; Steve Fuller, "'Never Let a Good Crisis Go to Waste': Moral Entrepreneurship, or the Fine Art of Recycling Evil into Good," *Business Ethics: A European Review* 22, no. 1 (2013):

118–129; Christopher Land, Scott Loren, and Jörg Metelmann, "Rogue Logics: Organization in the Grey Zone," *Organization Studies* 35 (2014): 233–253; Omar N. Solinger, Paul G. W. Jansen, and Joep P. Cornelissen, "The Emergence of Moral Leadership," *Academy of Management Review* 45, no. 3 (2020): 504–527.

12. According to Louis Fry, spiritual leadership revives the values of service, humility, charity, veracity, and work as a calling; see his article "Toward a Theory of Spiritual Leadership," *Leadership Quarterly* 14 (2003): 693–727. Laura Reave agrees with the idea of reviving values but lists different ones: respect, fairness, care, recognition, and reflection; see her article "Spiritual Values and Practices Related to Leadership Effectiveness," *Leadership Quarterly* 16 (2005): 655–687. In "Ethical Leadership," *Leadership Quarterly* 17 (2006): 595–616, Michael Brown and Linda Treviño say ethical leadership revives honesty, care, fairness, and acting on principle. In "Charismatic, Ideological, and Pragmatic Leadership," *Leadership Quarterly* 19 (2008): 144–160, Michael Mumford, Alison Antes, Jay Caughron, and Tamara Friedrich tell us that charismatic leaders draw followers to share established organizational values. In *Transforming Leadership*, James Burns tells us transformational leaders do the same as charismatic leaders with respect to moral values. Institutional leadership thinkers descending from Philip Selznick see that leaders "infuse" their organizations with values, but this noble line of thought does not spend much time saying *how* leaders do that (see, for instance, Philip Selznick, *Leadership in Administration: A Sociological Interpretation* [Berkeley: University of California Press, 1984]). In *The Dark Side of Transformational Leadership* (Hove, UK: Routledge, 2013), Dennis Tourish, who leads critical leadership studies, supplies negative accounts of value decay; Enron is his compelling main case.

13. The phrase belongs to Immanuel Kant. For an insightful analysis, see Isaiah Berlin, *The Crooked Timber of Humanity* (Princeton, NJ: Princeton University Press, 1990).

14. Kissinger, Gino, and Badaracco write about leaders breaking conventions and bending rules. When leaders are lucky, they are seen as geniuses, if not as fools or clowns. Olivetti gave workers two-hour lunch breaks, during which they attended lectures by poets and intellectuals; Olivetti had luck because the lunches raised the quality of work. Such conventional risk-taking earns respect, market growth, and profits but does not change moral orders. See Gino, *Rebel Talent*, 59–65, for the Olivetti case. Gino does include some *moral* risk-takers, such as Napoleon (1–6), among her conventional risk-takers, but without bringing out the nature of moral risk-taking. See also Kissinger, *Leadership*, and Badaracco, *Defining Moments*. Closer to us are those who write specifically about moral risk-taking in related fields: see Aditi Bagchi, "Managing Moral Risk: The Case of Contract," *Faculty Scholarship at Penn Law* 354 (January 1, 2011), https://scholarship.law.upenn.edu/faculty_scholarship /354, and David Stanford Horner, "Moral Luck and Computer Ethics: Gauguin in Cyberspace," *Ethics Information Technology* 12 (2010): 299–312.

15. See Christopher Michaelson, "Moral Luck and Business Ethics," *Journal of Business Ethics* 83 (2008): 773–787, and Patrick Taylor Smith, "Political Revolution as Moral Risk," *The Monist* 101 (2018): 199–215. The number of scholars who, like us, write about moral risk-taking in business remains small.

16. Steven B. Sample, *The Contrarian's Guide to Leadership* (San Francisco: Jossey-Bass, 2002), 86, 92–102, 108–112, 118.

17. For more on Ruskin's thinking about business, see Chia and Holt, *Strategy without Design*, 146–150.

18. See John Ruskin, "Unto the Last," in *English Prose of the Victorian Era*, ed. Charles Frederick Harrold and William D. Templeman (New York: Oxford University Press, 1938), 931–932.

19. See the correction of the common account of Maslow in Todd Bridgman, Stephen Cummings, and John Ballard, "Who Built Maslow's Pyramid? A History of the Creation of Management Studies' Most Famous Symbol and Its Implications for Management Education," *Academy of Management Learning & Education* 18, no. 1 (2019): 81–98.

20. Jacqueline Brassey and Michiel Kruyt, "How to Demonstrate Calm and Optimism in a Crisis," *McKinsey and Company Insights*, April 30, 2020, https://www .mckinsey.com/business-functions/organization/our-insights/how-to-demonstrate -calm-and-optimism-in-a-crisis?cid=other-eml-ofl-mip-mck&hlkid=7537ac721d804 dc792c5d4355e558349&hctky=andrew_cha@mckinsey.com_PROOF&hdpid =ab421275-338f-4358-9851-08a7151faffd.

21. Friedrich Nietzsche, *The Gay Science*, trans. with commentary Walter Kaufmann (New York: Vintage Books, 1974), §125, p. 181.

22. In *The Genealogy of Morals*, Nietzsche spells out the death of Christianity as arising from seeing truthfulness as divine: "What is it, in truth, that has triumphed over the Christian god? . . . 'The Christian ethics with its key notion, ever more strictly applied, of truthfulness.' . . . After drawing a whole series of conclusions, Christian truthfulness must now draw its strongest conclusion, the one by which it shall do away with itself. This will be accomplished by Christianity's asking itself, 'What does all will to truth signify?'" (*The Genealogy of Morals*, in *The Birth of Tragedy & The Genealogy of Morals*, trans. Francis Golffing [New York: Anchor Books, 1956], §27, p. 297). The will to truth signifies that we criticize everything in seeking truth. Nothing can be safe. The truth is that we cannot take any belief fully seriously. See also Nietzsche, *The Gay Science*: "We godless anti-metaphysicians still take our fire, too, from the flame lit by a faith that is thousands of years old, that Christian faith which was also the faith of Plato, that God is the truth, that truth is divine.—But what if this should become more and more incredible?" (§344, p. 283).

23. At his most positive, Nietzsche describes us as distrustful of ultimate convictions because we have been burned too many times and because we are jubilant over our newfound freedom from binding conviction. However, because we ride the mad and fiery horses of certainty, we are still drawn to our fanaticisms (see *The Genealogy of Morals*, §375, p. 337).

24. For a fuller account of the Stoic thought experiment and the whole Nietzschean thought experiment, see Charles Spinosa, Matthew Hancocks, and Billy Glennon, "What Calls for Thinking in Business: Consulting as a Heideggerian Philosopher," in *Handbook of Philosophy of Management*, ed. Cristina Neesham, Markus Reihlen, and Dennis Schoeneborn (Cham, Switzerland: Springer, 2018), https://doi.org/10.1007/978-3-319-48352-8_2-2.

25. Nietzsche, *The Gay Science*:

> What, if some day or night a demon were to steal after you into your loneliest loneliness and say to you: "This life as you now live it and have lived it, you will have to live once more and innumerable times more; and there will be nothing new in it, but every pain and every joy and every thought and sigh and everything unutterably small or great in your life will have to return to you, all in the same succession and sequence—even this spider and this moonlight between the trees, and even this moment and I myself. The eternal hourglass of existence is turned upside down again and again, and you with it." (§341, pp. 273–274)

We focus attention on this rendition of the eternal return, also favored by Bernard Williams, rather than on the slightly different version found in Friedrich Nietzsche, *Thus Spake Zarathustra*, trans. Thomas Common (Mineola, NY: Dover, 1999), 107–109.

26. William Shakespeare, *Macbeth*, in *The Riverside Shakespeare*, ed. G. Blakemore Evans (Boston: Houghton Mifflin, 1974), 5.5.24–28, p. 1337.

27. Nietzsche, *The Gay Science*, §341, pp. 273–274.

28. Seneca, "On Providence," 3–17. Among classics scholars, Seneca is known as the billionaire philosopher because of the landed wealth he acquired in Roman government service. For those interested in how a massively wealthy Stoic thinks about wealth, see his essay "On the Happy Life," in *Seneca*, 85–111.

29. Herman Melville, *Moby-Dick* (1851; New York: Penguin Books, 2003), 456.

30. To avoid confusion, when we say that an organization is morally and aesthetically *admirable*, we mean that it is widely admired by people with varied roles and perspectives from both inside and outside the community or organization. These people admire the organization's moral and aesthetic coherence (allowing for discordia concors) and that it thereby provides many with the possibility of attaining good lives they deem worthy.

We are definitely not saying that with admiration comes an obligation to embrace the morals or aesthetics of a community or an organization. We, Westerners, could, for instance, admire the moral and aesthetic sense of, say, a Japanese community or organization while embracing our own Western love for tough argumentation, continuous self-interrogation, and minimal respect for hierarchy. We also do this when we assess historically older communities. We could admire the moral-aesthetics of, say, ancient Sparta, its courageous heroism and the stories Spartans and other Greeks used to glorify Sparta's moral virtues. But if a new Sparta arose in our midst, we would reject it and even use force to change it. But because we admire it, we would not demonize it. In both the above cases of a Japanese moral and aesthetic sense and Sparta, Westerners do feel the moral sentiment of admiration; "appreciation" or "respect" are too thin to capture the moral sentiment. Those two communities represent relatively rare admirable, coherent, moral-aesthetic achievements. Many of today's organizations or communities that we would reject morally have not achieved a coherent set of moral-aesthetic standards. They remain trapped in expediency and so will not draw the moral sentiment of admiration.

In other words, admiration of moral-aesthetic standards implies the discernment and acknowledgement of coherent moral differences, but it does not entail acceptance. We admire moral worlds that provide coherent answers to what makes the good life. In organizational terms, the good life involves ways that advance human flourishing in a particular institutional domain, from education and health to commerce and defense. That flourishing is frequently summarized in mission or value statements about particular goals worth pursuing.

Meta's mission, for example, is "to give people the power to build community and bring the world closer together" ("FAQs," Meta, accessed July 21, 2023, https:// investor.fb.com/resources/default.aspx#:~:text=Meta%20Investor%20Relations% 3F-,What%20is%20Meta's%20mission%20statement%3F,support%20and%20 make%20a%20difference). Such explicit goals rest on a host of implicit premises that are taken for granted. At the beginning, Facebook took for granted that what was most important for community building was connectivity, not content. Over the course of time, however, content did become critical; hate speech, for example, undermines community. Commercial pressures may also cause an otherwise admirable company to give priority to certain practices, not necessarily with explicit awareness, that undermine its morally worthy ideals. If we determine that an admirable organization has done so, then while still admiring it, we will treat it like the new Sparta arising in our midst. Admirable organizations are not always *phronetic* (practically wise); no person or organization always is.

In short, admirability does not generate impeccability. Admirable organizations are not spotless and perfect. But they do articulate a coherent version of the good life, which they vigorously pursue through a series of particular judgments. To preserve admirability, leaders need to remain constantly alert to challenges, deviations, and likely errors.

31. Nietzsche, *The Gay Science*, §290, p. 232, emphasis in the original. The brilliant contemporary philosopher Alexander Nehamas treats this first life as Nietzsche's

only good life. He gives a great philosophical account of it in *Nietzsche: Life as Literature* (Cambridge, MA: Harvard University Press, 1985).

32. Nietzsche, *The Gay Science*, §295, pp. 236–237.

33. Nietzsche, *The Gay Science*, §303, pp. 243–244.

34. Richard Branson, *Losing My Virginity: How I Survived, Had Fun, and Made a Fortune Doing Business My Way* (New York: Crown Business, 1998).

35. Consider how Fastow seems to be living, as described in Quinton Mathews, "Interview of Andrew Fastow, Former Enron CFO," YouTube, December 23, 2020, https://www.youtube.com/watch?v=goQhGqQtFZ4.

36. Nietzsche, *The Gay Science*, §303, p. 243.

37. See, for instance, Fernando Flores and B. Scot Rousse, "Ecological Finitude as Ontological Finitude: Radical Hope in the Anthropocene," in *The Task of Philosophy in the Anthropocene: Axial Echoes in Global Space*, ed. Richard Polt and Jon Wittrock (New York: Rowman and Littlefield, 2018), 175–192.

38. See, for instance, Peter M. Senge, *The Fifth Discipline: The Art and Practice of the Learning Organization* (New York: Doubleday, 2006), and C. Otto Scharmer, *Theory U: Leading from the Future as It Emerges* (Oakland, CA: Barrett-Koehler, 2009).

39. Nietzsche thought that the improvising life was spreading from America to Europe and that, unsurprisingly, improvisers tend to become actors (*The Gay Science*, §356, pp. 302–304).

40. Don Sull makes an argument that suggests that Lakshmi Mittal might well be the improvisatory leader we are looking for. We are still investigating. See Donald Sull, *The Upside of Turbulence: Seizing Opportunity in an Uncertain World* (New York: HarperCollins, 2009), 4–6, 18–21, 121–122.

41. Michael Sandel tells us that "when we decide that certain goods may be bought and sold, we decide at least implicitly, that it is appropriate to treat them as commodities, as instruments of profit and use" (*What Money Can't Buy: The Moral Limits of Markets* [New York: Farrar, Straus and Giroux, 2012], 9). We and the ancient Romans disagree with Sandel's quite popular view. For an important discussion of the distinction between economic and moral commodification that is consistent with our basic argument, see Albert Borgmann, "Reality and Technology," *Cambridge Journal of Economics* 34 (2010): 27–35.

42. Here we have drawn heavily on H. F. Jolowicz and Barry Nicholas, *Historical Introduction to the Study of Roman Law* (Cambridge: Cambridge University Press, 1972), 137–158.

43. Bezos, "Obsessions 1998," in *Invent and Wander*, 39–40.

44. Roddick, *Body and Soul*, 110–111.

45. Maria Flores Letelier, Charles Spinosa, and Bobby J. Calder, "Strategies for Viral Marketing," in *Kellogg on Integrated Marketing*, ed. Dawn Iacobucci and Bobby J. Calder (Hoboken, NJ: Wiley, 2003), 90–134.

46. Stone, *The Everything Store*, 54.

47. Collins, *Good to Great*.

48. Sull, *The Upside of Turbulence*; see also Donald Sull and Kathleen M. Eisenhardt, *Simple Rules: How to Survive in a Complex World* (New York: Mariner Books, 2016). Despite our differences with Sull, we admire his thought and also feel obliged to point out that he might be describing a way to lead Nietzsche's risk-taking good life.

49. On mimetic desire, see René Girard, *Violence and the Sacred* (Baltimore: Johns Hopkins University Press, 1977), and Wolfgang Palaver, *René Girard's Mimetic Theory* (East Lansing: Michigan State Press, 2013). For an account of Girard's mimetic theory in the context of Silicon Valley, see Adrian Daub, *What Tech Calls Thinking* (New York: FSG Originals, 2020), 99–112.

50. See Linda A. Hill, Maurizio Travaglini, Greg Brandeau, and Emily Stecker, "Unlocking the Slices of Genius in Your Organization: Leading for Innovation," in *Handbook of Leadership Theory and Practice*, ed. Nitin Nohria and Rakesh Khurana (Boston: Harvard Business Review Press, 2010), 611–654.

51. Martin Heidegger, *Nietzsche*, vol. 2: *The Eternal Recurrence of the Same* (New York: HarperCollins, 1991).

52. Nietzsche, *The Gay Science*, §291, pp. 233–234.

53. Isaacson, *Steve Jobs*, 117–124.

54. Stone, *The Everything Store*, 84–86.

55. In many ways, our leader is a more insistent version of Donna Ladkin's dwelling leader, whom few would call patriarchal or heroic. See Donna Ladkin, "When Deontology and Utilitarianism Aren't Enough: How Heidegger's Notion of 'Dwelling' Might Help Organisational Leaders Resolve Ethical Issues," *Journal of Business Ethics* 65 (2006): 87–98, esp. 92–94 on "staying with."

56. See Alasdair MacIntyre, *Whose Justice? Which Rationality?* (London: Duckworth, 1988), 10–11.

57. Yuval Noah Harari, "The Dangerous Quest for Identity," *Time*, February 6, 2023, 36–37.

58. For a more extended account of how businesses already compete in the public discursive space as well as in the marketplace, see Haridimos Tsoukas, "David and

Goliath in the Risk Society: Making Sense of the Conflict between Shell and Green-peace in the North Sea," *Organization* 6, no. 3 (1999): 499–528.

59. Rowan Williams, *The Tragic Imagination* (Oxford: Oxford University Press, 2016), 30.

60. We look forward to taking up in another work the complex philosophical issues around gratitude and the sister notions of solidarity and love. Here, we rely primarily on our interpretation of Bernard Williams (more in chapter 6 with the discussion of gratitude toward Gauguin) and on Heidegger's thought of "a sending" for which we feel gratitude. For its focus on Heidegger's sending and gratitude, see Hubert Dreyfus and Sean Dorrance Kelly, *All Things Shining: Reading the Western Classics to Find Meaning in a Secular Age* (New York: Free Press, 2011). Note that Dreyfus and Kelly write of a generalized gratitude for a gift that has no giver. Our gratitude for any action or masterpiece always carries with it the distinct flavor of the action. Our gratitude for a feast feels different from our gratitude for wisdom. For the roots of an economy of gratitude in solidarity, love, and a collective person, see Max Scheler, *Formalism in Ethics and Non-formal Ethics of Values: A New Attempt toward the Foundation of an Ethical Personalism* (Evanston, IL: Northwestern University Press, 1973), 501–561.

61. Heideggerians are coming to develop the conceptual distinctions to enable the admiration of moral diversity, though obviously not all moral orders will be admired by those outside the order. For a first step, see Gregory Fried, *Heidegger's Polemos: From Being to Politics* (New Haven, CT: Yale University Press, 2000).

Chapter 3

1. For more on achieving a new normal, check out Carolyn Dewar, Scott Keller, Kevin Sneader, and Kurt Strovink, "The CEO Moment: Leadership for a New Era," *McKinsey Quarterly*, July 2020, https://www.mckinsey.com/featured-insights/leadership/the-ceo-moment-leadership-for-a-new-era. See also Sapana Agrawal, Aaron De Smet, Sébastien Lacroix, and Angelika Reich, "To Emerge as Strong Players in the New Normal, Companies Should Start Reskilling Their Workforces Now," *McKinsey and Company Insights*, May 2020, https://www.mckinsey.com/business-functions/organization/our-insights/to-emerge-stronger-from-the-covid-19-crisis-companies-should-start-reskilling-their-workforces-now.

2. Martha Nussbaum, *Upheavals of Thought: The Intelligence of Emotions* (Cambridge: Cambridge University Press, 2001), 90. We are leaving out Nussbaum's careful philosophical distinctions between moods and emotions. These distinctions are not germane to the practice we recommend.

3. Quoted in Robin McKie, "I Didn't Take Covid Seriously Enough, Admits Leading Statistician," *The Guardian*, February 6, 2022, https://www.theguardian.com/science

/2022/feb/06/i-didnt-take-covid-seriously-admits-leading-statistician-david-spiegel
halter?CMP=Share_AndroidApp_Other&fbclid=IwAR3rigSy9fEJVYpJ1Kx53r5aOvpg
XRkpAlbQ9aNPf7ApvYjV05CTZsH_Dek.

4. For views on authenticity in business studies, see Bruce J. Avolio, "Pursuing
Authentic Leadership Development," in *Handbook of Leadership Theory and Practice*,
ed. Nohria and Khurana, 739–768. For the more popular account, see Bill George,
Discover Your True North (Hoboken, NJ: Wiley, 2015). Beware that George's account
of authenticity is precisely the philosopher Søren Kierkegaard's account of the *inauthentic* dutiful judge in *Either/Or* (New York: Penguin Classics, 1992).

5. William Wordsworth, "Michael," in *William Wordsworth*, ed. Stephen Gill (Oxford:
Oxford University Press, 2010), 134–146.

6. Lionel Trilling, *Sincerity and Authenticity* (Cambridge, MA: Harvard University
Press, 1972), 34, 93.

7. See Charles Guignon, *Being Authentic* (New York: Routledge, 2004).

8. See Richard Polt, *Heidegger: An Introduction* (London: Routledge, 1999), 63.

9. Guignon, *Being Authentic*, 163.

10. Guignon, *Being Authentic*, 165. See also Haridimos Tsoukas, "A Dialogical
Approach to the Creation of New Knowledge in Organizations," *Organization Science*
20, no. 6 (2009): 941–957.

11. Guignon, *Being Authentic*, 166.

12. William James, *The Principles of Psychology*, vol. 2 (Mineola, NY: Dover, 2012),
463.

13. Ibarra, *Act Like a Leader, Think Like a Leader*, 118.

14. For a sympathetic philosophical exploration of the sort of "originary inauthenticity" that Ibarra describes, see Simon Critchley, *Infinitely Demanding: Ethics of Commitment, Politics of Resistance* (London: Verso, 2012), 84.

15. Richard Wollheim, *On the Emotions* (New Haven, CT: Yale University Press,
1999).

16. Collins, *Good to Great*.

Chapter 4

1. For earlier thinking on this issue, see Charles Spinosa, "Do You Believe in Trust
at First Sight?," in *How Can Brands Build Trust among Customers?*, ed. Fraser Allen
(Edinburgh, UK: White Light Media, 2019), 1–5.

2. We recommend such reasoning to identify virtues. Robert Solomon's book *A Better Way of Business* (Oxford: Oxford University Press, 1999) is a good Aristotelian starting point that sets out 40 virtues.

3. In the United States, virtue signaling has infected both the Left—saying nasty things about Trump—and the Right—wearing a MAGA hat.

4. There is some doubt that Amazon will keep this level trust. Guru Hariharan, the cofounder and CEO of CommerceIQ, is quoted as saying, "For 20 years, it was customer obsession at any cost. Now, it's customer obsession at the right cost" (quoted in Sebastian Herrera, "Amazon's Customer Satisfaction Slips with Shoppers," *Wall Street Journal*, November 21, 2022, https://www.wsj.com/articles/amazons-customer-satisfaction-slips-with-shoppers-11668986981?mod=hp_lead_pos11).

5. Gregory Bateson, *Mind and Nature: A Necessary Unity* (Toronto: Bantam Books, 2002), 72.

6. Fernando Flores, Maria Flores Letelier, and Charles Spinosa, "Developing Productive Customers in Emerging Markets," *California Management Review* 45, no. 4 (2003): 77–103. For alternative accounts, see W. Chan Kim and Renée Mauborgne, *Blue Ocean Strategy: How to Create Uncontested Market Space and Make the Competition Irrelevant* (Boston: Harvard Business School Press, 2005), 71–74, and C. K. Prahalad, *The Fortune at the Bottom of the Pyramid* (Upper Saddle River, NJ: Wharton School Publishing, 2006), 221–234.

7. Some leaders are hiring anthropologists. See Gillian Tett, *Anthro-Vision: A New Way to See in Business and Life* (New York: Avid Reader Press, 2021).

8. Geoffrey Chaucer, "The Franklin's Tale," in *The Works of Geoffrey Chaucer*, ed. F. N. Robinson (New York: Houghton Mifflin, 1957), ll. 739–742, p. 135.

9. Geoffrey Chaucer, "The Franklin's Tale," in *The Complete Poetical Works of Geoffrey Chaucer: Now First Put into Modern English*, ed. John S. P. Tatlock and Percy MacKaye (New York: Free Press, 1912), 251.

10. Cole Porter, "I've Got You under My Skin" (1936), Genius, accessed December 29, 2022, https://genius.com/Cole-porter-ive-got-you-under-my-skin-lyrics.

Chapter 5

1. For example, see Nicolai Chen Nielsen, Gemma D'Auria, and Sasha Zolley, "Tuning In, Turning Outward: Cultivating Compassionate Leadership in a Crisis," *McKinsey and Company Insights*, May 2020, https://www.mckinsey.com/business-functions/organization/our-insights/tuning-in-turning-outward-cultivating-compassionate-leadership-in-a-crisis.

2. Kim Scott, *Radical Candor* (New York: Pan Books, 2018), xi–xii, 10.

3. Brad Blanton, *Radical Honesty: How to Transform Your Life by Telling the Truth* (Stanley, VA: Sparrowhawk, 2003), viii.

4. We are drawing on the ancient tradition of speaking truth to power, which remained a strong tradition from about 400 BCE to 600 CE. The ancients called it *parrhesia*. Masterpiece creators are parrhesiasts. Michel Foucault wrote and spoke about this tradition a great deal in the last years of his life. For instance, see Michel Foucault, *The Government of Self and Others: Lectures at the Collège de France 1982–1983*, trans. Graham Burchell, ed. Frédéric Gros (New York: Picador, 2010).

5. Friedrich Nietzsche, *Beyond Good and Evil: Prelude to a Philosophy of the Future*, trans. with commentary Walter Kaufmann (New York: Vintage, 1989), §231, p. 162.

6. In *The Gay Science*, Nietzsche dismisses any simple moral universalism or relativism: "The usual mistaken premise [of the historians of morality] is that they affirm some consensus of the nations, at least of tame nations, concerning certain principles of morals, and then they infer from this that these principles must be unconditionally binding also for you and me; or, conversely, they see truth that among different nations moral valuations are *necessarily* different and then infer from this that *no* morality is at all binding. Both procedures are equally childish" (§345, pp. 284–285, emphasis in the original).

7. Nietzsche, *The Genealogy of Morals*, §12, pp. 255–256.

8. Nietzsche, *The Gay Science*, §374, pp. 336–337. In *The Will to Power*, Nietzsche says, "There are many kinds of eyes. Even the sphinx has eyes—and consequently there are many kinds of 'truths'" (*The Will to Power*, trans. Walter Kaufmann and R. J. Hollingdale, ed. Walter Kaufmann [New York: Vintage, 1968], §540, p. 291). Bernard Williams captures our view of Nietzsche's devotion both to truth seeking and to multiple truths in the chapters "Introduction to *The Gay Science*" and "'There Are Many Kinds of Eyes,'" in *The Sense of the Past: Essays in the History of Philosophy* (Princeton, NJ: Princeton University Press, 2006), 311–324, 325–330. In short, Nietzsche insisted on truth seeking and claimed that truth seeking leads to perspectivism, which is usually thought to contradict the law of noncontradiction basic to truth. He is thus a perfect example of F. Scott Fitzgerald's aphorism "The test of a first-rate intelligence is the ability to hold two opposing ideas in mind at the same time and still retain the ability to function."

9. Friedrich Nietzsche, *The Anti-Christ*, in *The Twilight of the Idols and The Anti-Christ: Or, How to Philosophize with a Hammer*, trans. R. J. Hollingdale (London: Penguin, 1968), §59, p. 194.

10. Stephen Neale, "The Philosophical Significance of Gödel's Slingshot," *Mind* 104, no. 106 (1995): 761–825. Neale says, "There is no knock-down argument against facts," but then he meticulously sets out the vexing barriers we need to overcome

to say a sentence is true because it corresponds to the facts (816). For the way back to facts, see John Perry's eloquent essay "Evading the Slingshot," in *Philosophy and Cognitive Science: Categories, Consciousness, and Reasoning. Proceedings of the Second International Colloquium on Cognitive Science*, ed. Andy Clark, Jesús Ezquerro, and Jesús M. Larrazabal (Dordrecht, Netherlands: Kluwer Academic, 1996), 95–114.

11. For a useful, short review of antirealist accounts of truth, see Richard L. Kirkham, *Theories of Truth: A Critical Introduction* (Cambridge, MA: MIT Press, 1992), 73–118. Though still refining our views, we, like the philosopher Alan R. White, tend to think that different theories of truth apply to different regions of inquiry: pragmatism (or instrumentalism) for everyday coping, coherence for literary inquiry, and a combination of correspondence and coherence for science, history, and philosophy: if coherence for discovery, then correspondence for justification, or vice versa. See Kirkham, *Theories of Truth*, 315, on White and his difference from us.

12. This position is more often associated with those who hold nonrealist theories of truth—people who believe truth is a matter of justification. But we think that in the vanilla form in which we make the claim here, it would also work for realist theories of truth where states of affairs in the world make the statement true. See Hilary Putnam, "Reference and Truth," in *Philosophical Papers*, vol. 3: *Realism and Reason* (Cambridge: Cambridge University Press, 1983), 69–86.

13. Ludwig Wittgenstein, *Philosophical Investigations*, trans. G. E. M. Anscombe (New York: Macmillan, 1958), §202 and §§243–265. See also Saul A. Kripke, *Wittgenstein on Rules and Private Language* (Cambridge, MA: Harvard University Press, 1982). For an alternative account of Wittgenstein on private language that insists on a stronger role for subjective meaning, see John McDowell, *Mind and World* (Cambridge, MA: Harvard University Press, 1994), 36–39, 92–95.

14. Saul Kripke has inspired our account with his famous argument about how the naming of natural kinds such as gold works. See Saul A. Kripke, *Naming and Necessity* (Cambridge, MA: Harvard University Press, 1980).

15. Hubert L. Dreyfus and Charles Spinosa, "Coping with Things-in-Themselves: A Practice-Based Phenomenological Argument for Realism," *Inquiry* 42 (1999): 49–78.

16. Walter Isaacson, *Einstein: His Life and Universe* (New York: Simon and Schuster, 2007), 212, 216–219. For our account, we draw on both Isaacson, *Einstein*, 211–224, and Carlo Rovelli, *Reality Is Not What It Seems* (New York: Riverhead, 2017), 91–92. Scholars debate whether Hilbert's paper from November 20 left out something crucial or "a trace term . . . unnecessary or obvious," but it is clear Hilbert gave the credit to Einstein (Isaacson, *Einstein*, 221–222).

17. Rovelli, *Reality Is Not What It Seems*, 91–92, and Isaacson, *Einstein*, 222. No one has found the primary source for the second Hilbert quotation.

18. Hilary Putnam, "The Meaning of 'Meaning,'" in *Philosophical Papers*, vol. 2: *Mind, Language and Reality* (Cambridge: Cambridge University Press, 1975), 227–229, for the division of linguistic labor argument.

19. Martin Heidegger, *Being and Time*, trans. John Macquarrie and Edward Robinson (New York: Harper & Row, 1962), 257–263. On disconfirmation, see Raymond S. Nickerson, "Confirmation Bias: A Ubiquitous Phenomenon in Many Guises," *Review of General Psychology* 2, no. 2 (1998): 175–220.

20. We add that we are not claiming that all truths are verifiable. We are not verificationists.

21. Philosophers and historians of science will note that with truth as uncovering and verifying, we are drawing on and altering for our own purposes Hans Reichenbach's "context of discovery" and "context of justification." His thinking is just too intuitively powerful to ignore. But his context of discovery is "about the search for the objective inductive relation between a theory and a body of evidence," whereas our discovery is about hermeneutical uncovering. See Clark Glymour and Frederick Eberhardt, "Hans Reichenbach" *Stanford Encyclopedia of Philosophy*, revised March 23, 2021, https://plato.stanford.edu/entries/reichenbach/.

22. That is why truth seeking and saying are both bracing and admirable. We know that Socrates faced judicial execution for truth-saying. So, it is likely, did Jesus. Dionysius was so unhappy with Plato's truth saying that he had him sold him into slavery. Consequences are a little less severe in our cancel culture.

23. Einstein began his first lecture in November 1915 at the Prussian Academy by detailing all that he had gotten wrong since 1907. He even mentioned the crucial mistake in 1912 of making the search for mathematical covariance a second priority. See Isaacson, *Einstein*, 215.

24. Tsoukas, "A Dialogical Approach to the Creation of New Knowledge in Organizations."

25. Maurice Merleau-Ponty, *Phenomenology of Perception*, trans. Colin Smith (London: Routledge, 1962), 354.

26. For a more worked-out position, see Bernard Williams, *Truth and Truthfulness: An Essay in Genealogy* (Princeton, NJ: Princeton University Press, 2002), 110–122.

27. William Shakespeare, *King Lear*, in *The Riverside Shakespeare*, 5.3.197–199, p. 1293.

28. Although living in a barrel seems like a joke, it gave Diogenes such a firm identity that when Alexander the Great met Diogenes, he said, "But truly, if I were not Alexander, I wish I were Diogenes." Building a distinctive truth-seeking and saying identity matters. If the barrel works, it works.

29. Francis X. Frei and Anne Morriss, "Begin with Trust," *Harvard Business Review* 98, no. 3 (2020): 112–121.

30. Michel Foucault, "On the Genealogy of Ethics: An Overview of Work in Progress," in *The Foucault Reader*, ed. Paul Rabinow (New York: Pantheon Books, 1984), 352.

31. See Vikram Dodd, "'She Just Did Not Get It': How Cressida Dick's Support as Met Chief Unraveled," *The Guardian*, February 11, 2022.

32. Chen Nielsen, D'Auria, and Zolley, "Tuning In, Turning Outward."

33. Foucault, *The Government of the Self and Others*.

34. Stone, *The Everything Store*, 84–86, 167.

Chapter 6

1. "The three American presidents since 2001 have said over and over that their primary duty was 'the safety of the American people.' No earlier presidents spoke in quite this way: the oath of office contains not a word about safety but commits the chief magistrate to uphold the constitution" (David Bromwich, "What Are We Allowed to Say?," in *How Words Make Things Happen* [New York: Oxford University Press, 2019], 104). For the recent situation, see also Jonathan Cole, "The Chilling Effect of Fear at America's Colleges," *The Atlantic*, June 9, 2016; and for a longer historical perspective, see Frederic Gros, *The Security Principle: From Serenity to Regulation* (London: Verso, 2019).

2. Karl E. Weick and Kathleen M. Sutcliffe, *Managing the Unexpected: Assuring High Performance in an Age of Complexity* (San Francisco: Jossey-Bass, 2001), preface.

3. Amy C. Edmondson, *The Fearless Organization: Creating Psychological Safety in the Workplace for Learning, Innovation, and Growth* (Hoboken, NJ: Wiley, 2018), xvi.

4. Julia Rozovsky, "The Five Keys to a Successful Google Team," *re: Work Blog*, Google, November 17, 2015, https://rework.withgoogle.com/blog/five-keys-to-a-successful-google-team/.

5. Aaron De Smet, Kim Rubenstein, Gunnar Schrah, Mike Vierow, and Amy Edmondson, "Psychological Safety and the Critical Role of Leadership Development," *McKinsey and Company Insights*, February 11, 2021, https://www.mckinsey.com/business-functions/organization/our-insights/psychological-safety-and-the-critical-role-of-leadership-development?cid=other-eml-ofl-mip-mck&hlkid=c70d9a6246C0948e683be97ef9660afdb&hctky=2248501&hdpid=1edc88af-5afd-42f3-b77a-e0f602bf3034.

6. Amy C. Edmondson and Mark Mortensen, "What Psychological Safety Looks Like in a Hybrid Workplace," *Harvard Business Review*, April 19, 2021, https://hbr.org

/2021/04/what-psychological-safety-looks-like-in-a-hybrid-workplace?utm_medium
=email&utm_source=newsletter_weekly&utm_campaign=insider_activesubs&utm
_content=signinnudge&deliveryName=DM129267.

7. Williams, *The Tragic Imagination*, 14.

8. Edmondson, *The Fearless Organization*, 4–5, 13, 18, 6.

9. Consider Brené Brown, *Dare to Lead: Brave Work. Tough Conversations. Whole Hearts* (London: Penguin, 2018). Brown is noteworthy for valuing courage and even truth saying (111 and, particularly in response to stress, 263 and 267); she also sees that values live in practices. But she starts out with premises like Edmondson's. For Brown, we live in "fear of being judged or misunderstood, of making a mistake, being wrong, and experiencing shame" (115). We fear these evaluations in the face of wanting connection and love: "Connection, along with love and belonging, is why we are here" (126). Consequently, we all are "vulnerable," which, for Brown, is a technical term (sometimes a state of affairs, sometimes a feeling). Saying "'I love you' first" (we assume without psychological safety) is the "very best example of vulnerability" (114). In contrast, for masterpiece creators, the emphasis is on leaning in to moral risk-taking in the face of a moral anomaly that blocks any right action. Moral-risk-taking leaders worry about becoming evil, not unloved. Of course, these leaders are extraordinarily vulnerable, but facing the distinctive moral risk they will take is their essence, not leaning in to their vulnerability.

10. Edmondson, *The Fearless Organization*, 110, 3–4, 6–8.

11. Edmondson, *The Fearless Organization*, 6, 110, for Dalio's "more extreme stance."

12. Edmondson, *The Fearless Organization*, xv.

13. Edmondson, *The Fearless Organization*, 178–180, 117–118.

14. See Edmondson, *The Fearless Organization*, 109–110, 112, for her account of the responsibility to speak up. Like Dalio, Reed Hastings says, "We now say that it is disloyal to Netflix when you disagree with an idea and do *not* express that disagreement" (Hastings and Meyer, *No Rules Rules*, 141).

15. Dalio, *Principles*, 312.

16. Matt Wirz, "Bridgewater Associates Raising New Money for Flagship Pure Alpha Fund," *Wall Street Journal*, September 11, 2016, https://www.wsj.com/articles/bridge water-associates-raising-new-money-for-flagship-pure-alpha-fund-1473628244.

17. Ray Dalio, "How to Build a Company Where the Best Ideas Win," TED2017, accessed January 31, 2022, https://www.ted.com/talks/ray_dalio_how_to_build_a _company_where_the_best_ideas_win.

18. Dalio, *Principles*, 52.

19. Dalio, *Principles*, 116; on Dalio's shaping of digital practices, see 540.

20. Dalio, *Principles*, 372, 373, 308.

21. Dalio, "How to Build a Company Where the Best Ideas Win."

22. Dalio, *Principles*, 257–258.

23. Roose, "Pursuing Self-Interest in Harmony with the Laws of the Universe."

24. Dalio, *Principles*, 344, 385–386, 454.

25. Adam Grant, *Originals: How Non-conformists Rule the World* (New York: Penguin, 2017); Kegan and Laskow Lahey, *An Everyone Culture*.

26. Shalimi Ramachandran and Joe Flint, "At Netflix, Radical Transparency and Blunt Firings Unsettle the Ranks," *Wall Street Journal*, October 25, 2018, https://classdat.appstate.edu/COB/MGT/VillanPD/OB%20Fall%202021/Unit%203%20-%20Cohesion/Org%20Culture%20Articles/At%20Netflix,%20Radical%20Transparency%20and%20Blunt%20Firings%20Unsettle%20the%20Ranks%20-%20WSJ%20Oct%202018.pdf.

27. Dalio, *Principles*, 30–32, 34.

28. Dalio, *Principles*, 118.

29. Laura Delizonna, "High-Performing Teams Need Psychological Safety: Here's How to Create It," *Harvard Business Review*, August 24, 2017, https://store.hbr.org/product/high-performing-teams-need-psychological-safety-here-s-how-to-create-it/H03TK7.

30. Stephen Greenblatt, *Will in the World: How Shakespeare Became Shakespeare* (New York: Norton, 2016), 173 and pictures, including Colaes Jansz Visscher's engraving of the heads, between pages 192 and 193.

31. Even in what many of us think to be our least political scholarly discipline, physics, truth saying can take a huge toll. In the 1950s, Niels Bohr forced Hugh Everett, who developed the many-worlds interpretation in quantum mechanics, to bowdlerize his work, and Everett then left academia. David Bohm, famous for the pilot wave theory that makes quantum mechanics deterministic, suffered a similar fate. See Tim Maudlin, "The Defeat of Reason," *Boston Review*, June 1, 2018, http://bostonreview.net/science-nature-philosophy-religion/tim-maudlin-defeat-reason.

32. Robert Austin, Daniel Hjorth, and Shannon Hessel, "How Aesthetics and Economy Become Conversant in Creative Firms," *Organization Studies* 39, no. 11 (2018): 1501–1519.

33. Doris Ruth Eikhof and Axel Haunschild, "For Art's Sake! Artistic and Economic Logics in Creative Production," *Journal of Organizational Behavior* 28 (2007): 523–538; Paul Thompson, Michael Jones, and Chris Warhurst, "From Conception to

Consumption: Creativity and the Missing Managerial Link," *Journal of Organizational Behavior* 28 (2007): 625–640; Barbara Townley, Nic Beech, and Alan McKinlay, "Managing in the Creative Industries: Managing the Motley Crew," *Human Relations* 62 (2009): 939–962; Boukje Cnossen, Ellen Loots, and Arjen van Witteloostuijn, "Individual Motivation among Entrepreneurs in the Creative and Cultural Industries: A Self-Determination Perspective," *Creativity and Innovation Management* 28, no. 3 (2019): 389–402, https://doi.org/10.1111/caim.12315; Silviya Svejenova, Carmelo Mazza, and Marcel Planellas, "Cooking Up Change in Haute Cuisine: Ferran Adrià as an Institutional Entrepreneur," *Journal of Organizational Behavior* 28, no. 5 (2007): 539–561.

34. Edmondson makes clear that job security is part of psychological safety (*The Fearless Organization*, 119–120).

35. Knight, *Shoe Dog*.

36. Bernard Williams, *Moral Luck: Philosophical Papers 1973–1980* (Cambridge: Cambridge University Press, 1981). See also Thomas Nagel, *Mortal Questions* (Cambridge: Cambridge University Press, 1979), 24–38.

37. Williams, "Postscript," 256.

38. For a fuller account of moral luck, leadership, and Churchill, see Spinosa et al., "Beyond Rational Persuasion."

39. Churchill, *Memoirs of the Second World War*, 266–267.

40. Winston Churchill, *The World Crisis*, vol. 1: *1911–1914* (1923; reprint, London: Bloomsbury Academic, 2015), 240.

41. Many thinkers who follow Aristotle's virtue ethics believe that cultivating the right character that manifests the main virtues of one's culture will lead to good actions and a good life. Under Bernard Williams's influence, Martha Nussbaum meticulously shows that Aristotle understood that even the virtuous life was subject to moral luck. See Martha Nussbaum, *The Fragility of Goodness: Luck and Ethics in Greek Tragedy and Philosophy* (Cambridge: Cambridge University Press, 1986), 318–371, 397–421.

42. Gary Hamel says explicitly that Google does not; see Gary Hamel and Bill Breen, *The Future of Management* (Boston: Harvard Business School Press, 2007), 115–116.

43. Milton, *Areopagitica*, 111.

44. See Dave Logan, John King, and Halee Fischer-Wright, *Tribal Leadership: Leveraging Natural Groups to Build a Thriving Organization* (New York: HarperBusiness, 2008).

45. Churchill, *Memoirs of the Second World War*, 266–267.

46. William Shakespeare, *Henry V*, in *The Riverside Shakespeare*, 4.3.3–39, p. 960.

47. "Henry V—Speech—Eve of Saint Crispin's Day—HD," YouTube, May 3, 2009, https://www.youtube.com/watch?v=A-yZNMWFqvM&t=65s.

48. For those who prefer the drier, rational appeal of a social scientist, consider this short passage from Max Weber, which says much the same as *Henry V*: "Only he has the calling for politics who is sure that he shall not crumble when the world from his point of view is too stupid or too base for what he wants to offer. Only he who in the face of all this can say 'In spite of all!'" (Max Weber, "Politics as a Vocation," in *From Max Weber: Essays in Sociology*, ed. H. H. Gerth and C. Wright Mills [New York: Oxford University Press, 1946], 128).

49. Shakespeare, *Henry V*, 5.2.269–270, p. 970.

Chapter 7

1. In *Tribal Leadership*, Logan, King, and Fischer-Wright characterize such cultures as like many different small towns (3).

2. Martin Heidegger made the claims about the fundamental role of coping practices in making sense of the world and about the critical importance of mood in *Being and Time*. His best account of style and culture appear in Martin Heidegger, "The Origin of the Work of Art," in *Poetry, Language, Thought* (New York: Harper & Row, 1971). The best introduction to Heidegger's thinking on these matters is Hubert L. Dreyfus, *Being-in-the-World* (Cambridge, MA: MIT Press, 1991). We also suggest Hubert L. Dreyfus, "Heidegger's Ontology of Art," in *A Companion to Heidegger*, ed. Hubert L. Dreyfus and Mark Wrathall (Oxford: Blackwell, 2005), 407–419. For an even simpler, more engaging introduction to the philosophy behind the thought here, see Tao Ruspoli's wonderful documentary *Being in the World* (New York: Mangusta Productions, 2010).

3. These claims about hammers and steps are illustrations and only parts of a philosophical argument. If you want something closer to the fuller philosophical argument, think about the fundamental concept of being. We only have a dim concept of what we mean by being, and that depends on us, in the first place, being.

4. Heidegger makes a fast move when he calls this way of mattering a mood. He is largely right, but his description misses some phenomena that become important when you are doing ground-level work. For instance, in a fear culture people determine the importance of things by virtue of how threatening they are. Things are important and inspire the feeling of fear when they are threatening. However, someone can live in a fear culture with a sense that things matter according to their level of threat and be lucky enough to face truly little that is threatening. Such a person will honestly say that she does not *feel* fear, but that does not mean that she does not evaluate what matters according to the degree of threat. The same is so for other cultures. Take a hope culture. People in such a culture see that what matters

is something that has the potential to change the world and that what does not matter is something that is simply normal. In successful biotechs with a pervasive mood of hope, you can find people on the manufacturing side of protein creation who say that they do not come to work with hope. Of course, they do hope that the company succeeds, but they are doing the normal stuff of growing and harvesting proteins as is done at any life-science company. They are still evaluating what matters by the standards of hope, but their activities are so far off from producing breakthroughs that they have no *feeling* of hope.

5. Some other theorists that take style as a basic organizing norm in culture are: Dick Hebdige, *Subculture: The Meaning of Style* (London: Routledge, 1979); Hans Ulrich Gumbrecht and K. Ludwig Pfeiffer, eds., *Stil: Geschichten und Funktionen eines kulturwissenschaftlichen Diskurselements* (Frankfurt am Main, Germany: Suhrkamp, 1986); Caroline van Eck, James McAllister, and Renée van de Vall, *The Question of Style in Philosophy and the Arts* (Cambridge: Cambridge University Press, 1995); Ivan Callus, James Corby, and Gloria Lauri-Lucente, *Style in Theory: Between Literature and Philosophy* (London: Bloomsbury, 2013); and Jasmin Herrmann, Moritz Ingwersen, Björn Sonnenberg-Schrank, and Olga Ludmila, *Revisiting Style in Literary and Cultural Studies: Interdisciplinary Articulations* (Berlin: Peter Lang, 2020). For a recent exploration of style in organization studies, see Daniel Hjorth and Robin Holt, *Entrepreneurship and the Creation of Organization: A Philosophical Investigation* (Abingdon, UK: Routledge, 2022).

6. For more on our second nature and how it gives us truth-grounding access to the world, see McDowell, *Mind and World,* 66–107. For McDowell, we make sense of the world by means of our second nature, our *Bildung*—we would say our skills and dispositions for coping with things—and this second nature then connects us with things. Without such a *Bildung*, we would remain trapped in concepts that refer only to other concepts.

7. Signature practices and conveying practices are much the same in form, but their context of use is different. We call dramatic, widespread practices "signature practices" when they manifest an established mood and style and when they are highly elaborated and connect to other practices. We call the core of these practices "conveying practices" when they change a culture. They tend to be simpler forms of the signature practices. They are dramatic and value producing, but the leader works to make them both widespread and connected with other practices. They do not start out that way. Most practices in a culture will naturally convey something of the culture's mood and style, but the practices we call "conveying" are dramatic. Moreover, when done well or poorly in business organizations, they significantly affect profitability.

8. Edgar H. Schein, *Organizational Culture and Leadership* (San Francisco: Jossey-Bass, 2010); Kim S. Cameron and Robert E. Quinn, *Diagnosing and Changing Organizational*

Culture (San Francisco: Jossey-Bass, 2011); and Roger Connors and Tom Smith, *Change the Culture: Change the Game* (New York: Penguin, 2011).

9. Joel Gelman, Linda K. Treviño, and Raghu Garud have a powerful academic study on how establishing basic honor-code practices leads people guided by the practices to take on more and more honor practices. That is how practices work. As we start seeing things through the lens of a certain practice, we see more and more opportunities for making that practice work better and also on new and unexpected occasions. See Joel Gelman, Linda K. Treviño, and Raghu Garud, "Values Work: A Process Study of the Emergence and Performance of Organizational Values Practices," *Academy of Management Journal* 56, no. 1 (2013): 84–112.

10. For more on moods, see Charles Spinosa, Christopher Davis, and Billy Glennon, "Transforming Crippling Company Politics," *Organizational Dynamics* 43 (2014): 88–95. A leader who creates an organization with any one of the positive moods will have an organization that the leader and others admire as they admire a work of art for its wonder and resonance. Such admiration is a meditative, arresting emotion directed at a particular organization. As a reminder, that admiration is different from the *mood* of admiration, which is a form of love. We can admire works of art that we do not love. In a *mood* of admiration, we feel affection or its absence toward our colleagues, organization, customers, and shareholders.

11. Ray Dalio's Bridgewater plays a starring role in Kegan and Laskow Lahey's book *An Everyone Culture.*

12. For these simple business focuses, we draw on Michael Treacy and Fred Wiersema's three main conventional strategies—operational excellence, product leadership, and customer intimacy—and add one of Michael Porter's generic strategies, the niche strategy. Because a strategy of competing by growing network effects is popular today, we also add it. With network effects, the product becomes more valuable the more people there are who use it. Consider Google, Meta, Twitter, and such. Note that we are looking at these "strategies" as business focuses. Masterpiece *strategies* are quite different and the subject of the next chapter. For more on these business focuses, see Michael Treacy and Fred Wiersema, *The Discipline of Market Leaders: Choose Your Customers, Narrow Your Focus, Dominate Your Market* (New York: Perseus, 1997), and Michael Porter, *Competitive Strategy: Techniques for Analyzing Industries and Competitors* (New York: Free Press, 1980).

13. Famously, Xerox PARC, Xerox's Research and Development Center, had a version of this practice for arguing on both sides (arguing *in utrumque partem*). See David Burkus, *The Myths of Creativity* (San Francisco: Jossey-Bass, 2013), 154.

14. Read any annual report written by Warren Buffett. He can be succinct because he is totally blunt and does not put on any airs. He says—even in his annual report—where he was wrong and another officer right and how he has come to see

things. He balances narrative with analysis. People with zeal serve a mission, and in its service, they do not try to look good. They serve with a kind of modesty that says the message they are uttering is far more important than they are. The modesty, the honesty about mistakes, and so forth draw admiration and trust.

15. On Gore, see Hamel and Breen, *The Future of Management*, 83–100, and Malcolm Gladwell, *The Tipping Point* (New York: Little, Brown, 2000), 183–192. On Morning Star, see Gary Hamel, "First, Let's Fire All the Managers," *Harvard Business Review*, December 2011, 48–60.

16. Ed Catmull and Amy Wallace, *Creativity, Inc.: Overcoming the Unseen Forces That Stand in the Way of True Inspiration* (New York: Random House, 2014), xv.

17. Catmull and Wallace, *Creativity, Inc.*, 90–91.

18. We are drawing on Catmull and Wallace's description of this practice throughout *Creativity, Inc.* but primarily on 85–105.

Chapter 8

1. Kim and Mauborgne, *Blue Ocean Strategy*.

2. Richard Rumelt, *Good Strategy Bad Strategy: The Difference and Why It Matters* (London: Profile Books, 2017), 27, 83–84.

3. Pankaj Ghemawat, *Commitment: The Dynamic of Strategy* (New York: Free Press, 1991), 121, 18.

4. Lockout occurs most typically with closing facilities when the cost of reopening would be prohibitive even if the market returned to pre-close-down valuations (Ghemawat, *Commitment*, 19–20).

5. Ghemawat, *Commitment*, 22, 45.

6. On changing a commercial philosophy, see Rumelt, *Good Strategy Bad Strategy*, 27.

7. Rumelt, *Good Strategy Bad Strategy*, 9–10, 23, 27, emphasis in original.

8. Rumelt, *Good Strategy Bad Strategy*, 79–81.

9. Rumelt, *Good Strategy Bad Strategy*, 84–85.

10. Rumelt, *Good Strategy Bad Strategy*, 92–93.

11. Haridimos Tsoukas, "Strategy and Virtue: Developing Strategy-as-Practice through Virtue Ethics," *Strategic Organization* 16, no. 3 (2018): 332.

12. Tsoukas, "Strategy and Virtue," 336–337.

13. Tsoukas, "Strategy and Virtue," 337–338.

14. For a wrenching example of an incumbent business that failed to take a lumpy, distasteful moral action quickly enough, see Don Sull's case study of Firestone's collapse in the face of Michelin's entry to the US tire market. Because Michelin's new radial tires lasted twice as long as US bias tires, radial tires became more popular and reduced the need for factories. In the name of the moral value of treating employees like family, Firestone failed its employees, customers, and shareholders (Sull, *The Upside of Turbulence*, 67–90).

15. For a more extended account of Roddick's moral risk-taking and change of the beauty industry, see Spinosa et al., "Beyond Rational Persuasion."

16. Roddick, *Body and Soul*, 9, 15–16.

17. Ball, *Madam C. J. Walker*, 49–48, 69.

18. Roddick, *Body and Soul*, 78.

19. Roddick, *Body and Soul*, 68–70, 74, 217, 221–223. We put Roddick's various ethical stands, such as against animal testing, under the overall moral norm of compassion.

20. Roddick, *Body and Soul*, 74.

21. Roddick, *Body and Soul*, 85–86.

22. Roddick, *Body and Soul*, 245.

23. Julia Robertson (CEO, Impellam), face-to-face interview with Matthew Hancocks, Impellam offices, Devonshire Square, London, October 11, 2022.

24. Robertson interview.

25. Julia Robertson founded her own business, The Agency, inspired by her belief that there was a "'better way' to do recruitment" (Julia Robertson, LinkedIn, accessed July 21, 2023, https://uk.linkedin.com/in/julia-robertson-73739616).

26. Robertson interview.

27. Erin Hatton, *The Temp Economy: From Kelly Girls to Permatemps in Postwar America* (Philadelphia: Temple University Press, 2011), 2. Robertson also drew on Stephen R. Barley and Gideon Kunda, *Gurus, Hired Guns, and Warm Bodies: Itinerant Experts in a Knowledge Economy* (Princeton, NJ: Princeton University Press, 2004); Vicki Smith and Esther B. Neuwirth, *The Good Temp* (Ithaca, NY: Cornell University Press, 2008); and Louis Hyman, *Temp: The Real Story of What Happened to Your Salary, Benefits, and Job Security* (London: Penguin Books, 2019).

28. Journalists uncovered the case of Staffline, where the sales executive Andy Coop offered to set up a separate payroll for agency workers on lower wages than those received by the company's direct hires (*Dispatches*, October 21, 2013; for a summary report, see "UK—Staffing Firms Criticised in National TV Programme," SIA, October

22, 2013, https://www2.staffingindustry.com/eng/Editorial/Daily-News/UK-Staffing-firms-criticised-in-national-TV-programme-27697). In addition, there were exposés in *The Guardian* about working practices for temps. For example, two agencies, Best Connection and Transline, were found to be charging temporary staff members £15 for the service of having their salary processed. See Simon Goodley, "Revealed: How Sports Direct Effectively Pays below Minimum Wage," *The Guardian*, December 9, 2015, https://www.theguardian.com/business/2015/dec/09/how-sports-direct-effectively-pays-below-minimum-wage-pay. These exposés led in 2016 to the British Parliament declaring the practices inhuman. See "Sports Direct Staff 'Not Treated as Humans,' Says MPs' Report," *BBC News*, July 22, 2016, https://www.bbc.co.uk/news/uk-england-derbyshire-36855374.

29. For example, see Adam Jay, "Corporate Services Pair Found Guilty," *Telegraph*, September 18, 2003, https://www.telegraph.co.uk/finance/2863499/Corporate-Services-pair-found-guilty.html.

30. The traditional strategist Richard Rumelt would call Robertson's visceral response a *diagnosis*. However, it was more the classic practical wisdom of sensing how internal goods were out of sync with external community goods.

31. Robertson interview.

32. In Rumelt's terms, Robertson's *guiding policy* is one of high-road employees for high-road employers.

33. Robertson interview.

34. Robertson describes in a podcast the "liberating" feeling of firing a low-road customer. See "A Conversation with Julia Robertson—Group Chief Executive Officer of the Impellam Group," *People Make the Difference—the Lorien Podcast*, Spotify, June 2022, https://open.spotify.com/episode/48ktltYQmg6ec2sjnG7nHl?si=3pXtqhNiT4uB3fJiY8_1pQ&nd=1.

35. On falling into resignation or fighting, see Logan, King, and Fischer-Wright, *Tribal Leadership*, 56–57.

36. Robertson interview.

37. For example, see Jill Treanor, "Former Chiefs Found Guilty of Fraud," *The Guardian*, September 17, 2003, https://www.theguardian.com/business/2003/sep/18/9; and for a high-profile example that exonerated company executives but implicated the company, see Sam Francis, "Did Blue Arrow Make Bank Fraud Untriable?," *BBC News*, April 14, 2014, https://www.bbc.co.uk/news/uk-politics-26178868.

38. The date of the end of the previous financial year before Robertson's tenure as CEO.

39. Robertson interview.

40. Adecco, *Making the Future Work for Everyone: 2017 Annual Report* (Zurich: Adecco Group, 2018), https://www.adecco-jobs.com/-/media/project/adeccogroup/investor -pdfs/2018/the_adecco_group_2017_annual_report.pdf/?h=738&w=2652&modi fied=20210621195725.

41. We construct our account of the Fastow case based on Mathews, "Interview of Andrew Fastow, Former Enron CFO."

42. "Andrew Fastow," Wikipedia, last edited December 25, 2022, https://en .wikipedia.org/wiki/Andrew_Fastow.

43. Roberts, *Churchill*, 588, 780.

Chapter 9

1. For a full account of footing, see Erving Goffman, *Forms of Talk* (Philadelphia: University of Philadelphia Press, 1981), 124–159, and Charles Taylor, *The Language Animal* (Cambridge, MA: Harvard University Press, 2016), 264–288.

2. Jocko Willink and Leif Babin, *Extreme Ownership: How U.S. Navy Seals Lead and Win* (New York: St. Martin's Press, 2015); Ben Horowitz, *The Hard Thing about Hard Things* (New York: Harper Collins, 2014).

3. Gianpiero Petriglieri, "Identity Workspaces for Leadership Development," in *The Handbook for Teaching Leadership*, ed. Scott Snook, Nitin Nohria, and Rakesh Khurana (Thousand Oaks, CA: Sage, 2012), 297, 303.

4. Churchill, *Memoirs of the Second World War*, 238.

5. Jay A. Conger, "Leadership Development Interventions: Ensuring a Return on the Investment," in *Handbook of Leadership Theory and Practice*, ed. Nohria and Khurana, 717.

6. Jeffrey Pfeffer, "Getting beyond the BS of Leadership Literature," *McKinsey Quarterly*, January 2016.

7. The quotation comes from Logan, King, and Fischer-Wright, *Tribal Leadership*, 62, though in their piety these authors recoil from the term *evil* (63).

8. Nietzsche, *The Gay Science*, §290, pp. 232–233, described in chapter 2.

9. We are describing the nuts and bolts of Wollheim's account of shifting a mood. Recall chapter 3, and see Wollheim, *On the Emotions*.

10. Lucius Annaeus Seneca, *Letters from a Stoic*, trans. and with an introduction by Robin Campbell (New York: Penguin, 1969).

11. Marcus Aurelius, *Meditations*, trans. Martin Hammond (New York: Penguin, 2006); Seneca, "On Anger," in *Seneca: Dialogues and Essays*, 47.

12. For more on such introspection, see Charles Spinosa, Matthew Hancocks, and Billy Glennon, "Coping with Time in Organizations: Insights from Heidegger," in *Skillful Performance: Enacting Capabilities, Knowledge, Competence, and Expertise in Organizations*, ed. Jorgen Sandberg, Linda Rouleau, Ann Langley, and Haridimos Tsoukas (Oxford: Oxford University Press, 2017), 261–281.

13. Max Weber, "The Sociology of Charismatic Authority," in *From Max Weber: Essays in Sociology*, trans. and ed. Hans Heinrich Gerth and Charles Wright Mills (Oxford: Oxford University Press, 1946), 245–264.

14. The leaderly style change and coaching described here is a version of the coaching successfully pioneered by Werner Erhard, where he had leaders identify their "rackets," instead of stories, and then create a way of living based on a new declaration of what matters. Erhard acknowledges that he developed this type of coaching out of an understanding of Martin Heidegger. Hubert L. Dreyfus was Erhard's primary teacher. See Bruce Hyde and Drew Kopp, *Speaking Being: Werner Erhard, Martin Heidegger, and a New Possibility of Being Human* (Hoboken, NJ: Wiley, 2019). Tracy Goss and Fernando Flores draw on this form of coaching. See Tracy Goss, *The Last Word on Power: Executive Re-invention for Leaders Who Must Make the Impossible Happen* (New York: Doubleday, 1996), and Fernando Flores, *Conversations for Action and Collected Essays: Instilling a Culture of Commitment in Working Relationships* (North Charleston, SC: CreateSpace Independent, 2012). Similarly, see Chauncey Bell, *Mobilize! Dancing in the World* (Hemel Hempstead, UK: Harvester Press, 2020), and James Flaherty, *Coaching: Evoking Excellence in Others* (Amsterdam: Elsevier Butterworth Heinemann, 2005). We stand on the shoulders of these leadership coaches and adapt their approaches with Stoic practices and our fundamentally important aestheticization. In particular, the coaching practice we describe is blunt and challenging in the mode of Stoic *ascesis* (the practice of severe self-discipline) and the courageous-speech tradition in coaching, consulting, and psychoanalysis. See Mick Cooper, *Existential Therapies*, 2nd ed. (London: Sage, 2017), esp. chaps. 3, 6, and 7; Roy E. Barsness and Brad Strawn, "Core Competency Seven: Courageous Speech/Disciplined Spontaneity," in *Core Competencies of Relational Psychoanalysis: A Guide to Practice, Study, and Research*, ed. Roy E. Barsness (Abingdon, UK: Routledge, 2018), 179–200; Erik de Haan, *Fearless Consulting: Temptations, Risks and Limits of the Profession* (Chichester, UK: Wiley, 2006); Erik de Haan, *Relational Coaching: Journeys towards Mastering One-to-One Learning* (Chichester, UK: Wiley, 2008), esp. 228–230. Unlike our predecessors, we coach our leaders to replace a foundational story with a legendary story and continue revising or shifting that story through a craftlike discipline. In contrast, our predecessors get rid of rackets and encourage leaders and others to make bold new declarations of what their lives are about and to navigate through life based on those declarations or fundamentally new ones. Of course, we, the authors, individually differ as coaches; each of us has his own style. But the core of our work builds upon adopting virtues skillfully when needed, managing

mood, listening for difference, telling the truth, and taking moral risks in which one changes one's own style to create a masterpiece organization and style of leadership.

15. "Jessica" is not this client's real name. We have promised anonymity, and we have altered some details accordingly.

16. We make a point of letting people know how much virtues matter by pointing out that the Christians' cultivation of the virtue of hope changed the ancient world dramatically. Remember that the best Greek and Roman afterlife was never as good as physical life, and the course of most lives in that era was determined by fate. Hope for a transformation on the order of Christian salvation made no sense. Of course, people could have expectations based on odds, but a larger hope—such as what stands behind the virtue of hope—came with the Christian community, and it changed the Western world. Secularly, some today live in the hope of a world-changing breakthrough, and most can comprehend such a disposition. Virtues really matter. New ones change the world.

17. We have not worked in any place like the postbellum South, where Madam C. J. Walker grew up and where lynchings, peonage, and Jim Crow laws attempted to make it impossible for Black people to cultivate virtues.

18. In this light, we recur to one of Nietzsche's aphorisms, which Walter Kaufman mentions in a footnote: "A very popular error: having the courage of one's convictions; rather it is a matter of having the courage for an *attack* on one's convictions!!!" (Nietzsche, *The Gay Science*, §99, p. 152, n. 42, emphasis in original).

19. If you do not know this song, try Paul McCartney's version. See "Paul McCartney —Till There Was You," YouTube, November 22, 2006, https://www.youtube.com /watch?v=vJaap5XwiPA.

20. This famous Clint Eastwood line is from *The Good, the Bad, and the Ugly* directed by Sergio Leone (Los Angeles: United Artists, 1966), 2:58. The actual line is: "God's not on our side because he hates idiots."

21. For more on the doctrine of continuous copy, see Joel B. Altman, "The Practice of Shakespeare's Text," *Style* 23, no. 3 (1989): 466–500.

22. Machiavelli, *The Prince*, 67.

Chapter 10

1. See Bernard Williams's highly illuminating account of Nietzsche on truth in "Introduction to *The Gay Science*," 311–324, especially 322, where Williams unpacks the quotation given in this chapter's epigraph.

2. Sull, *The Upside of Turbulence*; Sull and Eisenhardt, *Simple Rules*.

3. Hastings and Meyer, *No Rules Rules*, 173–176.

4. Gertrude Himmelfarb, *The Moral Imagination: From Adam Smith to Lionel Trilling* (Lanham, MD: Rowman and Littlefield, 2012). Edmund Burke first used the term *moral imagination*. Rowan Williams's tragic imagination is a form of the moral imagination, and we draw indirectly on his book *The Tragic Imagination* in our account.

5. Mark Johnson, *Moral Imagination: Implications of Cognitive Science for Ethics* (Chicago: Chicago University Press, 1993), 198.

6. Lionel Trilling, *The Liberal Imagination* (New York: Anchor Books, 1953), 105. In the *Huckleberry Finn* essay, Trilling claims that Huck's more profound feat of moral imagination is Huck becoming a servant of the "river-god" (100–113); we draw on Trilling's simpler case.

7. David Foster Wallace, "Transcription of the 2005 Kenyon Commencement Address" (Kenyon College, Gambier, OH, May 21, 2005, https://web.ics.purdue.edu/~drkelly/DFWKenyonAddress2005.pdf).

8. For recent explorations of how moral imagination offers ways out of dogmatic ethical divisiveness, see James Mumford, *Vexed: Ethics beyond Political Tribes* (London: Bloomsbury Continuum, 2020); David Bromwich, *Moral Imagination: Essays* (Princeton, NJ: Princeton University Press, 2014); and James Paul Lederach, *The Moral Imagination: The Art and Soul of Building Peace* (Oxford: Oxford University Press, 2005).

9. Jeffrey P. Bezos, "Amazon's 2004 Annual Report," Six-Page Narratives, accessed December 30, 2022, https://www.sec.gov/Archives/edgar/data/1018724/0001193125 18121161/d456916dex991.htm.

10. Thomas Carlyle, "On Heroes, Hero-Worship, and the Heroic in History," in *English Prose of the Victorian Era*, ed. Charles Frederick Harrold and William D. Templeman (New York: Oxford University Press, 1938), 202, emphasis in original.

11. Nietzsche, *Beyond Good and Evil*, "Nietzsche's Preface," 1.

12. Although Heidegger and Merleau-Ponty preceded him in making this claim, John McDowell has made it persuasively in the Anglophone world (see *Mind and World* and our chapter 7, n. 6).

13. "Universal History, the history of what man has accomplished in this world, is at bottom the History of the Great Men who have worked here" (Carlyle, "On Heroes, Hero-Worship, and the Heroic in History," 170).

14. Carlyle, "On Heroes, Hero-Worship, and the Heroic in History," 196–197, emphasis in original.

15. Carlyle, "On Heroes, Hero-Worship, and the Heroic in History," 197, 199.

16. Carlyle, "On Heroes, Hero-Worship, and the Heroic in History," 197–198.

17. Williams, "Postscript," 251–258, esp. 256 for involvement.

18. For a different defense of moral luck as central to agency, responsibility, and the common good, see also Margaret Urban Walker, "Moral Luck and the Virtues of Impure Agency," in *Moral Luck*, ed. Statman, 235–250.

19. It might be worth noting that in the early-modern world Machiavelli thought about gratitude and its importance in creating a stable state, but he could not bring himself to consider it the moral ground of any state he knew. He argued eloquently about the need for princes and republics to avoid ingratitude. At the end of his argument, he pointed out that in times of adversity princes and republics grant benefits to people to keep them loyal and advises that during peaceful times princes and republics should do the same in preparation for bad times. In short, he advised creating a well of gratitude as a tactic. Still, it is clear that he would like gratitude to be part of the everyday economy of moral behavior (Machiavelli, *The Discourses*, I.28–32, pp. 179–189). Perhaps, like one of our masterpiece-creating leaders, Machiavelli is attempting to make the prudential good of gratitude into a moral good.

20. Martha Nussbaum, "Martha Nussbaum: Applying the Lessons of Ancient Greece," BillMoyers.com, November 16, 1988, https://billmoyers.com/content/martha -nussbaum/; James G. March and Thierry Weil, *On Leadership* (New York: Blackwell, 2005), 18–25.

21. Williams, *The Tragic Imagination*, 31. See also Stanley Cavell, *The Claim of Reason* (Oxford: Oxford University Press, 1979).

22. Roberts, *Churchill*, 588, 780.

23. Søren Kierkegaard, *Fear and Trembling*, trans. Alastair Hannay (1985; reprint, London: Penguin, 2003), 83–103.

24. Churchill, *Memoirs of the Second World War*, 266–267.

25. Hannah Arendt, *Life of the Mind* (New York: Harcourt Brace, 1971); Robin Holt, "Hannah Arendt and the Raising of Conscience in Business Schools," *Academy of Management Learning & Education* 19, no. 4 (2020): 584–599; Marco Berti, Walter Jarvis, Natalia Nikolova, and Alexandra Pitsis, "Embodied Phronetic Pedagogy: Cultivating Ethical and Moral Capabilities in Postgraduate Business Students," *Academy of Management Learning & Education* 20, no. 1 (2021): 6–29; Mary Crossan, Daina Mazutis, and Gerard Seijts, "In Search of Virtue: The Role of Virtues, Values and Character Strengths in Ethical Decision," *Journal of Business Ethics* 113 (2013): 567–581; John Shotter and Haridimos Tsoukas, "In Search of Phronesis: Leadership and

the Art of Judgment," *Academy of Management Learning & Education* 13, no. 2 (2014): 224–243; Williams, *The Tragic Imagination*, 30.

26. Williams, *The Tragic Imagination*, 30.

27. Zygmunt Bauman, *Postmodern Ethics* (Oxford: Blackwell, 1993), 250.

28. Hannah Arendt, *Responsibility and Judgment* (New York: Schocken Books, 2003); Cornelius Castoriadis, *Philosophy, Politics, Autonomy: Essays in Political Philosophy* (Oxford: Oxford University Press, 1991); and James A. Colaiaco, *Socrates against Athens* (New York: Routledge, 2001).

Index

Note: Page references with *f* indicate illustrations, and a *t* indicates a table.

Stress, 101
Sull, Don, 54, 237n40, 238n48, 253n14
Supreme Court, 59

Tate, 162, 164–167, 169
Tate, Saxon, 165
Tate, Virginia ("Ginny"), 164–165
Technological ethos, x–xii
Teller, Astro, 108
Temp workers, 166–167, 169–171, 212,
    253–254n28
Tesla, 59
Tobacco companies, 59
Tocqueville, Alexis de, 7
Tories, 16
Tourish, Dennis, 233n12
Toy Story (film), 146
Tragic imagination, 61, 218–219,
    258n4
Transline, 254n28
Treacy, Michael, 251n12
Trendsetting style, 135*f*, 135–137
Treviño, Linda, 233n12, 251n9
Tribalism, 63, 182
Trilling, Lionel, 70, 205–206, 258n6
True to oneself, being, 69–70
Truss, Liz, xiv
Trust, 14, 79–87
    via anticipating customer anxiety,
        81–82, 87
    difficulty gaining or regaining, 79
    at first sight, 79–80, 87
    via listening for difference, 81–87
    via virtues, 79–80, 87, 241n2
Truth, 14, 89–103. *See also* Speaking
    truth to power
    and accepting when you are wrong,
        97, 244n22
    antirealist accounts of, 92, 243n11
    vs. candor, 89–90, 109
    and coherence, 92, 243n11
    communities' truths, 93

and correspondence to facts, 92,
    242–243nn10–11
of discovery, 90, 96, 100, 102, 209
and dogmatism, 92–94
Einstein as a seeker of, 94–97, 100
and feelings, ethics of, 100–102
and gender, 58–59
importance of, 90
and meaning, 92–93, 95, 243n11,
    243n14
moral approach to speaking, 61–62
multiple truths, 91, 242n8
Nietzsche on truth seeking, 210,
    234n22, 242n8
vs. perspectivism, 242n8
vs. radical honesty, 90–91
and reasoning, 98, 100
vs. relativism, 91
seeking and telling, 61–62, 90–91, 96,
    98–100, 204, 209–210
social psychological approach to
    speaking, 61
and verification, 95–96, 100,
    244nn20–21
Tuskegee Institute, 19–20
Twain, Mark: *Huckleberry Finn*, 206,
    258n6
Twitter (*now* X), 53, 110

Uber, 52
Ukraine, Russian invasion of, 60
Ultra Beauty, 162
Umpqua Bank, 51
Understanding, as a good, xi
Unkrich, Lee, 147
Urbino (Italy), 2
Utilitarians, 118

Values, 2, 132, 135*f*, 224n4
    decay of, 233n12
    and practices, 246n9
    reviving, 39, 233n12